UNION INTERNATIONALE DES SCIENCES PRÉHISTORIQUES ET PROTOHISTORIQUES
INTERNATIONAL UNION OF PREHISTORIC AND PROTOHISTORIC SCIENCES

PROCEEDINGS OF THE XVI WORLD CONGRESS (FLORIANÓPOLIS, 4-10 SEPTEMER 2011)
ACTES DU XVI CONGRÈS MONDIAL (FLORIANÓPOLIS, 4-10 SEPTEMBRE 2011)

VOL. 1

Actes de la session 17
Proceedings of session 17

The Intellectual and Spiritual Expression of Non–Literate Societies

Edited by

Chairman
Emmanuel Anati
Co-Chairman
Luiz Oosterbeek
Co-editor
Federico Mailland

BAR International Series 2360
2012

Published in 2016 by
BAR Publishing, Oxford

BAR International Series 2360

Proceedings of the XVI World Congress of the International Union of Prehistoric and Protohistoric Sciences
Actes du XVI Congrès mondial de l'Union Internationale des Sciences Préhistoriques et Protohistoriques

Secretary of the Congress: Rossano Lopes Bastos
President of the Congress National Commission: Erika Robrhan-Gonzalez
Elected Bureau (2011-2014):
President: Jean Bourgeois
Secretary General: Luiz Oosterbeek
Treasurer: François Djindjian
Series Editors: Luiz Oosterbeek, Erika Robrhan-Gonzalez
Volume editors: Emmanuel Anati, Luiz Oosterbeek, Federico Mailland

The Intellectual and Spiritual Expression of Non-Literate Societies

ISBN 978 1 4073 0947 7

© The editors and contributors severally and the Publisher 2012

The signed papers are the sole responsibility of their authors.
Les textes signés sont de la seule responsabilité de leurs auteurs.

Contacts: General Secretariat of the U.I.S.P.P. – International Union of Prehistoric and Protohistoric Sciences
Instituto Politécnico de Tomar, Av. Dr. Cândido Madureira 13, 2300 TOMAR Email: uispp@ipt.pt

The authors' moral rights under the 1988 UK Copyright,
Designs and Patents Act are hereby expressly asserted.

All rights reserved. No part of this work may be copied, reproduced, stored,
sold, distributed, scanned, saved in any form of digital format or transmitted
in any form digitally, without the written permission of the Publisher.

BAR Publishing is the trading name of British Archaeological Reports (Oxford) Ltd.
British Archaeological Reports was first incorporated in 1974 to publish the BAR
Series, International and British. In 1992 Hadrian Books Ltd became part of the BAR
group. This volume was originally published by Archaeopress in conjunction with
British Archaeological Reports (Oxford) Ltd / Hadrian Books Ltd, the Series principal
publisher, in 2012. This present volume is published by BAR Publishing, 2016.

Printed in England

BAR titles are available from:

        BAR Publishing
        122 Banbury Rd, Oxford, OX2 7BP, UK
EMAIL   info@barpublishing.com
PHONE +44 (0)1865 310431
FAX   +44 (0)1865 316916
        www.barpublishing.com

Contents

Contents i

List of Figures iii

List of Tables vii

Introductory note viii

Presentation 1
Emmanuel Anati

Les adaptations humaines et l'expression spirituelle des premiers Hommes
    anatomiquement modernes à la transition du Paléolithique moyen
    au Paleolithique supérieur 3
Janusz K. Kozlowski

The Lipari Middle Paleolithic and early navigation in the Mediterranean
    With an appendix on flint typology by *Federico Mailland* 5
Emmanuel Anati

The Paleolithic sanctuary at Har Karkom, Negev desert 13
Emmanuel Anati

The Karkomian flint industry: the context of the Har Karkom sanctuary
    at the transition between Middle and Upper Paleolithic 21
Federico Mailland

Geoglyphs on Har Karkom plateau: witness to the early start of the expression of
    conceptual ideas during the early Upper Paleolithic 29
Federico Mailland

Astronomical representations in rock art: some examples of the cognitive
    and spiritual processes of non-literate people 37
Fernando Coimbra

Ancient myths and scientific fiction: the representation of big head
    in the prehistoric art and its recreation in Western culture 45
Santiago Guimaraes

The pre-contact pueblo Kachina in the American Southwest: its iconography,
    first appearances and contexts of symbolic meanings 47
Jessica Joyce Christie

Deer representation in Sierra da Capivara National Park: morphology,
   syntax and archeological contexts: a visual analysis 57
Elaine Ignacio

Indigenous dolls and figurines: where sacred and social worlds merge
   and the implications for archeologists 59
Sharon Moses

Conveying an understanding of the landscape: the rock art of the Tagus
   and the Guadiana Valleys 67
Luiz Oosterbeek

The deer figures in Tagus rock art 71
Sara Garcês

The geometric art of the Iberian schist plaques 85
Cristina Lopes

Anthropozoomorphic figures and other monsters: mythical fantastic figures
   in Alpine rock art 89
Umberto Sansoni

Beliefs and Practices Connected with Megalithic Burial Customs
   in Eastern India 91
Ranjana Ray

Substrats néolithiques aux arts traditionnels des Balkans 97
Marcel Otte

List of Figures

Emmanuel Anati: The Lipari Middle Paleolithic and early navigation in the Mediterranean

Figure 1 – The village of Lipari from the mountain above 5

Figure 2 – The valley at the foot of which there have been findings 6

Figure 3 – The origin of the valley is a fossil volcanic crater 6

Figure 4 – Canneto, Lipari. 1: retouched Levallois point. 2-5: Mousterian points 7

Figure 5 – Canneto, Lipari: transverse scraper with abrupt retouch. Evident bulb
of percussion 8

Figure 6 – Canneto, Lipari: stone with natural hole, retouched, completed
and rounded 8

Figure 7 – Canneto, Lipari: 1, 3: Scrapers on blade; 2: scraper on flake 9

Figure 8 – Canneto, Lipari: Levallois flake (truncated) with evident bulb
of percussion and retouched platform 9

Figure 9 – Canneto, Lipari: 1: reutilized Levallois core with two notches; 2: flake
detouched by recurrent Levallois technique. Evident bulb of percussion 10

Figure 10 – Canneto, Lipari: retouched splinters 10

Figure 11 – Canneto, Lipari: 1-2, 4-6: retouched splinters; 3: borer on backed blade 11

Emmanuel Anati: The Paleolithic sanctuary at Har Karkom, Negev desert

Figure 1 – Location of Har Karkom in the Sinai peninsula 14

Figure 2 – Plan of the site HK/86b and the underlying terraces 15

Figure 3 – Plan of the site HK/86b: particular 16

Figure 4 – Flint orthostats of the site HK86b 16

Figure 5 – Photograph and tracing of a flint nodule with a natural form of
a human face, completed by man with secondary retouching, some flaking,
and a thin line to complete the eye 17

Figure 6 – A flint nodule in the form of a bird retouched in the tail and base
with flaking. Finely incised lines define the eyes and beak 17

Figure 7 – left: zoomorphic flint nodule retouched on the upper and lower edges,
and with a large flake on the right side; right: Flint nodule with three hammered
dots, which probably indicate the eyes and mouth of an anthropomorphic face 17

Figure 8 – Aerial view of the prehistoric trail (marked by dotted line)
which descends from the sanctuary towards the Paran desert 18

Figure 9 – Eastward view of the Paran desert, with the Paleolithic sanctuary
in the foreground 19

Figure 10 – View of the two "breasts," the two summits of Har Karkom, from the Palaeolithic sanctuary, site HK 86b 19

Federico Mailland: **The Karkomian flint industry: the context of the Har Karkom sanctuary at the transition between Middle and Upper Paleolithic**

Figure 1 – Har Karkom: map of sites with Karkomian flint industry. The star shows the position of the ceremonial site HK/86b 22

Figure 2 – HK/87b. 1: Châtelperron point; 2: point; 3, 5: points on denticulate blades; 4: leaf-shaped point 23

Figure 3 – HK/87b. 1: denticulate retouch on Levallois flake; 2: notch; 3: burin; 4: denticulate; 5: tanged tool; 6: side scraper; 7: blade; 8: borer; 9: end scraper 24

Figure 4 – HK/87b. 1, 7: points; 2: retouched Levallois point; 3, 5, 6: retouched flakes; 4: round scraper; 8: notch on denticulate; 9: retouched Levallois flake; 10, 11: continuous retouch flakes; 12: borer 24

Figure 5 – HK/191a. 1, 15: borer; 2: point on backed blade; 3: Levallois point; 4: point; 5, 12: denticulates; 6: end scraper; 7: transverse scraper; 8, 9, 16, 17, 18: backed blades; 10, 11, 19, 21: blades; 13, 14: notch; 20: double burin 25

Figure 6 – Ceremonial site HK/86b. 1: double borer on denticulate; 2: retouched point on Levallois flake; 3: small blade with abrupt retouch and blunted platform; 4: borer on transverse scraper on a Levallois flake; 5: transverse scraper on a Levallois flake; 6, 7: denticulate on Levallois support; 8, 9: denticulate; 10: notch on denticulate 25

Federico Mailland: **Geoglyphs on Har Karkom plateau: witness to the early start of the expression of conceptual ideas during the early Upper Paleolithic**

Figure 1 – Geoglyph of a rhinoceros 33

Figure 2 – Geoglyph of an elephant 33

Figure 3 – Remains of geoglyph (bathing elephant) 33

Figure 4 – Geoglyph of a quadruped. The ventral part was disturbed by the superimposition of another figure 33

Figure 5 – Anthropomorphic geoglyph 34

Fernando Coimbra: **Astronomical representations in rock art: some examples of the cognitive and spiritual processes of non-literate people**

Figure 1 – Typology of sun images from Saimaly-Tash 38

Figure 2 – Anthropomorphic sun standing on a bull 38

Figure 3 – Dancing to the sun god (?) 38

Figure 4 – Anthropomorphic motive holding a sun image 38

Figure 5 – Anthropomorphic sun image from Peyra Escrita 39

Figure 6 – Megalithic burial with seven skeletons forming a sun image 39

Figure 7 – Menhir with crescent moon 40

Figure 8 – Comet or meteor, being observed by a San group 42

Jessica Joyce Christie: **The pre-contact pueblo Kachina in the American Southwest: its iconography, first appearances and contexts of symbolic meanings**

Figure 1 – Katsina doll representing Talava (Morning Singer) 47

Figure 2 – Map of Ancestral Pueblo sites, contemporary Pueblos, and Pueblo-related cultures. Sites mentioned in the text are shaded 48

Figure 3 – Drawing of Ma 'lo Katsina mask 48

Figure 4 – Early pecked and abstracted masks possibly executed before A.D. 400 49

Figure 5 – Three Rivers, petroglyph portraying Katsina-style mask..50

Figures 6 – Cerro Indio, petroglyph of Katsina-style mask. Note the stepped motif
referencing clouds 50

Figure 7 – Petroglyphs of Koyemsi Katsina near Homol'ovi II on the Little
Colorado River, Arizona, and post-contact Koyemsi or Mudhead mask 50

Figure 8 – Section of a panel of painted Katsina masks and figures from the Village
of the Great Kivas site, Zuni-Cibola region; dated post-1325 to present......................51

Figure 9 – Sherd from a Talpa Black-on-white pot and rockart images with
horned Katsina masks, origin of ceramic sherd: Pot Creek Pueblo,
Rio Grande; origin of rockart from the Little Colorado River......................................51

Figure 10 – Paiyatuma and Ka'nashkule in Layer N-41 of the Kuaua murals,
Coronado State Monument, New Mexico 52

Figure 11 – Tablita with Qa'otiyo (Corn Boy) Katsina which combines
a tablita headdress with a Katsina mask 53

Figure 12 – Early Pueblo IV petroglyph mask in the form of a bowl
with cloud symbolism...53

Figure 13 – Tlaloc figure with stepped cloud motif, from Three Rivers,
New Mexico 54

Sharon Moses: **Indigenous dolls and figurines: where sacred and social worlds merge and the implications for archeologists**

Figure 1 – Author's photograph of Bering Strait traditional dolls and figurines –
ivory, mammoth tusk, seal fur and leather materials 64

Sara Garcês: **The deer figures in Tagus rock art**

Figure 1 – Map of the Tagus Valley Rock Art Complex rock art sites..............................71

Figure 2 – Rock number 60 of Alagadouro. Possible hunting scene (?) involving
an anthropomorphic presence of a different artistic style...73

Figure 3 – Deer figures from Chão da Velha rock art site..74

Figure 4 – a: Rock number 59 from Cachão do Algarve; b: Details of rock
number 59 from Cachão do Algarve – tracing of the mould 74

Figure 5 – Rock number 49 from Fratel. The black colour deer of the first group
(Full Neolithic) and gray colour deer in the second group (Late Neolithic).................75

Figure 6 – Rock number 155 from Fratel. This reproduction attempts to
demonstrate the level of possible associations between deer and zoomorphic
figures in general with this type of motif. The representation of the rock is
based only on a personal interpretation of the figures that exist within it
(because it was impossible so far to make the tracing of the rock mould).
However, Baptista (1981) argues that deer figure belongs to the period
Classic Subnaturalism or Evolved including spirals that seem to be
associated to them..76

Figure 7 – Rock of the Deer – Rovinhosa Valley, Ocreza River 77

Figure 8 – a) Panel 1 from Two Deer Rock – Rovinhosa Valley, Ocreza River;
b) Panel 2 – Rovinhosa Valley, Ocreza River 77

Figure 9 – Representations of deer pierced with weapons. a) Rock number 45
from Fratel; b) Rock number 56 from Cachão do Algarve...78

Figure 10 – Possible mating in rock number 155 from Fratel. According to
M.V. Gomes associated with the female to a male of the archaic period
of phase I (subnaturalistic) 78

Figure 11 – a) Rock number 60 from Alagadouro. Couple of deer and possible
hunter (?); b) Rock number 174-175 from Fratel. Possible hunting scene involving
anthropomorphic figures, one (or more) possible dog and deer (the zoomorphic
which is in the middle of the scene could possibly be interpreted as a deer?)..............79

Figure 12 – Example of deer/ circles and spirals association. a) Rock number 56 from Cachão do Algarve; b) Rock number 61 from Cachão do Algarve. c) Rock number 111 from Fratel d) Rock number 155 from Fratel. e) Rock number 211ª from Fratel. f) Rock number 43 from São Simão g) Rock number 119ª from São Simão. h) Rock number 386 from São Simão 80

Figure 13 – Phallic anthropomorphic sustaining a dead deer in his arms. Rock number 12 from São Simão. Interesting to consider the possibility of the antlers of the deer have been made in a later phase than the deer itself. The part that joins the two points appears to be different than the rest of the antlers. Coincidence or not, the antlers appears to have had an ultimate goal solar representation 81

Figure 14 – Anthropomorphic figurations sustaining solar figures in the air. Rock number 126 from Fratel and rock number 12 from Ficalho 82

Cristina Lopes: **The geometric art of the Iberian schist plaques**

Figure 1 – Standard nomenclature (From Gonçalves, 2004)...86

Figure 2 – (From Gonçalves, 2004) 86

Figure 3 – (From Gonçalves, 2004) 86

Figure 4 – (From Gonçalves, 2004) 86

Figure 5 – (From Gonçalves, 2004) 85

Ranjana Ray: **Beliefs and Practices Connected with Megalithic Burial Customs in Eastern India**

Figure 1 – A Bhumij gentleman from eastern India...92

Figure 2 – Cremation of the dead..93

Figure 3 – The ash from which charred bones are collected 93

Figure 4 – A megalith under which the pot with bones and ash are buried..........................94

Marcel Otte: **Substrats néolithiques aux arts traditionnels des Balkans**

Figure 1 – Le thème du serpent apparaît dans le folklore sous la forme de forces terrestres. Ici sous le manche de canne (b) et dès le néolithique sous la forme d'anse de vase (a) 98

Figure 2 – Le thème de l'arbre de vie perpétuelle apparaît dès le néolithique. Il se retrouve sous forme schématique dans le folklore actuel 99

Figure 3 – L'œuf, comme symbole de vie ultérieure, est un thème chargé d'espoir de vie dès le néolithique (b) et toujours dans le folklore actuel (a) 100

Figure 4 – Les motifs décoratifs observés sur les statuettes néolithiques (a) évoquent les costumes traditionnels des campagnes bulgares (b)..100

Figure 5 – Le thème du cheval correspond dans le folklore actuel à la force de traction de l'araire (c), si fondamentale pour le renouvellement de la vie. On le voit sous forme réaliste ou schématique dans le folklore actuel (a et b).............101

Figure 6 – Le thème de la spirale, signe de vie, de renouvellement par l'eau et la renaissance, se trouve aussi bien au néolithique (a et b) que dans les robes actuelles (c)...101

Figure 7 – Le thème de la femme décorée apparaît sur les céramiques néolithiques peintes (a) et sur les robes actuelles (b) 102

Figure 8 – Le thème de l'orant aux bras dressés se retrouve comme un fidèle qui implore ses dieux 103

Figure 9 – La structure du décor vestimentaire traverse tous les temps en marquant la distinction entre le plastron et la jupe, et en insistant sur les motifs rayonnants, spiralés et en étoile 104

Figure 10 – Le thème du bélier, symbole de la force animale vaincue, apparaît dès le néolithique (a et b) et se poursuit dans les fêtes du printemps actuelles sous forme de masques (c et d) 105

Figure 11 – Le dragon combine différents signes d'animaux dangereux, comme les carnassiers, le rapace et le serpent. On le retrouve aussi bien dans des décors peints néolithiques (b) et dans la statuaire (a et c) que dans les crosses de berger actuelles (e) 106

Figure 12 – La vaztika est un signe de vitalité par l'empennage donné à la croix qui lui donne son mouvement. Il se retrouve à l'identique sur les décors des robes néolithiques (a) et des robes actuelles (b) 107

List of Tables

Federico Mailland: **The Karkomian flint industry: the context of the Har Karkom sanctuary at the transition between Middle and Upper Paleolithic**

Table 1 Characters of the lithic industry in the different Karkomian sites 23

Table 2 Karkomian industry: descriptive statistics of lithic assemblage 26

Federico Mailland: **Geoglyphs on Har Karkom plateau: witness to the early start of the expression of conceptual ideas during the early Upper Paleolithic**

Chart 1 Quaternary paleoclimate, paleoenvironment, chronology & population of Har Karkom 31

Chart 2 Summary of the styles of Har Karkom geoglyphs 32

Introductory note

The International Union of Prehistoric and Protohistoric Sciences (Union Internationale des Sciences Préhistoriques et Protohistoriques – UISPP) was founded on May 28th, 1931, in Berne, and integrates all sciences related to prehistoric and protohistoric development: archaeology, anthropology, palaeontology, geology, zoology, botany, environment, physics, chemistry, geography, history, numismatics, epigraphy, mathematics and other. Research on adaptation mechanisms and human societies' behaviour dynamics are ate the centre of the scientific interest of UISPP. For this aim, UISPP periodically organises a world congress of prehistoric and protohistoric sciences, on which occasion the progress of knowledge is presented and common research goals are set. For these, UISPP creates scientific commissions devoted to specialised research themes.

The increasing specialisation of disciplines, of organisations and of scientific events requires a particular effort for their integration and communication, UISPP taking such responsibility. It secures the promotion of pluri-disciplinary and inter-institutional collaborations through the regional and thematic scientific commissions and affiliated organisations, sharing similar objectives, as well as with other scientific institutions.

UISPP is a member of the Unesco associate International Council of Philosophy and Human Sciences, since September 29th, 1955. As an international association of scholars, its aim is the collaboration of scholars from all countries through initiatives that may contribute for the advancement of prehistoric and protohistoric sciences, based on full academic freedom and refusing any sort of discrimination based on race, philosophical or ideological judgement, ethnic or geographic affiliation, nationality, sex, language or other, since discrimination is, by definition, the negation of the scientific approach. It also rejects any attempts of fictional rewriting of the past or of negationism, and it doesn't exclude any *bona fide* scholar from its scientific activities.

The XVI congress of UISPP was held in Florianópolis, Brazil, in 2011, with over 1.000 researchers, mainly from Latin America. In this occasion, the permanent council decided to organise the next two congresses with intervals of 3 years. The XVII congress will be organised in Burgos (Spain) in 2014 (August 31st-September 7th), and the XVIII congress will be organised in Melbourne (Australia) in 2017.

Information on the membership of UISPP, its scientific commissions, the next congress and other activities is available contacting uispp@ipt.pt.

The Bureau of UISPP

PRESENTATION

Emmanuel ANATI

President, CISPE, Centro Internazionale di Studi Preistorici ed Etnologici, Italy
Director, CCSP, Centro Camuno di Studi Preistorici, Italy
Director, Italian archeological project at Har Karkom, Negev, Israel

Dear Colleagues, it is a pleasure to welcome you to this session on 'the intellectual and spiritual expression of non-literate societies'.

Five years ago, at the XV UISPP Congress held in Lisbon in September 2006, I headed a session on prehistoric art and ideology. One of the resolutions at this session was to give birth to a new body within the UISPP called the International Commission on the Intellectual and Spiritual Expressions of Non-literate Peoples or CISENP (*Prehistoric Art and Ideology*, Proceedings of the XV World Congress, Vol. 16, Session C27, BAR International Series, Oxford, 2008, pp. 124). After receiving the blessing of UISPP, the Commission held a working session in Paris in October 2007 where the operational lines of the commission were set (*The Intellectual and Spiritual Expressions of Non-literate Peoples*, CISPE–CCSP, 2007, pp. 160).

The main idea was to consider various aspects of art, religion, cult structures and monuments, burial customs and funerary architecture, and other expressions of the spiritual and intellectual life of non-literate peoples as a cultural assemblage which could provide a dimension of the conceptual life of various horizons of human cultures. Rather than separating specialized sectors of rock art, mobiliary art, burials and other expressions of human creativity, as is sometimes customary, the Commission intended to persuade experts to concentrate on a wider debate and create a permanent dialogue on the global phenomenon of the intellectual manifestations and spirituality of pre-literate and non-literate societies. The purpose was to explore the human soul, using the material outputs.

Two more meetings were held between then and this Congress, along with two Symposia at Valcamonica (*Making History of Prehistory*, XXIII Valcamonica Symposium, 28 October–2 November 2009, pp. 430; and *Art and Communication in Pre-literate Societies*, XXIV Valcamonica Symposium, 13–18 July 2011, pp. 504). These meetings allowed the debate to expand to over 200 scholars and experts from 60 countries. A network of correspondence with professionals has been set up which is going to facilitate other meetings and develop updates and debates on both general and specific topics.

The present session has a rather limited participation due primarily to mistiming. After a period of uncertainty, it became clear to me that I could attend this Congress less than two months ago and many of the European and African colleagues in our research groups were already engaged elsewhere. It was possible, however, to gather 14 communications dealing with general problems as well as with specific topics concerning three continents, involving prehistoric and protohistoric studies, art history, cultural anthropology, ethnology and ethnography, and the history of religions. This is another aspect of our goals: developing cooperation and joint studies between different disciplines in the humanities and social sciences. Prehistoric research is enriched by the input of other disciplines and the benefits go in both directions. This occasion is particularly welcome as it allows a new and broader contact with South American colleagues who are often absent from European meetings.

In this session topics range from the Paleolithic to recent ethnography, and present several new discoveries and ideas. Recurring patterns of imaginary beings depicted in different ages and geographical areas pose intriguing questions. The observation of the sky and of the stars has given rise to beliefs and myths in different periods, and some of them still survive. Such topics concern both prehistory and our own popular beliefs. Old discoveries are awakening new theories of interpretation. Recent ethnographic cults and traditions, among American Indians and Balkan populations alike, are revealing ancient roots. Some depictions of rock art acquire new meaning by more detailed analyses both in Europe and Latin America.

A new contribution is that of the oldest known sanctuary, going back to the beginning of the Upper Paleolithic. The analysis of the context of its material culture is presented here for the first time. From the same locality pebble drawings or geoglyphs depicting figures of extinct fauna like the rhinoceros and the elephant which disappeared from that area nearly 30,000 years ago are also presented. Indeed, the presence of geoglyphs in the Near Eastern Paleolithic is a new and unexpected phenomenon. This newly described Near Eastern culture may provide far-reaching conclusions on the origins of art and religion. In this way this small session makes its own contribution to the Congress and to prehistoric studies. Hopefully it will awaken debate and stimulate research.

Most of the final texts of the papers have already been presented with their illustrations and they are ready to be printed. Texts of debates presented in a suitable form before the end of the Congress may eventually be added to the publication of the session.

May I conclude by thanking you for your presence and wishing you a stimulating and creative session.

LES ADAPTATIONS HUMAINES ET L'EXPRESSION SPIRITUELLE DES PREMIERS HOMMES ANATOMIQUEMENT MODERNES A LA TRANSITION DU PALEOLITHIQUE MOYEN AU PALEOLITHIQUE SUPERIEUR

Janusz K. KOZLOWSKI, Poland

Abstract: *L'archéologie, par l'étude de corrélations matérielles de domaines idéologiques, peut apporter la profondeur historique par les manifestations de la culture spirituelle des sociétés non-littéraires malgré l'absence des sources écrites.*

Comme nous avons documenté dans cette contribution, un important progrès dans les dimensions matérielles et idéologiques du vécu est observé avec l'apparition des Hommes Anatomiquement Modernes, qui a eu lieu en Afrique entre 300 et 200 Kyr BP. Ce progrès a continué surtout pendant leur diffusion en dehors de l'Afrique, vers le Proche Orient, Asie sud-orientale, et finalement l'Europe.

L'expansion sur les nouveaux territoires a nécessité de l'homme une habilité d'adaptation aux différents environnements. Les AMH pendant la période entre les deux maximums de la dernière glaciation – marquée par un rythme des oscillations climatiques profondes et assez fréquentes – ont du s'adapter a ces changements et ont été mieux préparées à la conquête des nouveaux territoires. Tenant compte de la faible densité de populations des AMH, surtout au début de cette conquête, il faut penser que la pression démographique n'a pas été à l'origine de leur diffusion. Il faut donc supposer que c'est le développement technologique et socio-économique qui a conditionné cette expansion. Les relations sociales entre les groupes humains basées sur leur propre identité et les systèmes de communication – y compris le développement de possibilités de communication orale – ont été également à l'origine de la diffusion des premiers AMH. Notons aussi que la recherche de certains matériaux rares (par ex. certaines roches pour la fabrication des outils et armes, matières colorantes utilisées dans la sphère de la culture symbolique, coquilles servant comme objets de parure, etc.) a pu expliquer l'origine de mouvements des groupes humains, outre la simple curiosité vers l'inconnu.

Ce qui accompagnait les déplacements des vagues successives des AMH c'était le développement des activités symboliques dans le quotidien de ces populations. Il est intéressant qu'avec la conquête des nouveaux territoires ces activités sont devenues de plus en plus complexes, conduisant à l'émergence de systèmes de symboles liés à la magie, aux rituels (par ex. d'initiation) et à une vision cosmologique.

Dans le développement de la pensée symbolique des premiers AMH nous pouvons distinguer plusieurs phases:
- *a) L'utilisation des colorants pour la peinture corporelle et peut-être aussi pour peindre des galets. Dans le cas de la peinture corporelle le but était de marquer l'identité des groupes ou des individus. La couleur rouge pourrait avoir aussi la signification symbolique, comme équivalent du sang.*
- *b) L'apparition des rituels funéraires, déjà connus par les Néandertaliens en Eurasie occidentale, mais probablement sans offrande.*
- *c) L'apparition des incisions sur l'os ou la pierre, représentées par les signes géométriques simples et répétées, dont la signification nous échappe. Ces incisions intentionnelles structurées et rythmées ont été aussi exécutées par les Néandertaliens (par ex. le motif de zig-zig gravé sur l'os de la couche 12 de la grotte Bacho Kiro antérieure à 45 Kyr BP).*
- *d) L'apparition des premiers objets de parure, en particulier de dents et coquilles percées, perles et pendeloques. Ces objets ont été les symboles de l'identité personnelle ou collective, plus durable que la peinture corporelle, mais probablement aussi l'expression de goût esthétique.*
- *e) L'apparition de l'art figuratif, aussi bien zoomorphe qu'anthropomorphe sous la forme de peintures, gravures et sculpture mobilière, semble être la dernière étape de développement de la pensée symbolique et de la spiritualité auxquelles s'ajoute un sens esthétique et peut-être les pratiques et croyances religieuses. L'origine de l'art figuratif était un phénomène polycentrique : il apparait parallèlement dans les zones marginales de la diffusion des AMH (en Australie et en Europe méditerranéenne et centre-occidentale). Cette apparition parait être instantanée (dans l'échelle de la chronologie du Paléolithique supérieur), et non le résultat des étapes successives de l'évolution artistique. Les plus anciens motifs dans l'art paléolithique occidental sont : les représentations des organes sexuels féminins, les représentations anthropomorphes mâles, fréquemment avec les têtes zoomorphes et les animaux (plutôt des espèces très rarement chassées comme les rhinocéros, lion des cavernes, ours des cavernes). Ce répertoire pourrait suggérer non seulement l'élaboration croissante du monde visuel artificiel mais aussi les relations sociales de plus en plus complexes entre les membres de sociétés préhistoriques et l'état de leur conscience.*

THE LIPARI MIDDLE PALEOLITHIC AND EARLY NAVIGATION IN THE MEDITERRANEAN

Emmanuel ANATI

President, CISPE, Centro Internazionale di Studi Preistorici ed Etnologici, Italy
Director, CCSP, Centro Camuno di Studi Preistorici, Italy
Director, Italian archeological project at Har Karkom, Negev, Israel

PREMISE

The discovery of Middle Paleolithic artifacts at Lipari, in the Aeolian Islands, is changing the history of this archipelago and of the whole of Sicily and provides new information on the early navigational ability of man in the Mediterranean. In his classic book *Sicily before the Greeks* (1961), Luigi Bernabo Brea, father of Sicilian prehistory, wrote: 'Man seems to have arrived very late in Sicily. There are in fact no traces in the island of Lower and Middle Paleolithic ... The earliest traces belong to the Upper Paleolithic ... Perhaps only at this time man crossed the Strait of Messina and entered the island.' Only recently the presence of sporadic finds from the Middle Paleolithic in Sicily has been suggested, while for the Aeolian Islands, off the Sicilian coast, the belief persisted that the first human presence dated back to the Neolithic.

The current sea-level has stabilized at the beginning of the Mediterranean Holocene, between 9,000 and 12,000 years ago, towards the end of the Paleolithic period. Before the conclusion of the last Ice Age, before the melting of the Pleistocene glaciers, the sea level was about 120 metres below the present level, and many coastal areas now submerged were above sea level.

There are conflicting opinions about the topographic changes that occurred in the Aeolian Islands, because of volcanic activity in addition to the effects of changes in sea level. Until a few years ago it was believed that the archipelago came into existence as a result of tectonic events in the final Pleistocene. Meanwhile this hypothesis was demonstrated to be wrong by the geological documentation of rocks and other sediments, thus bringing back the birth of the Archipelago at least to the Early Pleistocene.

The prevalent hypothesis is that, despite the topographic land changes due to tectonic activities and to the changes in sea level, in the last 100,000 years the archipelago has been a separate entity from the main island of Sicily. The sea corridor is likely to have been shorter than the current 20 km but not much. In any case man had to cross at least 14 km of sea to reach the Aeolian Islands. How? Probably by using rafts. This method was in use in various parts of the globe at least 60,000 years ago, when man crossed the sea to reach Australia.

Figure 1 – The village of Lipari from the mountain above

Figure 2 – The valley at the foot of which there have been findings

Figure 3 – The origin of the valley is a fossil volcanic crater

The discovery of Middle Paleolithic material culture in the Aeolian archipelago is therefore of importance for at least two reasons: for reviewing the origins of the population and history of this archipelago, and for the testimony it provides of the ability of Middle Paleolithic man to seafaring in the Mediterranean. To the best of our knowledge it is so far the oldest known documentation of seafaring in Europe.

THE FINDING

A fairly coarse lithic industry was discovered near the village Canneto in the island of Lipari in the Aeolian archipelago by Ms Maria Pia Fiorentino, who kindly invited me to study it. All of the artifacts analyzed in this report come from her collection. My visit and survey was supported by the local municipality of Lipari, followed by the analysis of the finds which were drawn and described by Ms Ida Mailland. Special thanks go to the Mayor of Lipari, Mariano Bruno, and to Alderman Giuseppe Finocchiaro, for their active interest and their contributions to our stay in Lipari. Thanks are extended also to Dr. Madeleine Cavalier and Dr. Maria Adelina Bernabò Brea, at the Lipari Museum, for having examined some of the lithic implements and to Dr. Maria Clara Martinelli of the local Direction of Antiquities for having read the Italian version of the present paper.

The on-site inspection at the site discovered by Ms Fiorentino, which took place 11–14 June 2010, allowed us to record the presence there of many stones of the same type of those collected by Ms Fiorentino, mostly marked by the action of rolling due to transport in water. Some of them have traces of intentional flaking, chipping and retouching, but due to the heavy state of wear none of the lithic implements seen by the present writer on the spot could be defined as typical tools. Probably Ms Fiorentino had successfully gathered the most obvious surface documentation.

The site, which was named Paleo-Canneto, is located at the mouth of a natural deep valley, coming down from the mountain and ending near the present sea-coast of Canneto. The examination of the state of wear of the lithic material allowed two possibilities; it could have been caused by sea waves rolling or by fluvial transportation. The angularity and the general characteristics of the findings excluded the possibility that it could have been caused by waves rolling and suggested the hypothesis that their wear could have been caused by fluvial stream transportation. It is unlikely, therefore, that the finds are in situ where they were found; presumably they were carried by torrential rain water from a location further upstream.

THE FINDINGS

The finds are fragments of natural local volcanic stones, defined by the municipal geologist as andesite. This kind of stone is currently found on the island in layers, also on the mountain above the Canneto valley, and is considered to be older than other volcanic rocks which are widespread on the island.

Among hundreds of items analysed, we found that only three of them had evident bulbs of percussion. Other fragments show distal protuberances but their state of erosion did not allow us to establish with certainty the presence of bulbs of percussion. Among the obvious tools, there is a front scraper on a heavy flake displaying the bulb of percussion, and the fragment of a thick blade with continuous retouching, also displaying a bulb of percussion. There are several retouched points of Mousterian type, some Levalloisian flakes, and end-scrapers on heavy flakes with steep retouching. Among the finds there are two nuclei, although atypical, belonging to a Mousterian typology. A peculiar find is a small stone with a natural hole which was retouched, completed and rounded in ancient times. The state of erosion due to the action of water transportation did not allow us to define several stones showing smoothed and worn traces of flaking. Several of the implements just displayed traces of flaking on tabular stones.

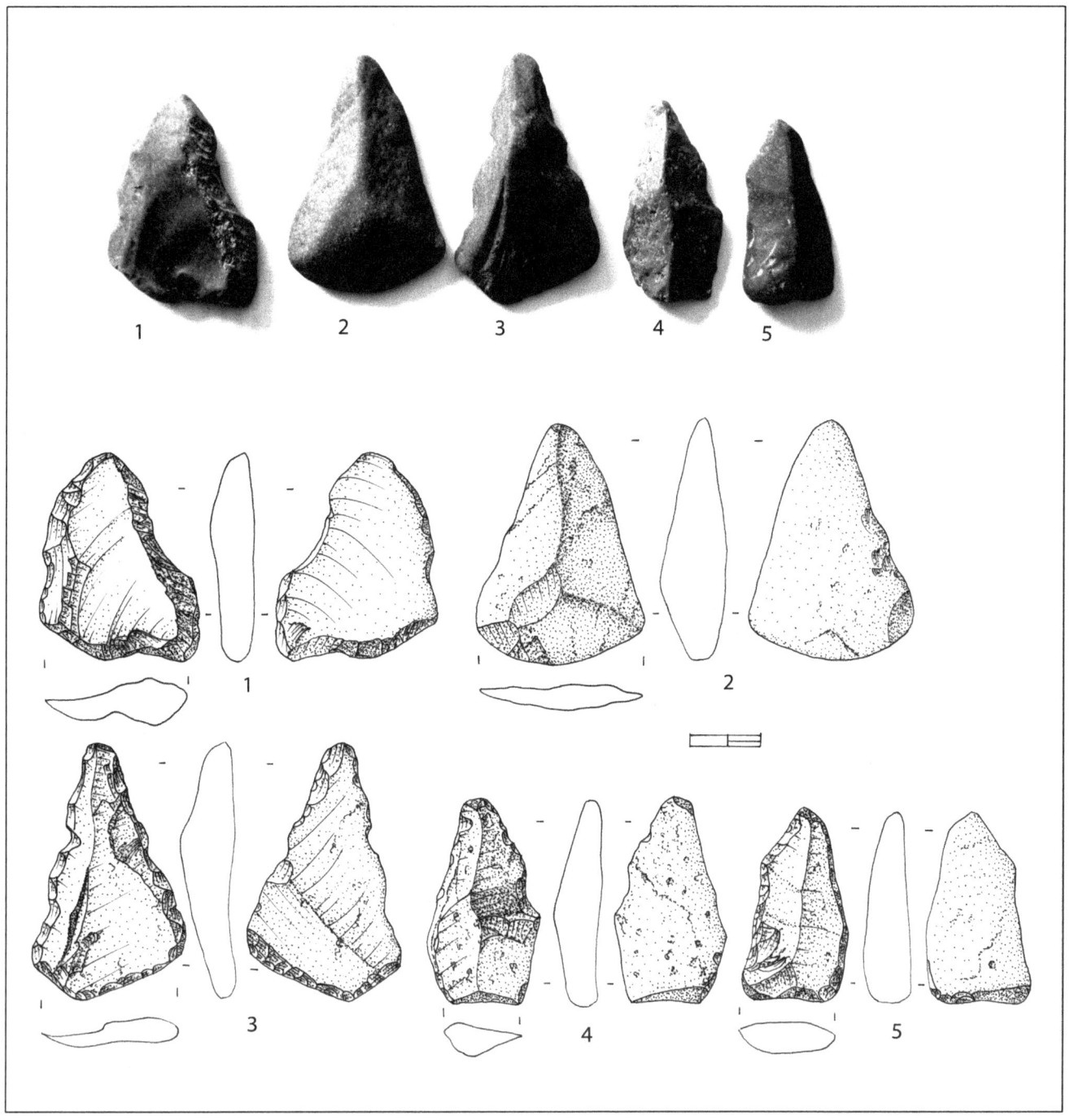

Figure 4 – Canneto, Lipari. 1: retouched Levallois point. 2-5: Mousterian points
(drawing Ida Mailland)

Despite the rather unusual character of the industry and its poor state of preservation, the typological and technical aspects seem to indicate that they belong to the Middle Paleolithic, an opinion shared by Dr. Federico Mailland, specialist in Paleolithic flint industries.

CONSIDERATIONS

The discovery of this site presents an unexpected archaeological innovation, if we consider that the presence of Paleolithic artifacts had never before been noticed in the archipelago and that they bear the testimony of human presence much earlier than ever supposed, in the Middle Paleolithic, likely to be over 50,000 years old.

So far, thanks to fundamental research of the late Luigi Bernabo Brea, it had been believed that the island of Lipari, like other Aeolian islands, had been reached by man for the first time in the Neolithic, around 5,000 years ago. This discovery increases the duration of human history by ten times.

How can we interpret this find? More extensive explorations to other areas of the archipelago should be

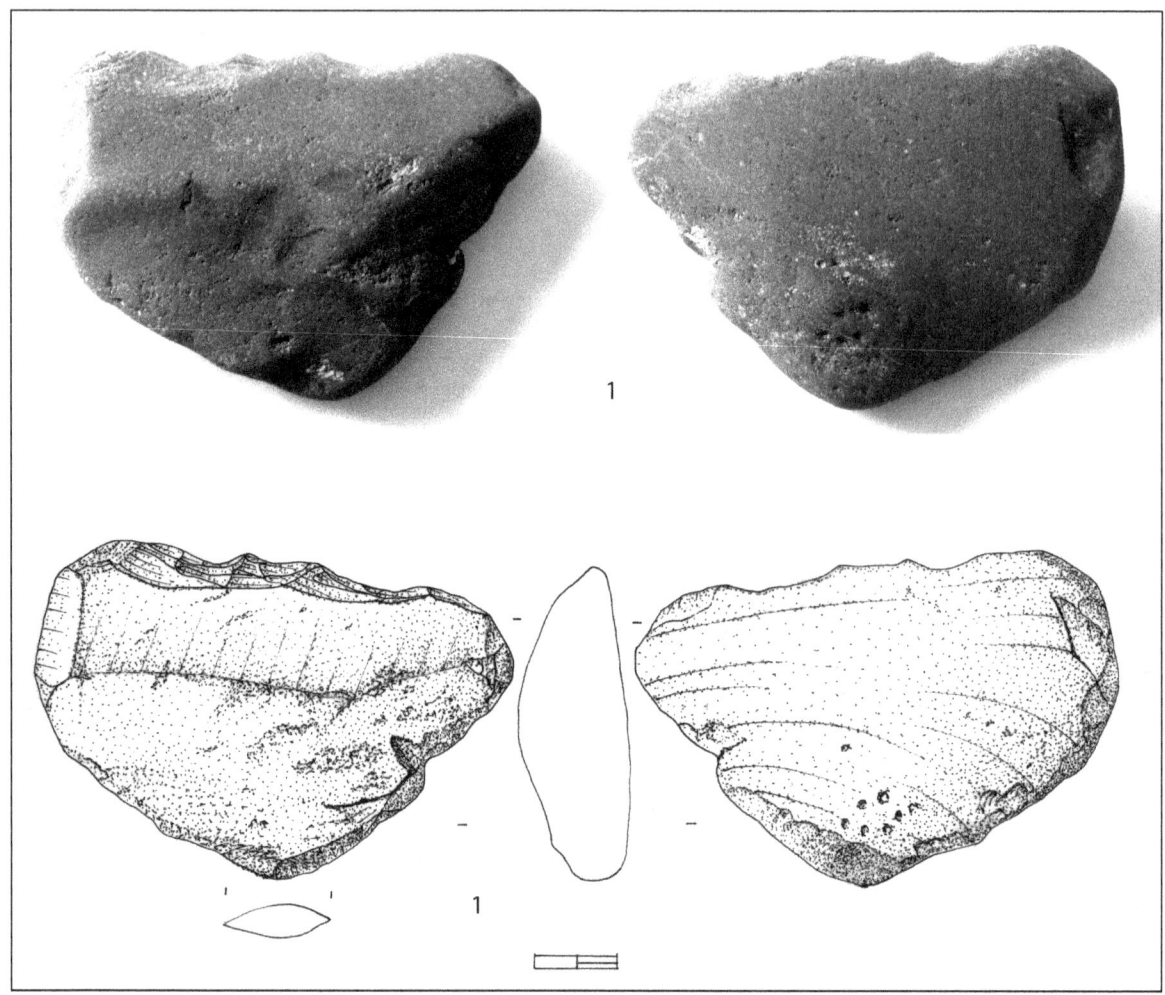

Figure 5 – Canneto, Lipari: transverse scraper with abrupt retouch. Evident bulb of percussion (drawing Ida Mailland)

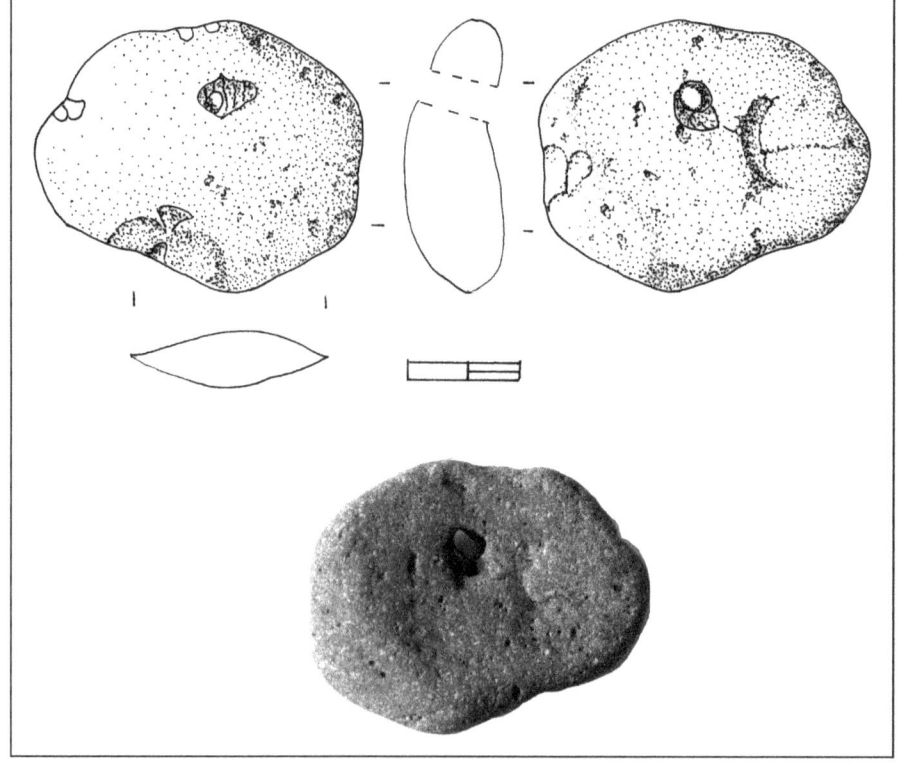

Figure 6 – Canneto, Lipari: stone with natural hole, retouched, completed and rounded (drawing Ida Mailland)

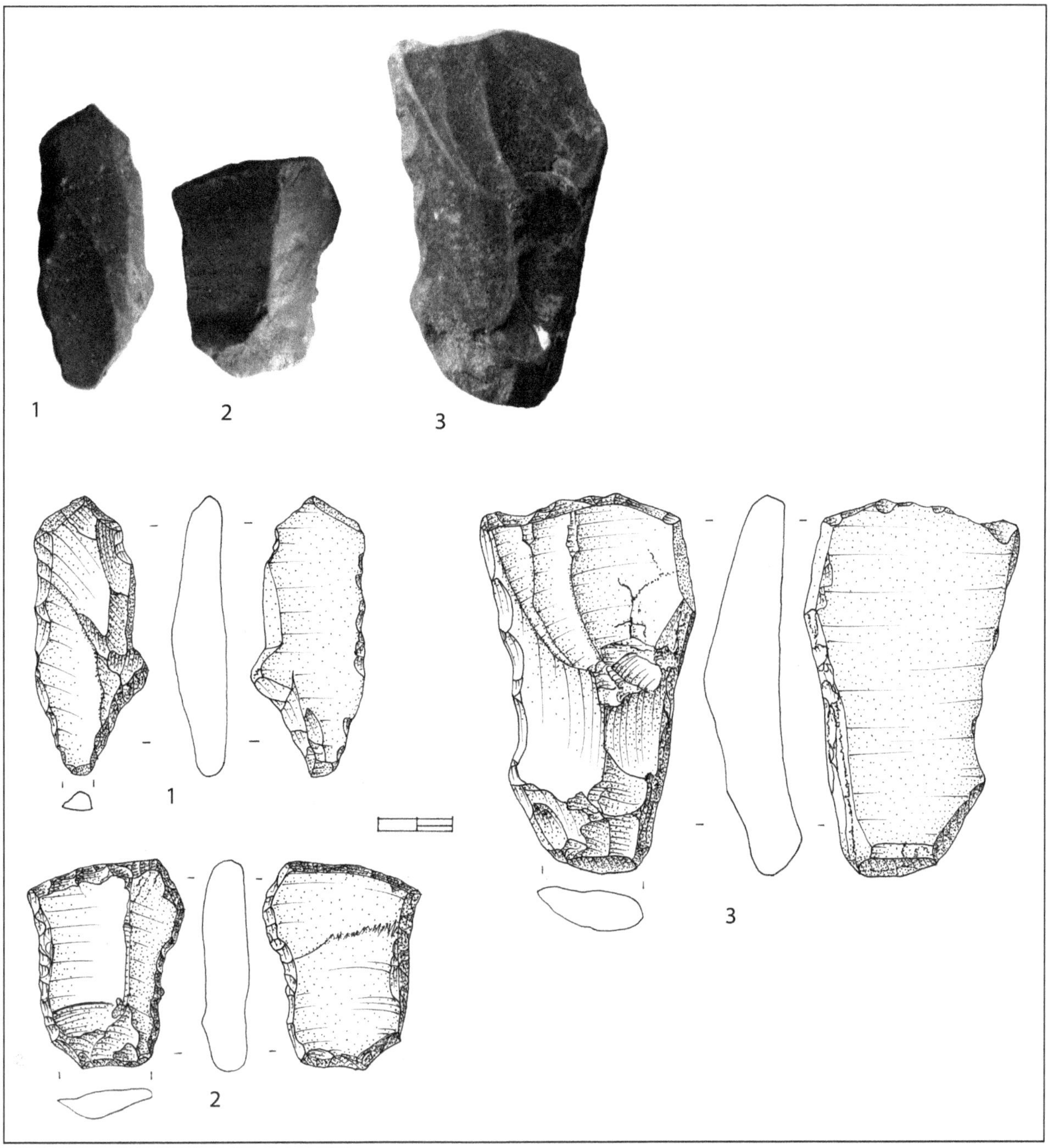

Figure 7 – Canneto, Lipari: 1, 3: Scrapers on blade; 2: scraper on flake (drawing Ida Mailland)

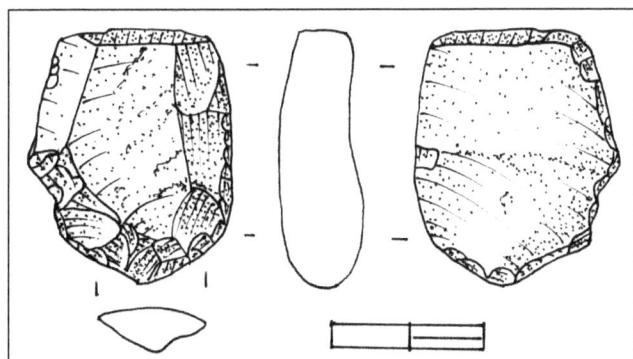

Figure 8 – Canneto, Lipari: Levallois flake (truncated) with evident bulb of percussion and retouched platform (drawing Ida Mailland)

encouraged, even if the archaeological survey carried on for four decades makes it unlikely to find other unexpected finds like this one. We cannot for the moment consider a continued, persistent presence of man since early times, as other Paleolithic traces in the Aeolian islands are unknown for the moment. It is likely that this discovery indicates an adventitious and short presence of a small human group.

The hypothesis that a major food resource along the coast was derived from the presence of marine mammals may suggest that such mammals found refuge in the islands, where they would remain undisturbed by the Neanderthal predators. This may suggest an explanation for the adventure of a small Middle Paleolithic human group

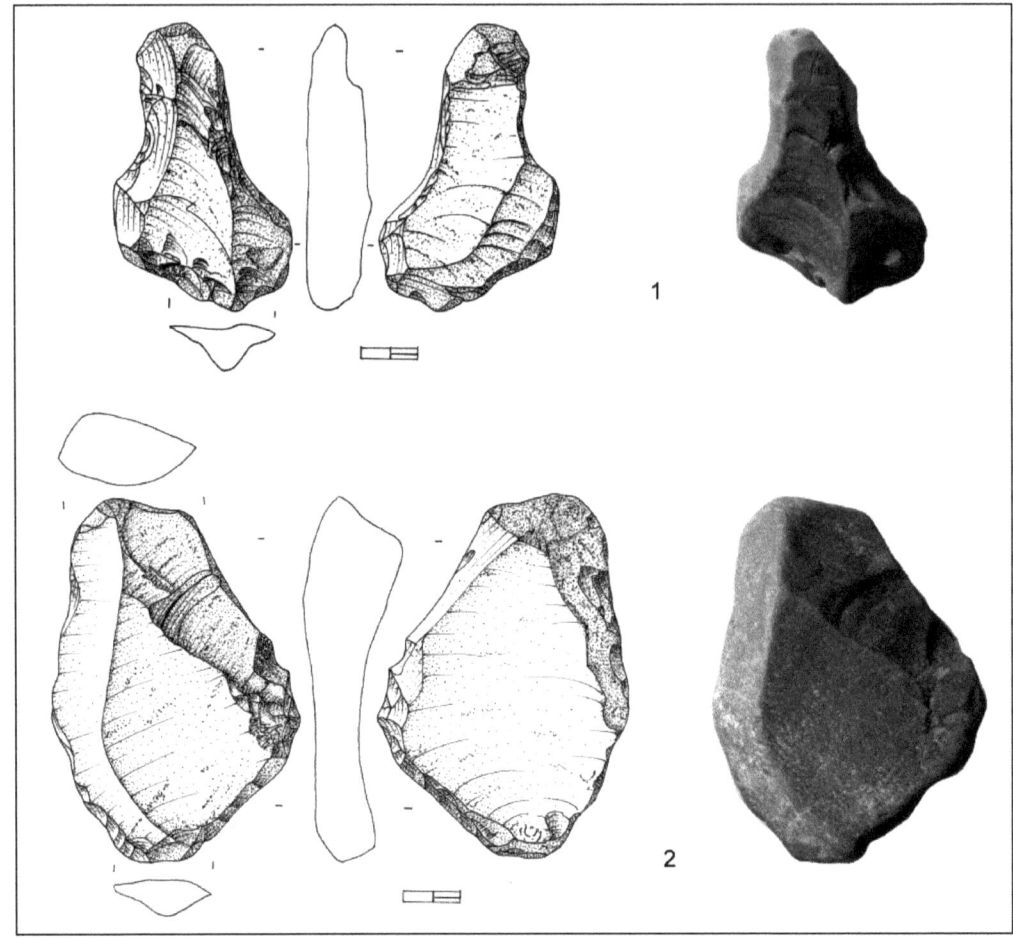

Figure 9 – Canneto, Lipari: 1: reutilized Levallois core with two notches; 2: flake detouched by recurrent Levallois technique. Evident bulb of percussion (drawing Ida Mailland)

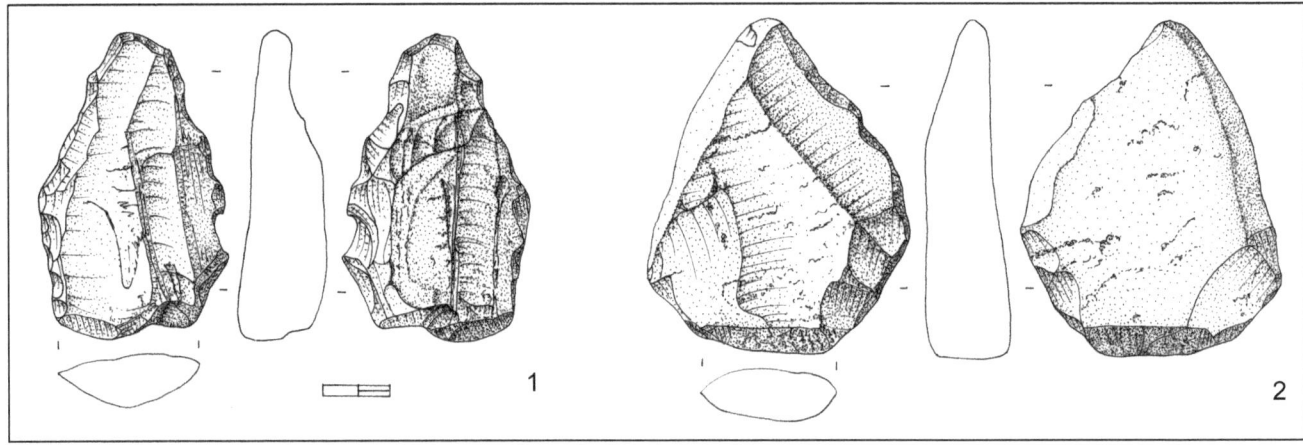

Figure 10 – Canneto, Lipari: retouched splinters (drawing Ida Mailland)

evidenced by this discovery. Such incursions of hunter-gatherers to nearby islands are recorded in various parts of the World, in off shore Australian islands, in the Fuegian archipelago at the southernmost end of South America, in the Canadian far north and elsewhere. It is not surprising that it took place also in Europe. But it is useful to have now a documentation on such early seafaring off the shores of Europe.

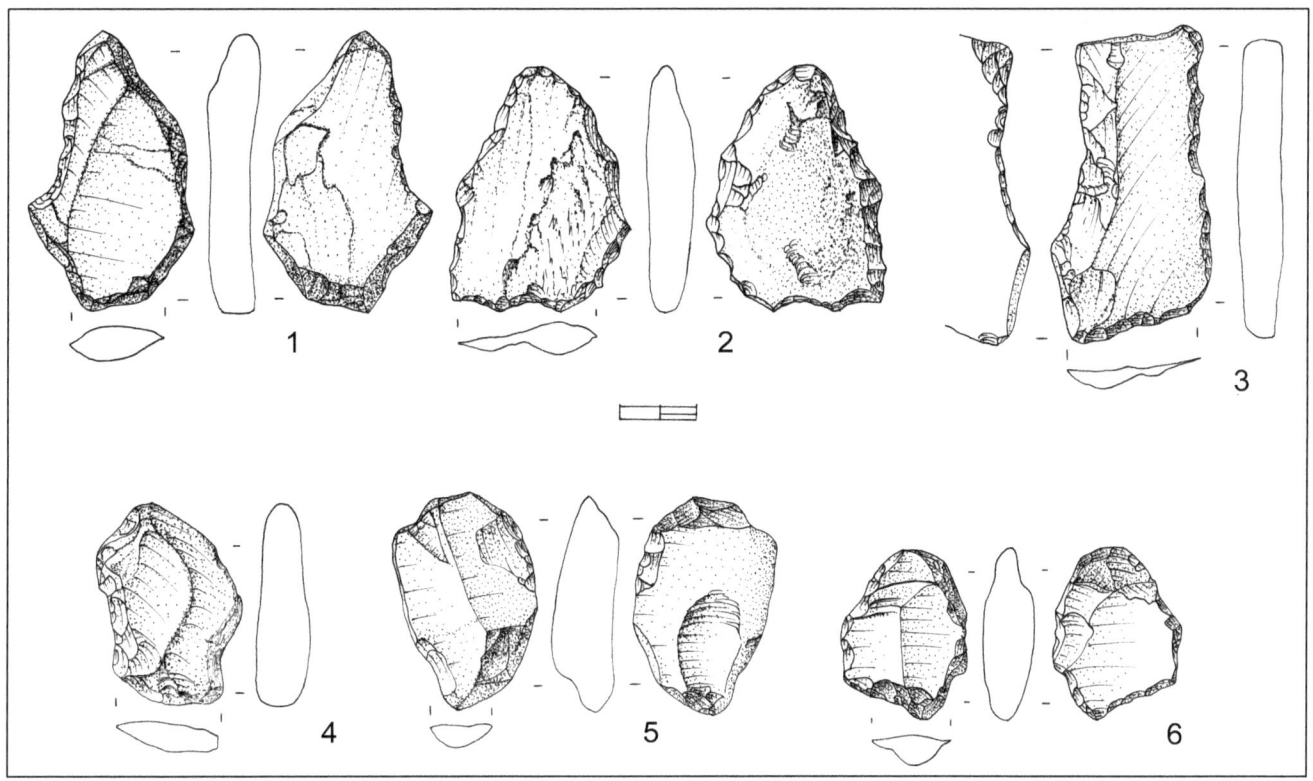

Figure 11 – Canneto, Lipari: 1-2, 4-6: retouched splinters; 3: borer on backed blade (drawing Ida Mailland)

APPENDIX:

THE LITHIC ASSEMBLAGE OF CANNETO (LIPARI)

Federico MAILLAND

Director, CISPE, Centro Internazionale di Studi Preistorici ed Etnologici, Italy

The lithic assemblage of Canneto consists of a small number of retouched tools made by andesite. This is an extrusive igneous, volcanic rock of intermediate composition between basalt and dacite. It is common both in the Aeolian archipelago and on Mt. Etna. The lithic implements are deeply eroded, most probably due to alluvial phenomena, and they have been transported down to the bottom of a narrow valley, where they have been found on the surface, from an upper location which has not yet been recognized. Obvious tools were collected from hundreds of similar chipped stones and fragments, but I had access only to collected tools.

A description of the lithic industry is reported as follows.

Cores: only one item may be defined as a true core. It is a unipolar Levallois core reutilized by flaking two notches on the two sides by bifacial retouch. The platform is also retouched (figure 9,1). A second tool, which could be interpreted as a core, is rather a deep flake detached by recurrent Levallois technique from an unipolar core. In fact, bulb of percussion is still present on the ventral face (figure 9,2).

Blades: they are defined according to the standard rules by length/width ratio $\geq 2:1$. Three items have been found, which classify the tools as having been made on laminar support: a side scraper with borer (figure 7,1); a scraper on blade with invasive retouch of the dorsal face, the platform was also retouched, by almost completely removing the bulb of percussion (figure 7,2). The third tool is a borer on backed blade with double side-scraper retouch (figure 11,3).

Flakes: the vast majority of the collected tools was produced on a flake support.

Points (n=5): four typical Mousterian points have been collected, three of them retouched on both margins (figure 4,2-5). One Levallois point (unipolar detachment) had been also retouched on both margins. Bulb of percussion well evident (figure 4,1).

Scrapers (n=3): one transverse scraper with abrupt retouch and bulb of percussion still evident (figure 5). One scraper with continuous retouch and borer (figure 7,3). One side scraper on a Levallois flake (truncated) detached by recurrent, unipolar technique. Bulb of percussion still present although retouched platform (figure 8).

Splinters (n=7): one denticulate (figure 10,1), two retouched Levallois flakes (figures 10,2 and 11,1). One splinter with removal of percussion bulb (figure 11,5) and 3 other retouched splinters (figures 11,2: 11,4 and 11,6).

The characteristics of the lithic industry have been summarized as follows: flakes 80%, blades 15%, Levallois index 30%, points 25%, scrapers 30%, borers 10%, denticulate 5%. When evident, the Levallois technique was always defined as recurrent, unipolar.

In conclusion, and within the limits of this scanty collection, due to the described characteristics, the lithic complex of Canneto may be classified under the complex of typical Mousterian, Levallois *facies*, according to the classification of Bordes.

Reference

BORDES, F. & BOURGON M. 1953 Levalloisien et Moustérien, Bulletin de la Société Préhistorique Française, 50: 226-235.

THE PALEOLITHIC SANCTUARY AT HAR KARKOM, NEGEV DESERT

Emmanuel ANATI

President, CISPE, Centro Internazionale di Studi Preistorici ed Etnologici, Italy
Director, CCSP, Centro Camuno di Studi Preistorici, Italy
Director, Italian archeological project at Har Karkom, Negev, Israel

Abstract: *The earliest known sanctuary at the mountain of Har Karkom, in the Negev desert, belonging to an early phase of the Upper Paleolithic, sheds new light on a mountain which was a cult place in the Chalcolithic period and the Bronze Age. Cult traditions have persisted for thousands of years. The choice of the cult place appears to have depended on the natural features of the landscape. The cult of ancestors was replaced, in later times, by other kinds of worship.*

INTRODUCTION

The discovery of a group of large flint standing stones and small flint figurines in the context of Paleolithic flint implements at Har Karkom, a mountain in the Negev desert, awakened a debate about its significance. The site, which was recorded as HK/86b, does not appear to have any economic or habitation function. We shall further consider the reasons that justify it being called a Paleolithic sanctuary. Whatever the case may be, why should Paleolithic people assemble about 40 such boulders and erect them in a small valley on the edge of a mountain? And why just there?

Since 1980 archeological research in the Israeli Negev desert, the northeastern territory of the Sinai Peninsula, has been the object of the Italian archeological research project of CISPE (International Centre for Prehistoric and Ethnological Research). A systematic survey of a research concession of 200 sq. km, in a desert territory where no relics of the past were previously known, has revealed more than 1,300 archeological sites and is now an exceptional natural museum. Over 300 of these sites belong to the Paleolithic period. The site HK86b is a unique case of a Paleolithic monumental installation.

THE CONTEXT

The research concession, which is located near the Egyptian border, between the towns of Eilat and Mitzpe Ramon, includes Har Karkom and the surrounding valleys. This mountain is a high plateau surrounded by precipices. It is located in a stony desert with an annual rainfall of less than 50 mm. The top of Har Karkom is just 847 m above sea level, overlooking the Paran desert which is about 500 m above sea level at the foot of the mountain and falls to around 250 m below sea level when it reaches the Arava valley near the Dead Sea (Figure 1).

In the Chalcolithic period and the Bronze Age over 120 sanctuaries, shrines, altars, circles of standing pillars and other cult structures indicate its role as a paramount sacred mountain in the middle of the desert. The assumption that Har Karkom is the mountain which the Bible calls Mount Sinai has generated debate among biblical scholars, geographers and archeologists. It is 200 km north of the monastery of St Catherine which is traditionally considered to be the location of Mount Sinai and such identification would mean reconsidering the generally accepted vision of the biblical itinerary of Exodus. Moving the location of the holiest site in the three major monotheistic religions about 200 km is not easily accepted by theologians, biblical scholars, geographers and archeologists. The debate is still open. In any case there is no doubt about the fact that Har Karkom was a very important holy mountain and a gathering or pilgrimage place in the Bronze Age. The problem is whether Har Karkom is the biblical Mount Sinai or a Mount Sinai. The detailed large-scale archeological surveys and excavations carried on all over the Sinai Peninsula in the 20th century have not so far revealed any other mountain having such a wealth of Bronze Age cult sites.

The discovery of a Paleolithic sanctuary marks a new aspect of this debate, as it indicates that the cult role of the mountain goes far back in time, practically since *Homo sapiens* stepped on it for the first time.

The flint industry found at site HK/86b belongs to the Karkomian culture, the same industry found in 22 living sites with clear plans of hut foundations in an area of 4 sq. km around the sanctuary. The flint industry is considered to belong to the early Upper Paleolithic. Along with flint tools and blades typical of the early phases of the Upper Paleolithic, it includes implements of flakes having a Middle Paleolithic character related to the Levalloisian flaking technique, a peculiarity which occurs in all the sites of the same cultural horizon.

In the Bronze Age, the Har Karkom plateau was reserved for religious activities and the habitation sites were at the foot of the mountain, where there are remains of more than 100 living sites. The high plateau has many Bronze Age places of worship: a temple, numerous small shrines,

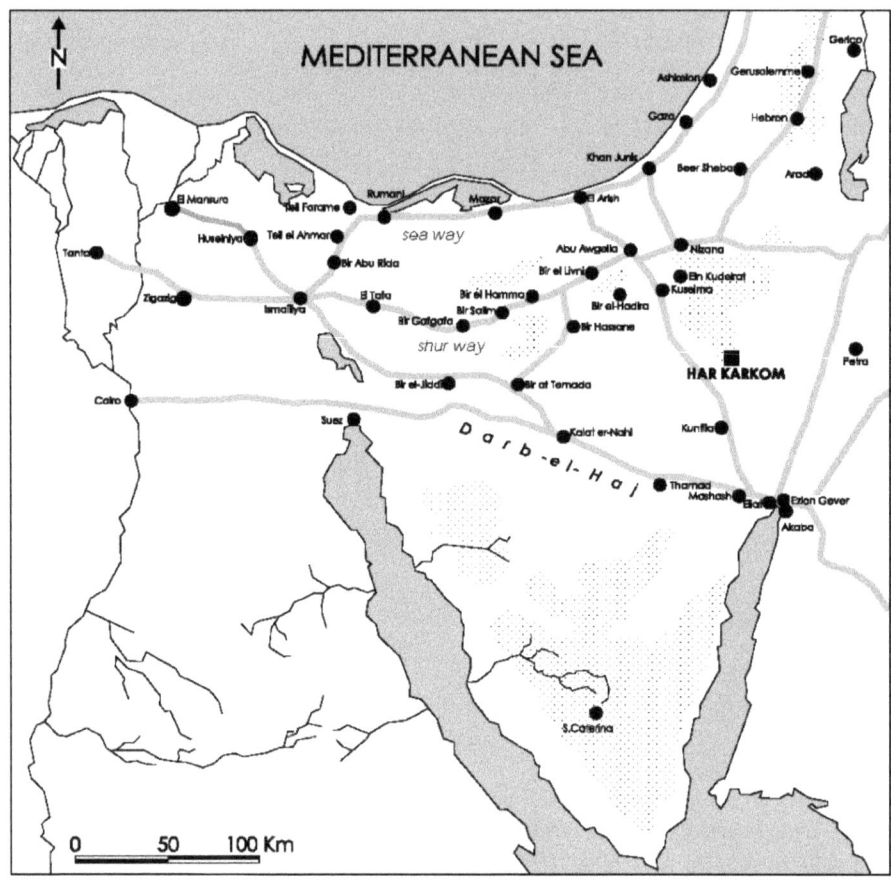

Figure 1 – Location of Har Karkom in the Sinai peninsula [after Anati 2006]

several altars, standing pillars or stele, platforms for offerings, cairns and stone circles. (Other temples and shrines are located at the foot of the mountain, near the habitation sites.) Since the last process of desertification started, dry conditions and strong winds carried away the light soil and paleo-soils emerged at the surface. Levels thousands of years old became exposed, with tools and traces of fireplaces in situ, as if they had been just abandoned. The high plateau is dotted with Paleolithic encampments in a state of unusually good preservation, with well-defined hut foundations clustered in small hamlets; remains of fireplaces, flint workshops and paleo-soils with incrustations of flint implements are still in situ, where they have been preserved for millennia.

Such excellent preservation generates doubts about the possibility that the people living in the many numerous Bronze Age living sites located in the surrounding valleys had free access to the mountain, as if so these Paleolithic sites would not have been so well preserved. Obviously the plateau with the Paleolithic remains did not receive many human visits, since the sites were abandoned thousands of years ago. It was deduced that in the Bronze Age the access to the mountain plateau must have been reserved for a selected few who built the shrines and altars, likely to have been leaders or priests.

The use of taboo for access to a sacred mountain is also referred to in the Bible in connection with Mount Sinai. The sacred mountain was forbidden to the common people; access was reserved for the high priest, in this case Moses. It is likely that thanks to this kind of prohibition the Paleolithic monuments, like this unique sanctuary, have been preserved until today.

While in later periods the mountain plateau was void of habitation sites, having only remains of worship places, during the Paleolithic it was a preferred location for living sites that are much more densely concentrated on the plateau than in surrounding valleys (239 Paleolithic sites were identified on the plateau in an area of about 8 sq. km). For many of these sites the entire plan of the hamlet could be reconstructed, including the location of huts, common areas, flint workshops, fireplaces and many other details, thus obtaining vast documentation on the habits and daily life of their inhabitants. The wealth of material culture, flint tools and other stone implements permitted the definition of the periods to which these settlements belong in the course of many millennia. Some belong to the Lower Paleolithic, but most of them belong to the Middle and early Upper Paleolithic and the different organization of the plans reveals different social structures, ranging from the large communal living structures of the Middle Paleolithic to the clusters of smaller huts in the early phases of the Upper Paleolithic. The Karkomian sites have this second type of typology and despite the persistent tradition of Middle Paleolithic flint flaking, it is considered to belong to the beginning of the Upper Paleolithic; the flint industry of the sanctuary belongs to this context.

In six out of 22 sites of this culture on the plateau, figurines have been found of flint nodules having natural vaguely anthropomorphic shapes, being completed or just partly shaped by human hands, with occasional incisions representing eyes, nose, breasts and other features to complete the natural shapes. These figurines are often grouped together with other flint pebbles having peculiar shapes but without manual intervention, hinting at the probable intentional collection of natural anthropomorphic and zoomorphic shapes by Paleolithic peoples.

THE SANCTUARY

Site HK86b is located in a small chalky valley on the edge of the precipice. Forty dark-brown flint boulders, mostly with anthropomorphic natural shapes, up to 1.40 m high, are concentrated in a relatively small space of around 15 x 30 m (Figures 2 and 3). Some of them were still standing, others had fallen down. Some of these boulders had been gathered in the immediate vicinity as they are of the same kind of flint surfacing in a local flint layer; others of a different kind of flint are likely to have been brought there from flint layers which are found at a certain distance.

Traces of geoglyphs (or pebble drawings) on the paleo-soil are found at some 30 m from the standing stones above the northern edge of the valley. They consist of alignments of flint pebbles, including cores and flakes. Some of them have been formed into round or oval lines. Flint implements are found on the hard soil. Several flint figurines of different size have been collected, mainly in the area of the geoglyphs.

According to the position of the standing stones (monoliths or orthostats) and of the small stones at their feet used to hold them standing, the original Paleolithic paleo-soil appears to have been eroded and to have been slightly higher than the present surface in certain spots. Elsewhere, the original paleo-soil with incrustations of flint implements and with traces of geoglyphs appears to coincide with the present stepping ground level.

The standing flint stones, mostly having anthropomorphic shapes (Figure 4), and concentrated in this small valley on the edge of the cliff, create a breathtaking landscape. Arriving from the surrounding hilly plateau one suddenly sees an unexpected group of dark 'beings' made of stone in a half-hidden whiteish narrow valley. Some of them are arranged in a sort of circle, others accompany the beginning of the trail that starts there to descend through the precipice to the Paran desert below. Whatever the function of this installation may have been, it is structured according to a conceptual order. On one side there are flint monoliths with anthropomorphic shapes, appearing as silent guardian spirits. On the other side there is paleo-soil with geoglyphs or alignments of flint stones on the paleo-soil; also there is a concentration of flints, including flint pebbles probably collected because of their anthropomorphic and zoomorphic natural shapes. Some of them have been retouched by flaking (Figures 5-

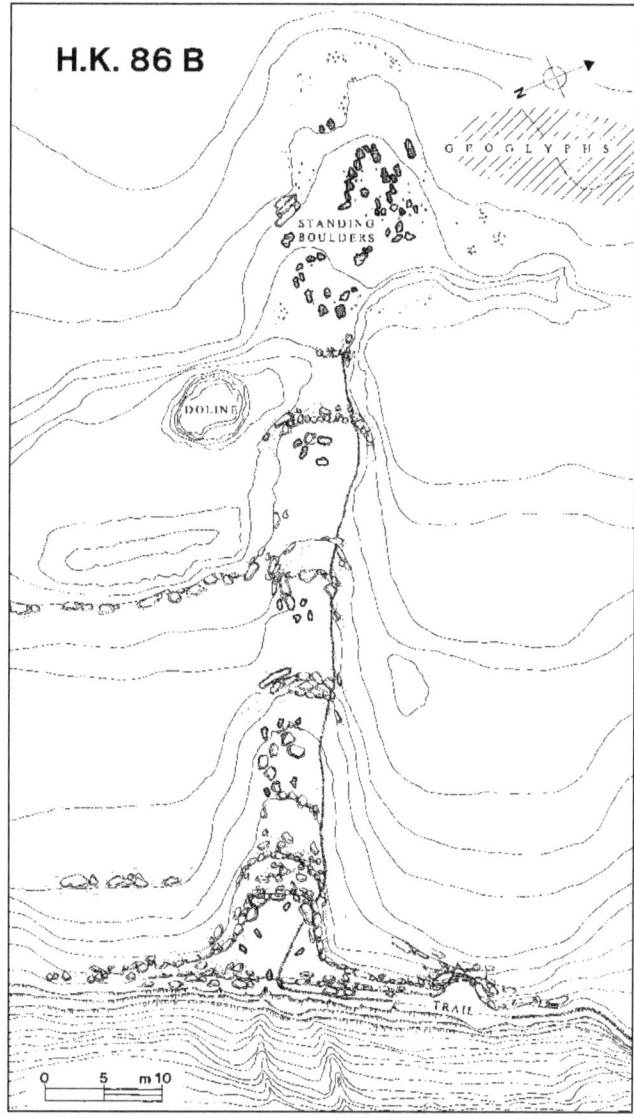

Figure 2 – Plan of the site HK/86b and the underlying terraces (drawing L. Cottinelli)

7) to enhance the shape and adding engraved lines to mark the eyes or other details to complete the natural shapes. Both these figurines and the standing monoliths have natural anthropomorphic and zoomorphic forms, and their presence is the result of the same process. They have been collected because of their natural form and have been enhanced by the active action of human hands.

Several of the monoliths weigh over 200 kg. Man selected them, brought them to the place, organized them and occasionally retouched them. Some of them have thin engravings of parallel lines and of crossing lines like tattoos on the stone body. Others have flaking to reshape details. This installation is likely to have been created with some purpose in mind.

What events or performances may have taken place in this 'sanctuary'? We can only assume, by comparison with more recent similar tribal shrines, that it might have been a place for initiation, meditation, socialization or the evocation of traditions and myths. We can say that much

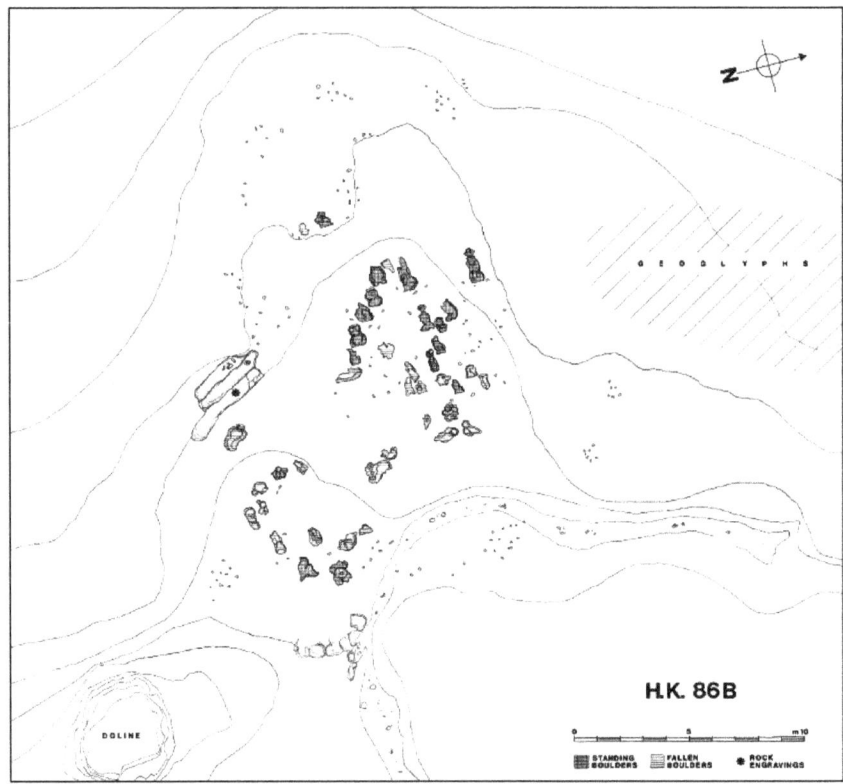

Figure 3 – Plan of the site HK/86b: particular (drawing L. Cottinelli)

Figure 4 – Flint orthostats of the site HK86b
(after Anati 2001)

energy was invested in the installation work of setting up the monoliths and making geoglyphs. The findings illustrate a concern for the exploration and understanding of nature, the meaning of natural forms, the human–animal and human-environment relations. The installation has a conceptual background.

Another question arises. The peculiar choice of site, the erection of orthostats, their position which looks to us like aesthetic environmental architecture performed by humans selecting and using natural forms: can all this be considered art or proto-art? There is not a true creation of forms, but there is a search for and selection of natural forms: man has chosen the forms he has sorted and has located them in specific places. Can such an installation be considered as art? The installation emphasizes a concern for the character and forms of nature, and an interest in collecting stone shapes (and perhaps objects of wood and other organic materials that have not been preserved). With their form, the collected monoliths evoke anthropomorphic and some also zoomorphic beings.

In the Bronze Age the mountain of Har Karkom was a holy mountain with numerous remains of hamlets at its foot which testify to the presence of people in the middle of the desert. It was a sort of prehistoric Mecca. As mentioned already, site HK86b is much older, belonging to the Karkomian culture in the early Upper Paleolithic. We cannot say if there was an uninterrupted cult tradition, but we may be certain that the people who created the Bronze Age cult sites were aware of this earlier site and probably they were influenced by it.

The precise date of this site has not been established so far, as no organic material was found for C-14 analyses.

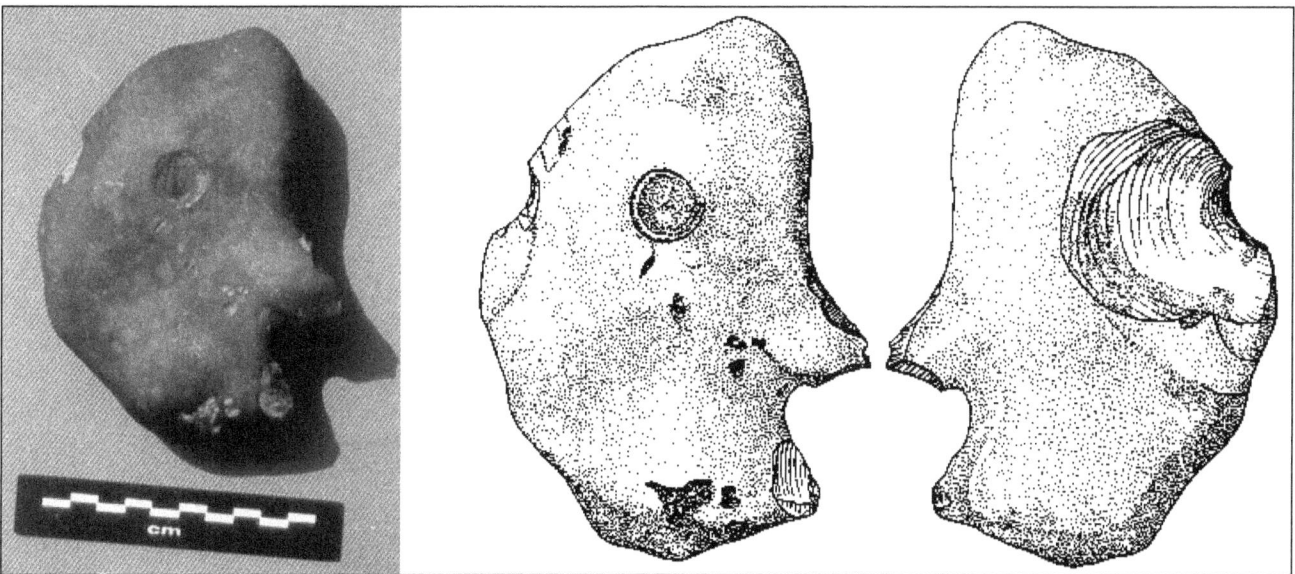

Figure 5 – Photograph and tracing of a flint nodule with a natural form of a human face, completed by man with secondary retouching, some flaking, and a thin line to complete the eye. (drawing Ida Mailland) (after Anati 2001)

Figure 6 – A flint nodule in the form of a bird retouched in the tail and base with flaking. Finely incised lines define the eyes and beak (after Anati 2010)

The tentative dating to between 45,000 and 35,000 years ago is a working hypothesis; it may be reductive and the installation could be older. According to the flint industry it is likely to be older than the cave art found in Europe. In this respect, the selection of natural shapes and their partial reshaping by flaking and incisions is a peculiar feature of the Karkomian culture which makes us define the shaped objects as proto-art, rather than art. Human and animal figures will remain thereafter, all over Eurasia, throughout the entire Upper Paleolithic period, the main subject matter of figurative images.

THE ROLE OF THE LANDSCAPE

This HK86b site lies in a half-hidden valley on the edge of the precipice and it is surrounded by several habitation

Figure 7 – left: zoomorphic flint nodule retouched on the upper and lower edges, and with a large flake on the right side; right: Flint nodule with three hammered dots, which probably indicate the eyes and mouth of an anthropomorphic face (after Anati 2010)

Figure 8 – Aerial view of the prehistoric trail (marked by dotted line) which descends from the sanctuary towards the Paran desert (after Anati 2001)

sites of the same period, with the same kind of lithic industry. It is likely to have served these several hamlets and to have been created as a joint effort of a certain number of adult people. It lies on the mountain, facing a broad panorama, overlooking valleys and hills all the way to the Edom and Moab mountain ranges over 60 km to the east. It looks towards the east where the sun rises. The choice of the site must have taken into consideration the immense open view of the landscape and the position on the cliff on the edge of the precipice. It is halfway between the hilly country, the hunting ground below and the mountain tops above, at the point where the trail coming from the hunting ground below reaches the plateau where the living sites are located (Figure 8).

From many sites in various continents we know that the landscape inside caves has interested and inspired prehistoric and tribal man and he has produced his graphic art as part of the landscape. He has not made art to describe what was there already but has added to and completed the landscape with his creations. According to hunter-gatherer populations, inside the caves every stalagmite, every natural shape, was not casual, but created by the ancestral spirits with a purpose, and they conveyed messages which the humans had to decipher. Natural monumental installations offered by the landscape are often completed by man, not only in caves but also in the open air. This significant expression of the primary concept of landscape appears to be a common feature of more recent hunter-gatherer groups in various parts of the world.

The narrow valley develops into a small crevice and a now dry cascade down the precipice. Its location on the edge of the mountain is between two large curves. When looked at from the Paran desert, these cliffs look like a couple of wide-open legs over 1 km long; the valley and its small crevice are at their junction. The black stones stand there, springing out of the vagina of the mountain. Without a somehow speculative analysis of this setting the so-called 'Paleolithic sanctuary' would remain meaningless. This unique site looking east dominates the immensity of the Paran desert below the cliff (Figure 9), likely to have been grassland at that time, and the edge of the mountain in the shape of open legs.

Looking west, one sees the two hill-tops of the mountain similar to women's breasts facing the sky (Figure 10). The landscape appears to have been conceived as a huge female body. The standing dark stones emerge between the legs, in the vagina of the female mountain. This deeply conceptual installation was conceived by Paleolithic hunter-gatherers.

With the help of our knowledge of the attempts to decipher the landscape by more recent hunter-gatherers, we may try a tentative reconstruction of the conceptual background of this installation. The location of the 'sanctuary' was selected because of the meaning attributed to the landscape. Why just there? Because it had a meaning in this setting, because the standing stones completed or added meaning to the landscape. Ancestral spirits are reborn, they come out of the womb of the mountain where they are to join the community of their living offspring.

The similarity to an Aboriginal site in the Kimberley may reveal common denominators in the reading of the

Figure 9 – Eastward view of the Paran desert, with the Paleolithic sanctuary in the foreground (after Anati 2001)

Figure 10 – View of the two "breasts," the two summits of Har Karkom, from the Palaeolithic sanctuary, site HK 86b (after Anati 2001)

landscape among early hunters. There, on the seashore, a group of standing stones are considered to be the ancestral spirits coming from the sea to enter the 'promised land' where their offspring have survived ever since and still live.

At Har Karkom, people coming out of Africa reached the mountain overlooking grassland which may have been a wealthy hunting ground. From the Paleolithic sanctuary, some 40,000 years ago, they looked at their 'promised land'. And they were accompanied by their ancestors reborn from the vagina of the holy mountain. The standing stones and the accompanying material culture are the archeological testimony. But without understanding the landscape setting they would have been almost meaningless. In this contest the geoglyphs may signify the itinerary, a mythical itinerary, or the trail to help the ancestral spirits find their way to join their living offspring. Similar depictions of mythical itineraries are commonly produced in commemorative ceremonies by various tribal populations, from the American Plain Indians to the San people of southern Africa, to the Australian Aborigines of the Central Desert.

CONCLUSIONS

It seems that the Har Karkom Paleolithic sanctuary emphasizes how prehistoric man studied and tried to decode the landscape. The analytical and metaphorical process is analogous to that of the Canadian Inuit, the Australian Aborigines and other present-day hunter-gatherers in various parts of the world. For them not a single feature of the landscape is meaningless, as every form has a reason for being. Here the interplay between natural forms and human intervention reflects one of the major trends which shaped the destiny of *Homo sapiens*: the total synergy and interplay between man and his natural environment in order to understand the messages and the meaning of the landscape.

References

ANATI, E. 2001 The Riddle of Mount Sinai, Archaeological discoveries at Har Karkom. Edizioni del Centro. Capo di Ponte.

ANATI, E. 2006 Har Karkom. A Guide to Major Sites. Edizioni del Centro. Capo di Ponte.

ANATI, E. 2010 La riscoperta del Monte Sinai. Ritrovamenti archeologici alla luce del racconto dell'Esodo. Edizioni Messaggero. Padova.

THE KARKOMIAN FLINT INDUSTRY: THE CONTEXT OF THE HAR KARKOM SANCTUARY AT THE TRANSITION BETWEEN MIDDLE AND UPPER PALEOLITHIC (NEGEV, ISRAEL)

Federico MAILLAND

Director, CISPE, Centro Internazionale di Studi Preistorici ed Etnologici (Italy)
Co-Director, Italian archeological project at Har Karkom (Negev, Israel)

Abstract: This report describes the flint industry found at the Paleolithic Sanctuary of Har Karkom and in 21 living sites around it. The character of the flint industry allows us to consider the chronological location of a unique testimony of prehistoric spirituality. The survey of the sanctuary and of the living sites led to considering them as short-lasting stations, which may have hosted groups of 20–30 individuals each.

The collection of over 800 flint implements from these sites allowed us to describe the lithic industry as characterized by tools and blades typical of the early phases of the Upper Paleolithic, which included also flakes made by a Levallois-type technique.

The main features include a slight prevalence of flakes (53.6%) over blades (42.2%), over 13% presence of denticulates on either support, notches and lateral borers. Also frequent are Mousterian-type points and Levallois points, with obverse platform blunting. This particular flint industry is called Karkomian, which due to its peculiar features appears to reflect a transitional facies between Middle and Upper Paleolithic. In the absence of human or other organic remains, considering the general cultural context of the Middle East and other Levantine transitional Paleolithic industries, it is tentatively considered to date around 40,000 BP.

PALEOLITHIC REMAINS AT HAR KARKOM

The mountain of Har Karkom is located in southern Negev, east of Sinai peninsula and was the object of a 30-year survey by the Italian archeological project directed by Emmanuel Anati (Anati & Mailland 2009). Har Karkom had intense frequentation during the Paleolithic period, as revealed by the remains of hundreds of Paleolithic sites on the flat surface of the plateau. Their careful survey was rendered possible by the unusually good preservation state of the Paleolithic campsites, because in later times the Har Karkom plateau was reserved for religious activities and the habitation sites were at the foot of the mountain. Remains of Paleolithic hut floors, fireplaces, flint workshops, remains of paleosoils with flint implements, are still *in situ*, where they have been preserved for millennia. Moreover, due to the erosive phenomena the soil is presently lower than in the ancient times and this revealed the ancient remains on the plateau surface. The area was carefully surveyed and the Paleolithic sites were classified according to the lithic industry left at the sites.

The Har Karkom population paralleled the curve of climate which had a long pluvial period between 70,000 and 28,000 years BP. In fact, the most intense frequentation of the mountain and of the surroundings was shown from the late Middle Paleolithic until the early Upper Paleolithic, with findings of Middle Paleolithic industry in 137 sites and of early Upper Paleolithic in 139 sites, the vast majority of them on top of the mountain (Anati and F. Mailland 2009a). Middle Paleolithic sites were characterized by a Mousterian flint industry, mostly on flakes obtained by the Levallois technique of flint knapping. Aterian-like tanged flint implements were also present. The majority of Upper Paleolithic sites were characterized by a leptolithic flint industry typical of the Levantine Aurignacian.

The investigation of the ceremonial site called a 'Paleolithic sanctuary' at the site HK/86b by the Italian archeological project directed by E. Anati (Anati et al. 1996; Anati and F. Mailland 2009b) led to the discovery of an interesting flint industry, characterized by a persistence of Middle Paleolithic flint knapping, associated with an incoming leptolithic flint flaking technique. Due to its particular features, the culture associated with this flint industry was called Karkomian, and is believed to represent a transition between Middle Paleolithic and Upper Paleolithic. This flint industry was found in the ceremonial site, and in 21 living sites all around the sanctuary, all of them having in common the remains of clusters of small hut floors, with a large central hut for the daily activities of the clan, surrounded by a few smaller huts, where family units of a few individuals spent the night. Many Karkomian campsites were provided with fireplaces located outside the huts; smaller areas cleared of stones, with flint cores, flakes and implements scattered among the surroundings, have been interpreted as flint workshops, where refitting of flint cores was often feasible. The findings are consistent with groups of 20–30 individuals and the paucity of flint implements is consistent with short-lasting stops of even just a few days. They are located in the eastern part of the plateau, on a north-south line, and face a small valley near the ravine border, where the ceremonial site is located (Figure 1). The sanctuary and the living sites have in common the transitional characteristics of flint knapping, as well as in some of them clusters of 'figurines', small flint stones (about 10–20 cm long) with anthropozoomorphic shapes, some of them roughly retouched to provide some anatomical parts, including

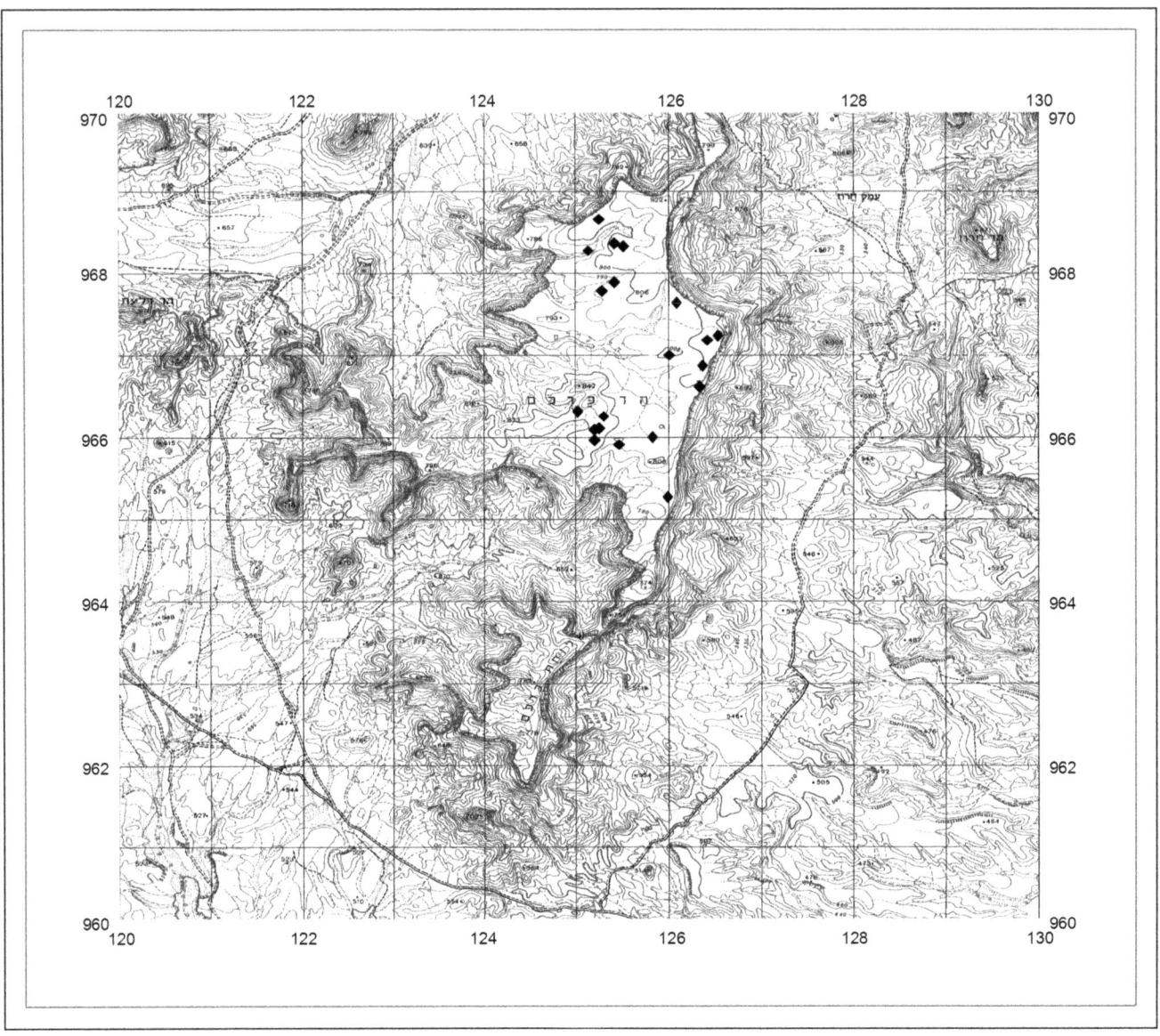

Figure 1 – Har Karkom: map of sites with Karkomian flint industry.
The star shows the position of the ceremonial site HK/86b

eye, mouth, breast and pubic triangle, indicating a sort of proto-art, which implies the presence of conceptual ideas at a very early phase of Upper Paleolithic (F. Mailland 2007; I. Mailland 2009).

THE KARKOMIAN FLINT INDUSTRY

The flint collection from 13 Karkomian sites, including the ceremonial site HK/86b and 12 living sites, allowed the classification of 813 flint artefacts: moreover, it was possible to make a statistical comparison among these sites and a descriptive analysis of the whole lithic assemblage.

The characters of the lithic industry in the Karkomian sites are reported in Table 1. The findings are illustrated in Figures 2–6. The characters appeared as sufficiently homogeneous among the different sites, certain differences being due to the small number of artefacts per individual site. Levallois technique was evident in all sites, at 1.69–4.88% of all flint artefacts, and was on average 3.20% of the overall sample. Blades varied between 18.87% and 63.01% of all flint artefacts; conversely, flakes varied between 32.88% and 75.47%. A characterristic common to all sites was the abundant presence of denticulate retouch and of transverse scrapers.

A descriptive analysis of the whole lithic assemblage is reported in Table 2.

Definitions and descriptions of the artefacts are as follows.

Cores: out of the 33 cores, 18.2% are defined as Levallois cores, having been used to detach flakes by Levallois technique. Another 18.2% are polyhedrons, a kind of bolas used for hunting. Finally, 21.2% were reutilized cores, i.e. retouched to use them as implements, including an end scraper and a denticulate.

Table 1 Characters of the lithic industry in the different Karkomian sites (percent calculated on total artefacts of the site)

Site HK/	87b	17	191a	74c	74d	75e	86b	Pool*	Total
Total n° artefacts	146	68	59	123	106	103	110	98	813
Blade/flake index	1.92	0.68	1.38	0.51	0.25	1.22	0.52	0.76	0.79
Blades	63.0%	38.2%	55.9%	30.8%	18.8%	54.3%	33.6%	41.8%	42.19%
Flakes	32.8%	55.8%	40.6%	60.9%	75.4%	44.6%	64.5%	55.1%	53.6%
Cores + nodules	4.11%	5.88%	3.39%	8.13%	5.66%	0.97%	1.82%	3.06%	4.18%
Levallois	4.11%	4.41%	1.69%	4.88%	2.83%	1.94%	0.91%	4.08%	3.20%
Backed / total blades	38.0%	42.3%	45.4%	0.00%	45.0%	19.6%	2.70%	12.2%	25.3%
Denticulate	8.90%	19.1%	5.08%	21.1%	1.89%	11.6%	7.27%	29.5%	13.0%
Points	12.3%	11.7%	8.47%	10.5%	3.77%	2.91%	7.27%	12.2%	8.73%
Borers	4.11%	8.82%	13.5%	4.88%	0.00%	5.83%	2.73%	13.2%	5.90%
Notches	2.05%	5.88%	3.39%	1.63%	0.00%	2.91%	11.8%	5.10%	3.94%
End scrapers	8.90%	7.35%	5.08%	7.32%	13.2%	25.2%	10.0%	8.16%	10.9%
Side scrapers	37.5%	21.0%	54.1%	13.3%	23.7%	17.3%	8.45%	22.2%	21.5%
Transverse scrapers	8.33%	15.7%	25.0%	12.0%	10.0%	17.3%	2.82%	16.6%	11.9%

* Due to the paucity of the findings, the artefacts of the sites HK/73a, HK/74d, HK/75a, HK/75c, HK/75g and HK/210 have been pooled.

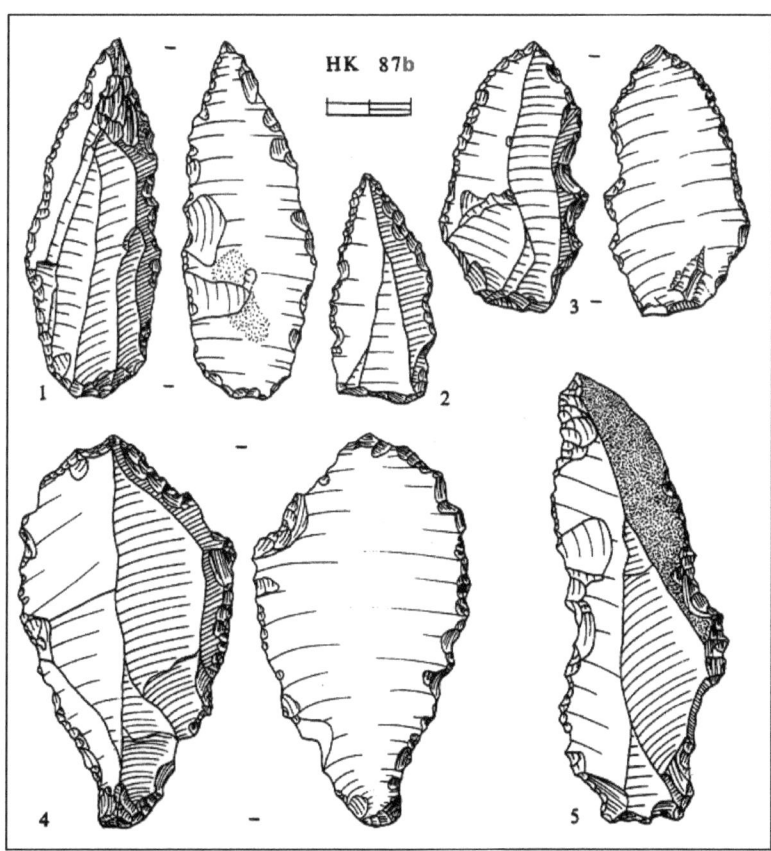

Figure 2 – HK/87b. 1: Châtelperron point; 2: point; 3, 5: points on denticulate blades; 4: leaf-shaped point (drawing Ida Mailland)

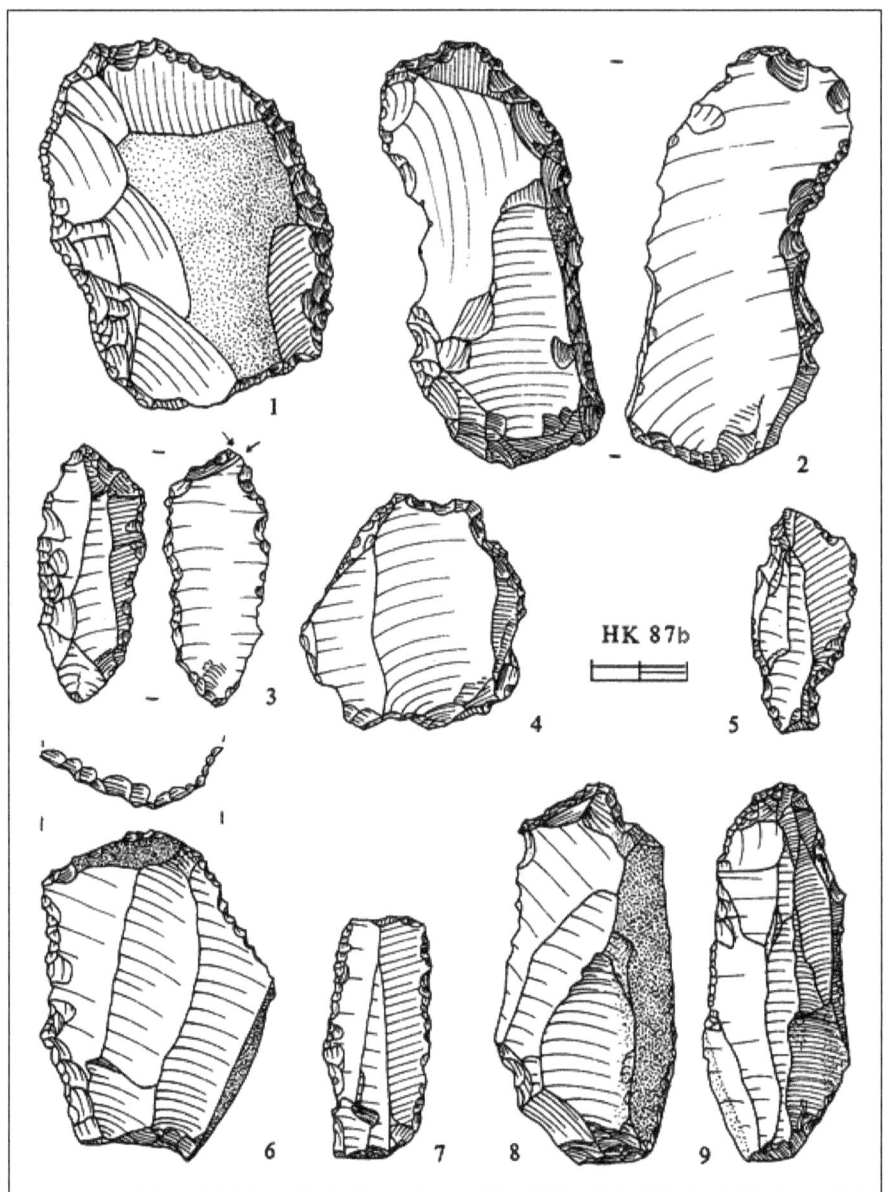

Figure 3 – HK/87b. 1: denticulate retouch on Levallois flake; 2: notch; 3: burin; 4: denticulate; 5: tanged tool; 6: side scraper; 7: blade; 8: borer; 9: end scraper (drawing Ida Mailland)

Figure 4 – HK/87b. 1, 7: points; 2: retouched Levallois point; 3, 5, 6: retouched flakes; 4: round scraper; 8: notch on denticulate; 9: retouched Levallois flake; 10, 11: continuous retouch flakes; 12: borer

Figure 5 – HK/191a. 1, 15: borer; 2: point on backed blade; 3: Levallois point; 4: point; 5, 12: denticulates; 6: end scraper; 7: transverse scraper; 8, 9, 16, 17, 18: backed blades; 10, 11, 19, 21: blades; 13, 14: notch; 20: double burin

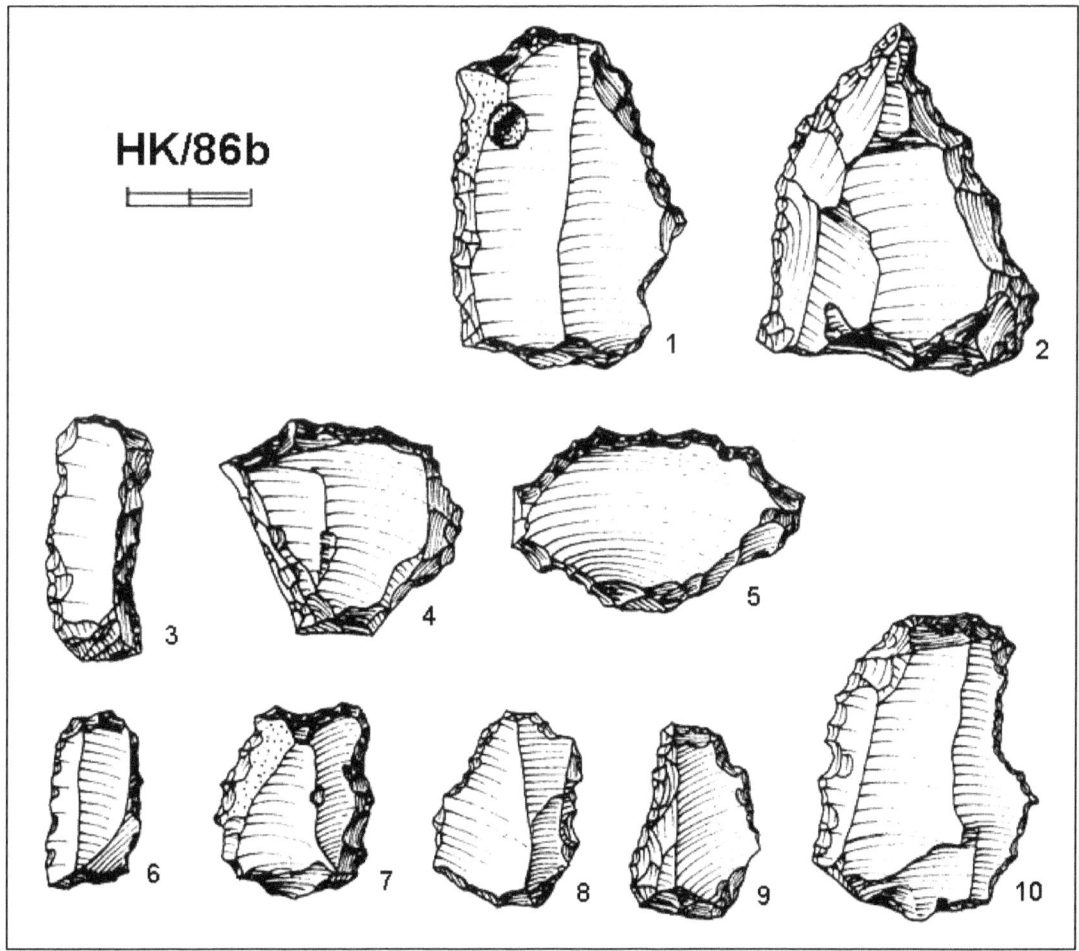

Figure 6 – Ceremonial site HK/86b. 1: double borer on denticulate; 2: retouched point on Levallois flake; 3: small blade with abrupt retouch and blunted platform; 4: borer on transverse scraper on a Levallois flake; 5: transverse scraper on a Levallois flake; 6, 7: denticulate on Levallois support; 8, 9: denticulate; 10: notch on denticulate

Table 2 Karkomian industry: descriptive statistics of lithic assemblage

Technology	typology/retouch	n	% on tech class
Cores	Levallois	6	18.2%
	polyhedron	6	18.2%
	reutilization of debitage	7	21.2%
	Total cores	**33**	**100.0%**
Nodules	hammerstone	1	100.0%
	Total nodules	**1**	**100.0%**
Blades (all lengths)	backed	87	25.4%
	backed point	6	1.7%
	Châtelperron point	4	1.2%
	Emireh point	3	0.9%
	other points	13	3.8%
	end scraper	40	11.7%
	borer	20	5.8%
	notch	18	5.2%
	denticulate	53	15.5%
	inverse	3	0.9%
	tanged	2	0.6%
	blunted platform	6	1.7%
	other retouched blades	14	4.1%
	unretouched blades	75	21.9%
	Total blades	**343**	**100.0%**
Flakes	all Levallois flakes	18	4.1%
	side scraper	42	9.6%
	transverse scraper	52	11.9%
	end scraper	28	6.4%
	round scraper	19	4.4%
	Levallois point	15	3.4%
	Emireh point	4	0.9%
	tanged point	4	0.9%
	leaf-shaped point	3	0.7%
	other points	23	5.3%
	borer	28	6.4%
	notch	14	3.2%
	denticulate	51	11.7%
	inverse	8	1.8%
	tanged	6	1.4%
	blunted platform	3	0.7%
	continuous retouch	57	13.1%
	other retouched flakes	90	20.6%
	unretouched flakes	44	10.1%
	Total flakes	**436**	**100.0%**
Total flints		**813**	

Blades (n=343) are defined according to the standard rules: length/width ratio ≥2:1. They have been divided into two groups according to their length: blades (>6 cm, n=179), small blades (≤ 6, n=164), only few small blades having a <4 cm length. Blades of different size present finely retouched, mostly denticulate, or naturally sharp margins; some of them show also an inverse retouch. The implements, as sharp as knives, may have been used for activities such as cutting animal skin or sectioning meat. Backed blades are defined as having a triangular section.

Flakes: (n=436) were obtained by Levallois technique in the proportion of 4.1%.

Points: (n=61) 26 of them were made on laminar support and include six backed points, four Châtelperron points and three Emireh points. Some of them present a finely denticulate retouch and notches; others are endowed with marginal retouch. Emireh points are defined after Garrod (Garrod 1955) as triangular points made by a Levallois-like technique, finely retouched on both margins, sometimes with inverse retouch on one edge. The platform is always thinned by means of careful retouch on both dorsal and ventral face. Points on flakes totalled 45, including 15 Levallois points, four Emireh points and four tanged points. Three leaf-shaped points are characterized by an invasive retouch on the dorsal face of a thin flake.

Tanged tools are few and mostly include flake points and a couple of end scraper. Obverse platform blunting is present on points. Overall, tanged tools and blunted platform form slightly more than 2% of all flint implements, with a prevalence of a blunted platform for blades and of tanged implements for flakes. Side scrapers, end scrapers, round scrapers: the definitions are those in general use. Transverse scraper is defined as an end scraper made on a flake with length<width. Almost 12% of all flakes were transverse scrapers, with triangular or trapezoidal shape and maximum width at the distal end. They were mostly further retouched, to obtain a borer on one side. Double transverse scrapers had both proximal and distal retouch.

Denticulate, notches: the definitions are those in general use. Denticulate was the most frequent retouch, being present on 15.5% of blades and 11.7% of flakes. Notches are present on 5.2% of blades, even associated with denticulate retouch; notches are present on 3.2% of flakes.

Borers are defined as tools from a flake or a blade, having been retouched to a small triangular-shaped projection. Borers were obtained on 5.8% of blades, over a half of them on backed blades. Borers are also present on 6.4% of flakes, 2.5% on transverse scrapers.

Burins are infrequent. Overall, they represent <1% of all flint tools and are mostly present on blades.

Abrupt retouch was noticed in six blades (1.75% of blades, all length) and in two end scrapers on flake (0.46% of flakes).

DATING THE KARKOMIAN INDUSTRY

In the absence of organic remains, considering the general cultural context of other Levantine transitional Paleolithic industries, Karkomian is tentatively considered to date not later than 40,000 BP. This corresponds to the maximum wet in the Negev, according to the curves of climate elaborated on the palynomorphs (Horowitz and Weinstein-Evron 1986, Issar 1995 & 2004). That was also the period of the maximum level of Lake Lisan (164 m under sea level), now known as the Dead Sea, when the Lisan basin probably extended to what are now the valleys of Lake Tiberias and the Jordan river on north and the Arava on south.

COMPARISON WITH OTHER TRANSITIONAL CULTURES

Sites with transitional flint industry between Middle and Upper Paleolithic are known in the Syro-Palestinian area.

The site of Boqer Tahtit is the most important in the Negev. Unearthed in the area of Sde Boqer, north of Har Karkom, Boqer Tahtit represents a level characterized by a transitional flint industry in the middle of a stratigraphic series of levels of Middle Paleolithic and Upper Paleolithic, respectively (Marks 1976). Radiocarbon dating of Boqer Tahtit gave the value of 47,000–40,000 years. Among the other findings, in that level many flint points were found obtained by an apparent Levallois flaking technique, not retouched on the margins, with only the platform retouched by an obverse blunting. Those points are similar to those found in the site of Erq-el Ahmar in the Judah desert, belonging to the Levantine Mousterian complex.

In Lebanon, the site of Ksar' Aqil also presents a transitional flint industry, in a period dating between 40,000 and 30,000 years BP (Bergman 1981; Broglio and Kozlowski 1987). In the first phase, the Levallois technique of flint flaking is prevalent, with production of leptolithic elements consisting of 59% of artefacts. Chanfrein blades (burins obtained by a flat transverse knapping) are reportedly the most typical tools. That phase is associated with human remains of Neanderthal type, while in a second phase the flint industry, less frequently obtained by the Levallois technique, is associated with human remains of the Cro-Magnon type.

CONCLUSION

A transitional flint industry between Middle and Upper Paleolithic characterized the culture of ancient human groups who climbed up the Har Karkom mountain at the time of the maximum wet in the Negev desert. At that time, a rich grassland was present in the valleys around Har Karkom, rainfalls were common not only in winter but also in the warm season, the temperature fell and large mammals lived in that environment. This permitted prehistoric hunters to live, who frequented what is presently a desert area. Though no human or other organic remains were found at Har Karkom, we have much indirect evidence of their lives, and the comparison with data coming from stratigraphic excavations at other sites allows a tentative dating around and not later than 40,000 years BP.

In the absence of human remains, it is not possible to hypothesize whether they were the last Neanderthal men or if they were the first *H. sapiens sapiens*, or other. They left an extraordinary monument in the ceremonial site HK/86b, the Paleolithic sanctuary that is the most ancient worship place known so far, where manifestations of art, or proto-art, imply the expression of conceptual ideas and the capability of people living in the very early Upper Paleolithic period to create symbols of spirituality.

References

ANATI, E.; COTTINELLI, L.; MAILLAND, F. 1996 Il Santuario più antico del mondo. Archeologia Viva, vol.15/16 pp. 26, 38. Giunti, Firenze.

ANATI, E.; MAILLAND, F. 2009a Map of Har Karkom (229). Archeological Survey of Israel. CISPE (Centro Internazionale di Studi Preistorici ed Etnologici), Esprit de l'Homme, Geneva.

ANATI, E.; MAILLAND, F. 2009b HK/86B, Palaeolithic ceremonial site at Har Karkom, holy mountain in the desert of Exodus, XXIII Valcamonica Symposium 'Making history of prehistory – the role of rock art', pp. 41–5. Capodiponte (BS), Italy, 28 October–2 November 2009.

BERGMAN, C.A. 1981 Point types in the Upper Paleolithic sequence at Ksar'Aqil, Lebanon. Colloques internationaux du C.N.R.N. n. 598. Préhistoire du levant, pp. 320–30. Maison de l'orient. Lyon 10-14-06-1980. C.N.R.S. Paris.

BROGLIO, A.; KOZLOWSKI, J. 1987 Il paleolitico (uomo, ambiente e culture). Jaca Book, Milano.

GARROD, D.A.E. 1955 The Mugharet el-Emireh in lower Galilee. Type-station of the Emiran Industry. J.R. Anthrop. Inst., 55, pp. 141–62.

HOROWITZ, A.; WEINSTEIN-EVRON, M. 1986 The late Pleistocene climate in Israel. Bulletin de l'Association française pour l'étude du Quaternaire, ½, pp. 84–90.

ISSAR, A.S. 1995 Impacts of climate variations on water management and related socio-economic systems. A review of reinterpretation of existing information. International hydrological programme, IHP-IV Project H-2.1. UNESCO, Paris.

ISSAR, A.S. 2004 Climate changes in the Levant during the late Quaternary period. In Climate Changes during the Holocene and their Impact on Hydrological Systems. International *Hydrology* Series. Cambridge University Press, Cambridge.

MAILLAND, F. 2007 Witness of Palaeolithic conceptual expressions at Har Karkom, Israel. In E. Anati and

J.-P. Mohen (eds), Les expressions intellectuelles et spirituelles des peuples sans écriture, pp. 76–82. CISPE and Edizioni del Centro, Capo di Ponte.

MAILLAND, I. 2009 Har Karkom – proto-arte agli albori del Paleolitico Superiore, XXIII Valcamonica Symposium 'Making history of prehistory – the role of rock art', pp. 41–5. Capodiponte (BS), Italy, 28 October–2 November 2009.

MARKS, A.E. 1976 Terminology and chronology of the Levantine upper Paleolithic as seen from the central Negev, Israel. U.I.S.P.P. IX Congrès, 15 September 1976.

GEOGLYPHS ON HAR KARKOM PLATEAU: WITNESS TO THE EARLY START OF THE EXPRESSION OF CONCEPTUAL IDEAS DURING THE EARLY UPPER PALEOLITHIC

Federico MAILLAND

Director, CISPE, Centro Internazionale di Studi Preistorici ed Etnologici, Italy
Co-Director, Italian archeological project at Har Karkom, Negev, Israel

Abstract: Remains of geoglyphs have been present on Har Karkom plateau since ancient times. The particular environment of stony desert, the flat surface and the contrast between the dark-brown flint stones and the white yellowish limestone provide the optimal conditions for pebble drawing. Climate fluctuations in the area allowed life during a long pluvial period between 70,000 and 28,000 years BP, which corresponded to an intense frequentation of the site during the Middle and early Upper Paleolithic. Interestingly, the finding of a Paleolithic 'Sanctuary' dating back to 40,000 years BP and a kind of proto-art related to it witness the early start of expression of conceptual ideas and the capability to create symbols of spirituality during the very early Upper Paleolithic period.

A second, shorter pluvial period started around 10,000 BP and lasted until the end of 4,000 BP. In correspondence with this humid period, an agriculture economy started to flourish in the area all around Har Karkom and remains of hundreds of villages reveal the improved climatic conditions, mostly during the Chalcolithic and Early Bronze Ages. During the fourth and third millennia BCE, the Har Karkom mountain became an enormous, unique worship place. At that period, only rock art, funerary sites and worshipping activities are seen on top of the mountain. The role of a funerary site continued during the Roman and Islamic times and the villages were placed on the terraces along the wadis. As a result, Har Karkom plateau was never settled, which contributed to preserving the ancient sites, and erosive phenomena have revealed to us the ancient remains on the plateau surface.

Geoglyphs at Har Karkom were made by various techniques, either by putting stones in alignments, or by clearing the brown stones from the ground surface, thus allowing the brilliant, clear loess appear. At least 25 sites have been found on the plateau, an area of 8 sq. km, representing animals, rarely humans, geometric figures or imaginary figures. Some of them are very large, even 30 m or 60 m long, and were performed by completing with stone alignments some natural limestone outcrops which suggested particular shapes. Interestingly, large mammals are represented, including a rhinoceros, two elephants and maybe a phacocerus. A figure of an elephant was later disturbed by a cyst grave during the Chalcolithic or Early Bronze Age. Another figure, interpreted as a hippopotamus, was disturbed by a later figure of an ostrich, made by a different technique. There is no way to date the geoglyphs, but relative dating may be proposed for some of them. In fact, large mammals such as those represented on the top of Har Karkom lived in the area during the Pleistocene, and were extinct before 28,000 BP. Thus, at least some of the geoglyphs of Har Karkom date back to the Paleolithic period, which makes them the oldest pebble drawings known so far.

Geoglyphs may be interpreted as a less durable form of figurative art than painting and sculpture, and this finding is not surprising. The discovery of Paleolithic geoglyphs on Har Karkom plateau suggests a number of questions: why the early humans represented their figures by pebble drawing, and what is the message left by the ancestors to modern people?

The geoglyphs on Har Karkom plateau are witness to the early start of expression of conceptual ideas during early Upper Paleolithic

INTRODUCTION

Har Karkom is an extraordinary mountain in the middle of what is today a desert area, in southern Negev (Israel). The environment is characterized by a stony desert, and Har Karkom is a *mesa*, with a flat surface of about 8 sq. km, fully covered by a layer of tabular flint, brown in colour, a few centimetres deep. Under the tabular flint there is a layer of *loess*, variable in deepness, which is characterized by very fine particle size, and appears as the result of the degradation of the underlying limestone formation. The contrast between the dark-brown flint stones and the white yellowish *loess* provides optimal conditions for pebble drawing.

Remains of geoglyphs have been present on Har Karkom plateau since ancient times. Some of them were preliminarily discovered by Emmanuel Anati (Anati 1994) by flying over the Har Karkom plateau with an ultra-light. Others were reported throughout the years by the teams who made the ground survey of the plateau and the surrounding valleys, and are mentioned in the recently published corpus of the surveyed area (Anati and Mailland 2009). Nevertheless, many of them are very large, even 30 m long, and their interpretation is difficult.

Recently, a team coordinated by the author started the careful, systematic investigation of Har Karkom geoglyphs by means of aerial photographs taken in zenithal position. The study started in 2007 and is still ongoing. Since the very beginning, the investigation led to the astonishing evidence that at least some geoglyphs represented large mammals that were extinct in the whole southern Levant during the late Pleistocene. A paper on the preliminary findings was reported at the XXIII Valcamonica Symposium (Mailland 2009). The hypothesis of having found geoglyphs drawn during the Paleolithic period was discussed there for the first time. If confirmed, that would make them the oldest geoglyphs known so far.

The aim of this report is to update the corpus of Har Karkom geoglyphs with the new findings and further discuss the hypotheses on their dating.

HAR KARKOM: CLIMATE FLUCTUATIONS AND ENVIRONMENT

Pollen analyses were performed in different regions of Israel (Horowitz and Weinstein-Evron 1986) by means of core samples which penetrated the sequences of the Quaternary periods, and in particular the Middle and Upper Pleistocene and the Holocene, from Lake Hula and Lake Lisan (Issar 1995). The analyses allowed the investigation of the paleoclimate on the basis of the quantity of fossil palynomorphs and of the vegetation present in different areas of the country, including the Negev, in the different periods. Depending on the Mediterranean sea-level changes (transgressions and regressions), consequent to the great climate fluctuations in Europe, there were in Israel pluvial periods, not only in winter but also in the warm season, with regular, abundant rain, in correspondence to the glaciations in Europe. Similarly, there were interpluvial periods, characterized by a dry climate in the whole country, in correspondence to interglacial periods in Europe and Mediterranean sea transgression. In between, intermediate periods have been described, defined as interstadial, characterized by a decrease of rainfall in the north of the country, while in the Negev there was an arid climate and a desert environment.

The climate changes in the Negev, compared with the archeological findings of the Har Karkom area, are reported in Chart 1. As expected, there is a strict correspondence between climate, environment and the population of Har Karkom in ancient times.

Climatic conditions were much better than now during the Upper Pleistocene and a pluvial period characterized the whole Negev between 70,000 and 28,000 years BP. All around the mountain, there are valleys that were transformed into a rich grassland during the pluvial. In correspondence with the favourable climate, the surface of the plateau carries signs of intense frequentation during Middle and early Upper Paleolithic. Hundreds of Paleolithic sites are still present on the surface with their hut floors and their flint workshops, and they have been classified according to the flint industry left *in situ*. The arid climate following 28,000 BP rendered the site inhospitable and life impossible for several millennia. Following another improvement in climate which involved southern Levant and northern Africa, the Negev started to be settled around 10,000 BP. One pre-pottery Neolithic site was unearthed at the foot of Har Karkom mountain, characterized by an agricultural economy which bears witness to the improved climatic conditions. Semi-nomadic settlements became numerous during the Chalcolithic and Early Bronze Age in the valleys around Har Karkom, while the whole mountain became an enormous, unique worship place. In that period, only rock art, funerary sites and worshipping activities are seen on top of the mountain. At the end of the third millennium BCE, the climate became suddenly very arid for a millennium. The area was settled again during the Roman period, but at that time the centre of activities was the well of Beer Karkom, 8 km north of the mountain, and the Roman villages were placed on the terraces along the *wadis*.

As a result, Har Karkom was never settled, which contributed to the preservation of the ancient sites. The area is presently a desert, and the climate corresponds to an interstadial period; erosive phenomena revealed the ancient remains on the plateau surface.

THE GEOGLYPHS

Geoglyphs at Har Karkom were made by various techniques, either by putting stones in alignments, or by clearing the brown stones from the ground surface, thus allowing the brilliant, clear loess to appear. Some of them were performed by completing with stone alignments the natural limestone outcrops which suggested particular shapes. All animal figures were drawn half face, independently of the drawing style. But the two anthropomorphic figures so far recognized were drawn facing front. Occasionally, rock engravings were found on stones belonging to the geoglyphs or in their vicinity. There is no material to date the geoglyphs of Har Karkom, but their ancient age is not in discussion. In at least two cases, other structures or other figures made by a different technique overlap geoglyphs drawn in more ancient times.

Based on the drawing techniques, five styles have so far been defined in Har Karkom geoglyphs, which are described below and summarized in Chart 2.

Style I

It is characterized by full figures, performed by completing natural limestone outcrops with stone alignments. Large mammals are represented, animals extinct at the end of the Pleistocene. Located in Paleolithic sites or in their immediate vicinity. The most interesting examples of this style are as follows.

WGS84 coordinates 30°17'48.00'N, 34°44'48.42'E
(Figure 1)

Profile drawing of a rhinoceros, 31.7 m long and 12.2 m high. The figure has an orientation south-north, with the head on the south and the legs on the west. The figure was made of limestone, taking advantage of some natural limestone outcrops over the brown tabular flint layer. Characterized by a large body, dorsal and ventral lines, the head provided with a large lower horn and a small upper one above the animal's nose. The animal has short, thin legs; the male sex and the outline of the right thigh are visible. The figure has a spear in the heart. Some of the white stones have late rock engravings from the Islamic period.

Chart 1 Quaternary paleoclimate, paleoenvironment, chronology & population of Har Karkom

Quaternary periods		Glacial/pluvial epochs		Level of Mediterranean sea	Hula & Lisan basins	Negev HK climate	Chron. until (→yr BP)	Archeological findings at HK	Population (number of sites)
		Europe	Near East						
PLEISTOCENE	Lower	archaic glaciations	pluvial	transgressions & regressions	decrease increase	humid / dry	2,000,000		
							700,000		
		glacial Mindel 1	pluvial	regression	increase	wet	500,000	Lower Paleolithic	sporadic
		interstadial	interstadial			dry			
	Middle	glacial Mindel 2	pluvial			wet			
		interglacial Holstein	interpluvial	transgression	decrease	arid	200,000	Hiatus	0
		glacial Riss 1-3	pluvial	regression	increase	humid	125,000	Lower Paleolithic	45
		interglacial Eemian	interpluvial	transgression	decrease	arid	80-70,000	Hiatus	0
	Upper	glacial Würm 1 & 2	pluvial	regression	lake Lisan is formed	maximum wet →	40,000	Middle Paleolithic	137
		glacial Würm 3 & 4	pluvial	regression	Lisan ↑ 164m u.s.l.	wet	28,000	Early Upper Paleolithic	139
			interpluvial	transgression	Lisan ↓ 350m u.s.l.	arid	14,000	Late Upper Paleolithic	1
HOLOCENE		interstadial	pluvial	regression	Dead sea	humid	4,500 BC	Mesol. Neol.	13
						humid	1,900 BC	Chalc. EB	212
						arid	37 BC	IA II Hell.	2
		interstadial	interstadial	intermediate		dry	AD 640	Rom. Byz.	65
						dry	Present	Islamic	83

Chart 2 Summary of the styles of Har Karkom geoglyphs

Style	Location	Technique	Description	Figures
I	Paleolithic sites	full figures by completing natural limestone outcrops with stone alignments	large size mammals	
II	Paleolithic site	mixed technique, clearing up surface and adding stone alignments/white spots	large size mammal	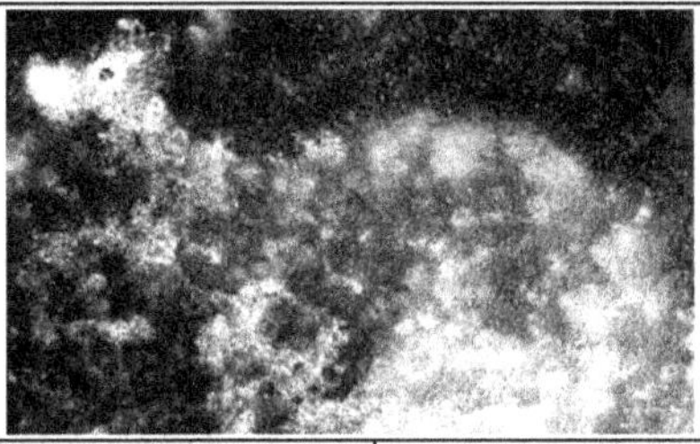
III	A – Paleolithic sites B – BAC sites	alignment of white stones on the brown ground, or alignment of brown stones on a white-yellowish ground	Animals, imaginary and geometric figures	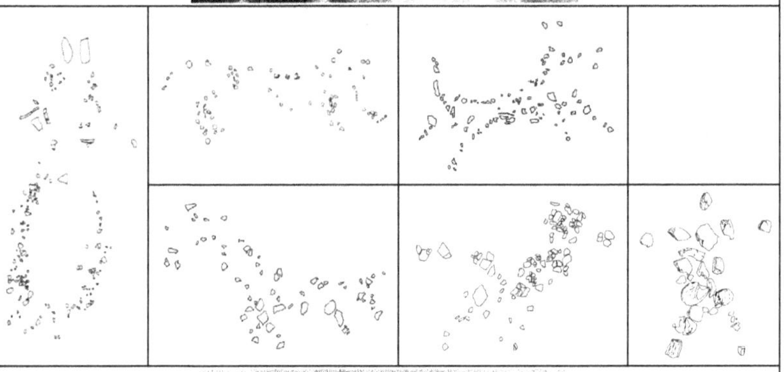
IV	Paleolithic site	negative contour	Animal (bird)	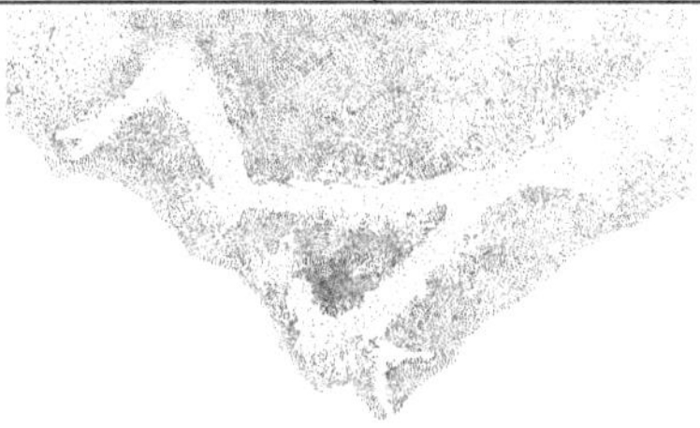
V	BAC site	full, negative figure by clearing stones from the surface	Animal (quadruped)	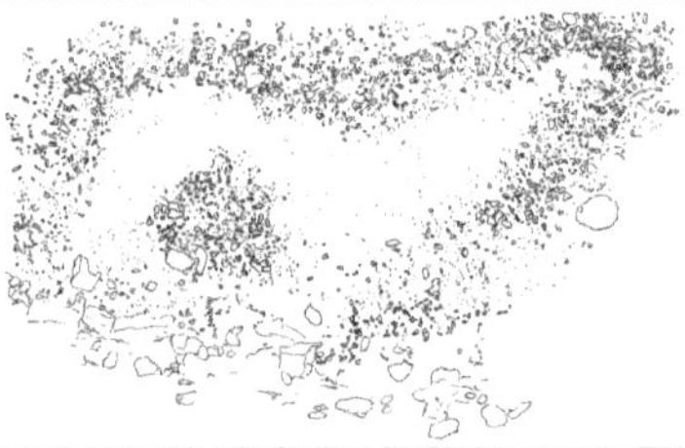

WGS84 coordinates 30°17'46.40"N, 34°44'48.11"E (Figure 2)

Not far from the previous figure, there is a profile drawing of an elephant, 19 m long. The figure has an orientation north-south, with the head on the north and the legs on the west. The figure was disturbed in ancient times by the later addition of a cyst grave, possibly during the Chalcolithic period. Currently, the dorsal line and the posterior legs are clearly visible. Other lines in the anterior part appear as a trunk and two tusks. The eye is represented by an oval, flat stone, 50–60 cm long, deeply eroded like very ancient carvings.

Figure 1 – Geoglyph of a rhinoceros

Figure 3 – Remains of geoglyph (bathing elephant)

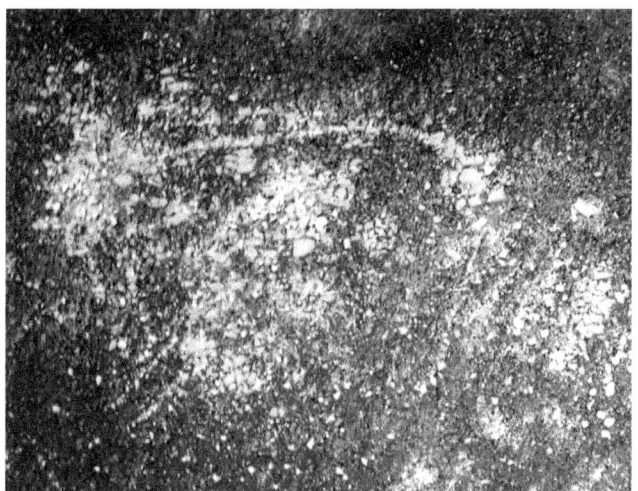

Figure 2 – Geoglyph of an elephant

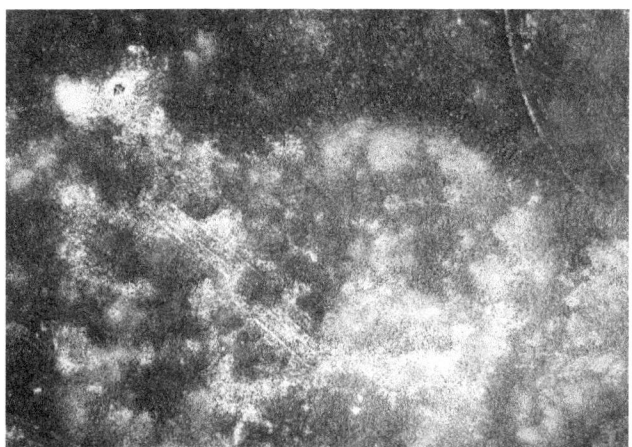

Figure 4 – Geoglyph of a quadruped. The ventral part was disturbed by the superimposition of another figure

WGS84 coordinates 30°17'48.02'N, 34°44'45.21'E

Profile drawing of a quadruped, rendered as a contour, with the exception of the muzzle, represented as full figure. This geoglyph has an orientation south-north, with the head on the south and the legs on the east. Two stone alignments under the animal's mouth may represent the tusks. The figure has been interpreted as a wild pig, maybe a *phacochoerus* sp.

WGS84 coordinates 30°17'58.8'N, 34°44'30.3'E
(Figure 3)

Remains of a small geoglyph, which originally would have represented a bathing elephant, rendered full figure. It is still possible to recognize the dorsal line, part of the body, the head and the erect trunk. The residual figure is 2.5 m long and has an orientation head-tail west-east.

Style II

Images made by a mixed technique, in part clearing the brown surface of the *hammada* and in part adding stone alignments and limestone white spots to the figure. Located in Paleolithic sites. The most representative depiction of this style is a large mammal, as follows.

WGS84 coordinates 30°18'11.7'N, 34°45'03.6'E
(Figure 4)

Large geoglyph, representing a quadruped, well preserved in its dorsal line and back, and rendered by spots made of white stones. The head, made by clearing the surface of stones, is also well preserved. This figure is about 50 m long and the line head-tail is orientated south-north. The ventral part was disturbed by the superimposition of another figure from style IV.

Style III

Contour drawings made of alignments of white stones on the brown ground, or alignments of brown stones on a white-yellowish ground. Animals and geometric and imaginary figures are represented. They are located in the context of either Paleolithic (IIIA) or Chalcolithic/Early Bronze age (BAC) (IIIB) sites.

WGS84 coordinates 30°18'31.5'N, 34°44'58.7'E

Between the Paleolithic campsites in the northern part of the plateau there is a funny figure, with a vaguely anthropomorphic shape, rendered by aligning white stones on the dark flint layer of the surface. It is 7.2 m long and the line head-feet is orientated west-east. We can distinguish an upper part representing the trunk: there is no head, the eyes are represented by two large slabs, 60 cm long, and the arms begin directly from the trunk, with no shoulders. The lower part has curved legs, and ends in two very small standing stones (the feet?).

WGS84 coordinates 30°17'46.1'N, 34°44'45.1'E

Near the figures of style I there is a figure of a quadruped, rendered by aligning white-yellowish stones on the brown surface. The body of the animal is represented by two lines, dorsal and ventral, the four legs by short lines of stones. The animal figure has a long, curved neck, also rendered by two parallel stone alignments, which end in the head turned bottom, with an aggressive bearing. A short tail is also represented. The figure is 10.5 m long and the line head-tail is orientated south-north.

WGS84 coordinates 30°17'29.9'N, 34°44'45.7'E

In the middle of remains from the Bronze Age was found the geoglyph of a quadruped, represented by contour lines of white stones on a brown ground. It has been rendered by a dorsal line and a ventral line, four lines for the legs, a square head and a long tail. It has been interpreted as a feline, maybe a leopard. It is 14.5 m long and the line head-tail is orientated southwest-northeast. Interestingly, this figure is surrounded by three small, rectangular stone platforms, 2.5–3 m long.

WGS84 coordinates 30°17'30.4'N, 34°44'16.6'E

Small anthropomorphic geoglyph drawn on a promontory of the plateau facing the western valley. It has been drawn by putting stones 30–50 cm long on the soft ground. It probably represents a female figure, as a circle of stones under the inguinal part of the figure may represent the vaginal opening. The arms are rendered by a unique, straight line and the head is represented by a vaguely anthropomorphic stone. A disturbed figure nearby may have been a male anthropomorphic figure.

Style IV

Drawings made by negative contour. The most interesting figure belonging to this style is a bird, as follows.

WGS84 coordinates 30°18'11.7'N, 34°45'03.6'E

Bird figure overlapping a large mammal of style II. The bird is 25 m long and the line head-tail is orientated southwest-northeast.

Style V

Full, negative figure obtained by clearing stones from the surface. So far one figure was identified, as follows.

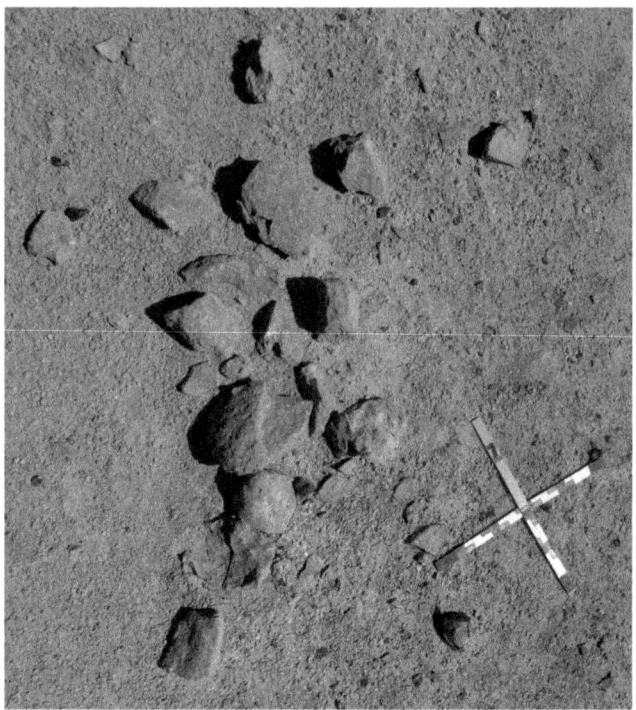

Figure 5 – Anthropomorphic geoglyph

WGS84 coordinates 30°18'04.1'N, 34°44'01.4'E

At the western foot of Har Karkom, a figure of a quadruped, probably a sheep, was rendered by clearing the ground surface of the brown stones, letting the brilliant white-yellowish colour of loess appear. The figure, drawn on the slope, is about 5 m long and the line head-tail is orientated northwest-southeast. It is located in the context of a BAC site.

DATING HAR KARKOM GEOGLYPHS

Dating geoglyphs has been tried in the past using different techniques. The White Horse in Uffington village (Oxfordshire) was dated by means of optical stimulated luminescence of feldspars and quartz present in the chalk and the date confirmed by archeological findings (Miles 2003). Dating of Serpent Mound (Ohio) was based on C^{14} measurements of organic material included in the patina, probably formed after drawing the geoglyphs (Dorn 1992; Fletcher 1996).

Neither method seems suitable for Har Karkom. In fact, ancient organic material was not preserved in the stony desert environment, and optical stimulated luminescence is apparently not applicable to the case. Thus, there is no way to get an absolute dating of the Har Karkom geoglyphs, but we used a different approach.

According to paleontological studies, large mammals were well represented in the Syro-Palestinian area in the Upper Pleistocene. Rhinoceros, elephant and phacocheros species were present on Mount Carmel (Israel) during the late Pleistocene (Bate 1937). Rhinoceros was also found in the late Pleistocene levels in Ksar'Aqil (Lebanon) (Hooijer 1961), Jebel Qafzeh (Israel) (Bouchud 1974) and Azraq (Jordan) (Clutton-Brock 1970). Paleontological findings agree with the a.m. climate studies, as a long-lasting pluvial period characterized the Upper Pleistocene between 70,000 and 28,000 BP. Thereafter, the large mammals were extinct, likely due to the climate changes from humid to dry and to the consequent environment changes from grassland to desert.

Accordingly, the figures of large mammals drawn by pebbles on Har Karkom were likely done during the Paleolithic period, when those animals lived in the area. Only small and medium-sized animals lived there during the Holocene, including ibexes, antelopes, reptiles and ostriches, that is the animals depicted in rock engravings of the Bronze Age Complex. At that time, the big mammals had already been absent for millennia.

If dating at least some of the Har Karkom geoglyphs to the Paleolithic period is confirmed, this makes them the oldest pebble drawings known so far. Geoglyphs may be interpreted as a less durable form of figurative art than painting and sculpture, and under this view the findings at Har Karkom are not surprising. Since the beginning of the Upper Paleolithic, humans were capable of performing paintings, engravings and later on sculptures. At Har Karkom, a form of mobiliary proto-art has already been documented at the very beginning of the Upper Paleolithic, with a relative dating of as much as 40,000 years BP (Mailland 2007). This accords with the period of the highest Dead Sea level, and therefore of the maximum rainfall, according to Issar (1995, 2004), when the whole Negev was a rich grassland, and indeed rhinoceros and the other large mammals were present in the area.

CONCLUSION

The discovery of Paleolithic geoglyphs on Har Karkom plateau poses a number of questions on the reasons why the early humans made those pebble drawings, and what is the message left by the ancestors to modern people. The flat plateau was a perfect environment for landscape drawings, since remote times, when the humans started to express conceptual ideas and created symbols of spirituality. The technique of completing natural forms had been used since Paleolithic times in other forms of art, like rock paintings or rock engravings. According to a common view, the artist completed the form suggested by the natural geomorphology of the rock, by adding paintings and tracings. This process is inherently characteristic of the human mind and is not dissimilar to that of modern artists. In the same manner, prehistoric artists would have seen some shapes in the natural limestone outcrop of the plateau and felt the need to complete the figures suggested to their minds. The representation of animal figures by pebble drawing could be interpreted as a form of magic, designed to ensure a successful hunt, or as an indication of shamanistic practices, totemism or animal worship.

Interestingly, the large size of the animals represented in the landscape renders it very problematic to recognize those figures from the ground. For many of them, the best view is from an altitude of 50–100 m. Does this mean that the ancient geoglyphs were drawn to be seen from the sky? Should we add a new chapter to the story of conceptual ideas and symbols of spirituality?

References

ANATI, E. 1994 Spedizione Sinai: nuove scoperte ad Har Karkom. Studi Camuni, Vol XI Ed. It., Edizioni del Centro, Capo di POnte.

ANATI, E.; MAILLAND, F. 2009 Map of Har Karkom (229). Archeological Survey of Israel. CISPE (Centro Internazionale di Studi Preistorici ed Etnologici), Geneva.

BATE, D.M.A. 1937 Palaeontology: The Fossil Fauna. Part II. In D.A.E. Garrod and D.M.A Bate, The Stone Age of Mount Carmel. Oxford University Press, Oxford.

BOUCHUD, J. 1974 Etude préliminaire de la faune provenant de la grotte du Djebel Qafzeh prés de Nazareth (Israel). Paléorient, 2(1), pp. 87–102.

CLUTTON-BROCK, J. 1970 The Fossil Fauna from an Upper Pleistocene Site in Jordan. J. Zool., 162, pp. 19–29.

DORN, R.L.; CLARKSON, P.B.; NOBBS, M.F. et al. 1992 New Approach to the Radiocarbon Dating of Rock Varnish, with Examples from Drylands. Annals of the Association of American Geographers, 82(1), pp. 136–51.

FLETCHER, R.V., CAMERON, T.L., LEPPER, B.T. et al. 1996 Serpent Mound: A Fort or Ancient Icon? Midcontinental Journal of Archeology, 21(1). University of Iowa.

HOOIJER, D.A. 1961 The Fossil Vertebrates of Ksar'Akil, a Palaeolithic Rock Shelter in the Lebanon. Zoologische Verhandelingen, 49.

HOROWITZ, A.; WEINSTEIN-EVRON, M. 1986 The late Pleistocene climate in Israel. Bulletin de l'Association française pour l'étude du Quaternaire, ½, pp. 84–90.

ISSAR, A.S. 1995 Impacts of climate variations on water management and related socio-economic systems. A review of reinterpretation of existing information. International hydrological programme, IHP-IV Project H-2.1. UNESCO, Paris.

ISSAR, A.S. 2004 Climate changes in the Levant during the late Quaternary period. In Climate Changes during the Holocene and their Impact on Hydrological Systems. International Hydrology Series. Cambridge University Press, Cambridge.

MAILLAND, F. 2007 Witness of Palaeolithic conceptual expressions at Har Karkom, Israel. In E. Anati and J.-P. Mohen (eds), Les expressions intellectuelles et spirituelles des peuples sans écriture. CISPE and Edizioni del Centro, Capo di Ponte.

MAILLAND, F. 2009 Geoglyphs on the Har Karkom plateau (Negev, Israel), XXIII Valcamonica Symposium 'Making history of prehistory – the role of rock art'. Capodiponte (BS), Italy, 28 October – 2 November 2009, pp. 208–14.

MILES, D. *et al.* 2003 Uffington White Horse and its Landscape: Investigations at White Horse Hill, Uffington, 1989–95 and Tower Hill, Ashbury, 1993–4. Oxford Archeology.

ASTRONOMICAL REPRESENTATIONS IN ROCK ART: EXAMPLES OF THE COGNITIVE AND SPIRITUAL PROCESSES OF NON-LITERATE PEOPLE

Fernando COIMBRA

Quaternary and Prehistory Group, Centre for Geosciences
uID 73 – FCT Portugal
coimbra.rockart@yahoo.com

Abstract: The countless cases of astronomical representations in rock art around the world seem to prove that one of the early cognitive abilities of non-literate people was to observe the sky. Indeed, the depiction of astronomical bodies like the sun, the moon and, less occasionally, cometary phenomena, constitute examples of the cognitive processes of those early societies and allow argument about their ways of thought regarding those celestial bodies, which become 'translated' not only into spiritual issues (myths and rituals), but also in a pragmatic way in the use of calendars.

Key words: astronomical representations, sun, moon, comet, rock art

Résumé: Les cas innombrables de représentations astronomiques en art rupestre dans tout le monde semblent prouver qu'une des plus anciennes capacités cognitives des peuples sans écrite était observer le ciel. Vraiment, la représentation de corps astronomiques comme le soleil, la lune et, moins fréquemment, phénomènes cométaires, constitue des exemples des procès intellectuelles de celles sociétés primitives et permet discuter sur leur modes de pensée en ce qui concerne ces corps célestes, ce que vient « traduit » non seulement en termes spirituelles (mythes et rituels), mais aussi dans un mode pragmatique dans l'usage de calendriers.

Mots clefs: représentations astronomiques, soleil, lune, comète, art rupestre

INTRODUCTION

The countless cases of astronomical representations painted or carved on rocks all over the world, with different chronologies, seem to prove that one of the early cognitive abilities of non-literate people was to observe the sky. Indeed, the depiction of astronomical bodies like the sun, the moon and, less occasionally, cometary phenomena, constitute examples of the intellectual processes of those early societies and allow argument about their ways of thought regarding those astral orbs.

According to C. Ruggles and H. Burl (1995) the activities of prehistoric peoples, including art, were strongly dependent on their perceptions of the world, being expressed in ritual and belief systems where celestial phenomena were a part of those perceptions. But intellectual aspects of ancient sky observation, mainly the moon, can be seen in a more pragmatic way, like the making of calendars.

The first part of this article considers several depictions of the sun and their associations with other engravings, which lead one to think about the existence of a prehistoric sun worship and early ways of thought regarding the construction of a primitive 'religion'. In the second part, moon representations are mainly considered in the context of megalithic art, but other examples are also studied, especially a group of paintings in a rock shelter from southern Portugal, which may be interpreted as a calendar. Finally, some unambiguous depictions of comets and meteors are analyzed, arguing about the impression that they probably left on the minds of the observers, due to the visual impact that they produced.

It is necessary to stress that the aim of this article is to bring to analysis and discussion some examples of the cognitive and spiritual processes of non-literate people based on astronomical representations in rock art, and that it is not intended to be a short or a long inventory of such depictions, which would be impossible in only one paper. This way, the present article focuses on some reflections made upon images of the sun, the moon, comets and meteors in rock art.

I - THE SUN

According to C.M. Silva and M. Calado (2003), among the nomadic Paleolithic hunter-gatherers time and space have linear characteristics, but for sedentary people time becomes cyclic and space is valuable in a particular way. Indeed the progressive process of the sedentary lifestyle allows the continuing observation of the sun and the moon as they rise or set on the horizon, probably with the intention of counting time. In this way landscape, which includes celestial bodies, inserts an extra dimension into the symbolic dialogue between man and nature, resulting in making space sacred and time a ritual (Oliveira and Silva 2010).

Clive Ruggles (1998) argues that astronomy appears as an integral part of all native cosmologies, meaning that it is meaningless to study sacred landscapes separately from the sky. Indeed, during prehistory, religious thought and

Figure 1 – Typology of sun images from Saimaly-Tash. (Drawing by Martynov, 1999)

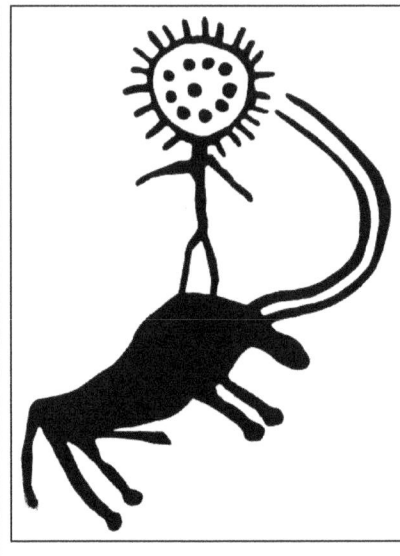

Figure 2 – Anthropomorphic sun standing on a bull (Drawing by Davis-Kimball & Martynov, 1993)

Figure 3 – Dancing to the sun god (?) (Drawing by Martynov *et al.*, 1992)

astronomical observations were very close and several myths from later pre-classical and classical civilizations seem to have their origin in early astronomical events.[1]

In this article we are not going to discuss if there is, or not, a solar religion. Our aim is just to analyse some depictions of the sun in rock art, trying to understand the spiritual processes of early societies in connection with this celestial body.

For example, in the mountains of Saimaly-Tash (Kyrgyzstan) there are many anthropomorphic sun images (Figure 1), dating from the beginning of the second millennium BC, which, according to some researchers, constitute possible representations of a solar deity (Martynov *et al.* 1992; Davis-Kimball and Martynov 1993; Martynov 1999; Coimbra 2009).

The same kind of motif appears also at Tamgaly, Kazakhstan, where an anthropomorphic sun stands on a big bull, seeming to show its power over nature (Figure 2). Again in Saimaly-Tash, one curious scene shows a kind of dancing to a 'sun-god', which seems to be presented to the population by a kind of 'priest' holding the celestial body (Figure 3). These engravings 'enable us to see the world through the eyes of our ancestors' (Davis-Kimball and Martynov 1993: 213). Other authors have similar ideas about rock art images, mentioning that they constitute 'images from ancient worlds as human minds envisioned them' and 'direct material expressions of human concepts, of human thought' (Taçon and Chippindale, 1998: 2).

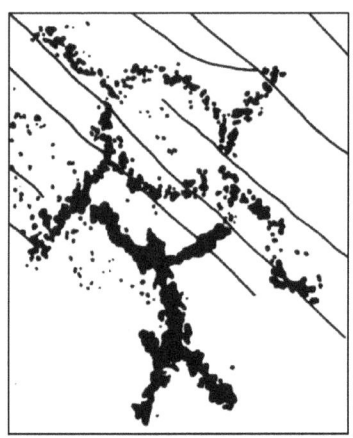

Figure 4 – Anthropomorphic motive holding a sun image (Drawing by Baptista, 1981)

Without establishing cultural parallels between Asia and western Europe, it is interesting to observe that sun images held by human figures can be seen also in the Tagus Valley (Portugal), dating from about 3000 BC (Figure 4). Besides that, anthropomorphic images of the sun seem to be present also in the eastern French Pyrenees, at Peyra Escrita, Formiguera (Figure 5), according to the interpretation of J. Abélanet (1990).

According to M. Green (1991: 24), 'megalithic sun imagery ... is the earliest unequivocal evidence we have for solar veneration in Europe'. The same author argues that 'solar motifs engraved in passage graves could have been placed there as a comfort to the dead, as a reminder that rebirth and renewal would take place' (Green 1991: 27). A suggestive example of this idea occurs at cairn T

---

[1] Several examples can be seen in Coimbra, 2010.

Figure 5 – Anthropomorphic sun image from Peyra Escrita. (Drawing by Abélanet, 1990)

Figure 6 – Megalithic burial with seven skeletons forming a sun image. (Drawing by Viana, 1950)

from Loughcrew, where a decorated stone, with sun imagery, in its last chamber was lit by the equinoctial sunrise[2] (Green 1991), as an awakening for the dead.

Another interesting case is a megalithic burial near Elvas (Portugal), where seven skeletons are displayed with the legs bending to the same side (Viana 1950), looking like a sun (Figure 6).

The sun seems to be one of the most powerful 'deities' worshipped in prehistoric times, which can be observed by the huge number of its representations in primitive art.[3] This importance can be understood by some cases of the survival of sun worship in recent times.

An interesting example comes from the rock art sanctuary of Saimaly-Tash, where 'not long ago pilgrims were still coming every August, bringing a kid or a lamb and seven flat cakes. The animals were slaughtered on the bank of the lake at sunset, then the meat was boiled and eaten, chapters from the Qur'an were read, and prayers were recited in supplication for health and prosperity' (Davis-Kimball and Martynov 1993: 215). This sunset ritual seems to continue a reverence for the sun god, which survives until recent times and proves its importance in the past. The same authors mention that till recently the engravings from this sanctuary were thought to have magical powers and also say that 'even today, Russian festivals in Siberia retain their pagan roots. Springtime carnivals are related to the cult of the sun and the Lord of the Heavens. During the festival, stuffed effigies of the fire god are burned and flat, round pancakes symbolizing the sun are eaten' (Davis-Kimball and Martynov 1993: 221).

The history of mankind is full of examples of the survival of symbols, myths and rituals, which have been used from prehistory till recent times. These survivals are explained by psychoanalysts like C.G. Jung, by the collective unconsciousness, the area of the mind which retains and transmits the psychological heritage common to all mankind.

However, the importance of the sun must be understood, in a general way, especially in cold, wet and dark climates, where its presence would be welcome. But the sun 'may in hot dry lands be seen as a threat and could be feared as an enemy' (Green 1991: 16), since extreme heat and drought would destroy the harvests. Indeed, according to Herodotus, the tribe of the Atarantes of Libya cursed the sun, but invoked the sky for its rainmaking properties (Green 1991), indispensable for agriculture.

II – THE MOON

Rock art depictions of the moon are much rarer than representations of the sun. The full moon could be obviously represented by a circle, but this geometric figure can also represent the sun, a well or a hut (Anati 1994) and so on, according to different cultures. Thus, in a general way, the only unambiguous representations of the moon in rock art are crescents. According to C. Oliveira and C.M. Silva (2010), in the Neolithic, the widespread cult of the mother-goddess was clearly related to the vital cycles of nature, including the agricultural ones, and to the calendar naturally based on the moon's phases. The need for knowing the exact time of the year for sowing, in order to get a good harvest and not starve,

---

[2] The solstice and equinoctial alignments of several megalithic monuments across Europe constitute other examples of the intellectual abilities of prehistoric people regarding the sun and the moon, but they are not fully developed in this article because they would be a theme for another paper.

[3] For example in the so called menhir-statues from Valcamonica the position of the sun is always dominant over the other depictions.

led to the appearance of calendars based often on the moon, as a result of pragmatic observations of the sky. For example, at Vale d'el Rei (Pavia, Alentejo, Portugal), the full moon rises directly on the symmetrical axis of a horseshoe-shaped megalithic enclosure (Oliveira and Silva 2010), thus associating this site with the moon for calendars or rituals. Furthermore, research done in the Alentejo region indicates the existence of several megalithic enclosures with significant alignments of the moon and the sun, which may constitute calendars (Silva 2000; Silva and Calado, 2003; Calado 2004; Alvim 2005; Oliveira and Silva 2010).

These alignments permit the argument that 'in moments of season change ... this fact was perceived by the builders of the enclosures and that the monuments materialized this phenomenon', being probably the existence of rituals which 'occurred in periods of full moon when it rises and sets at the same moment and in the opposite direction of the sunset and sunrise' (Alvim, 2005). Oliveira and Silva (2010: 86) argue that 'the importance of the Moon in the magic-symbolic contexts of the Neolithic-Chalcolithic is recognized not only in the Spring Moon orientation of the funerary monuments, but also in its representation in megalithic engravings', in the shape of crescent moons (Figure 7).

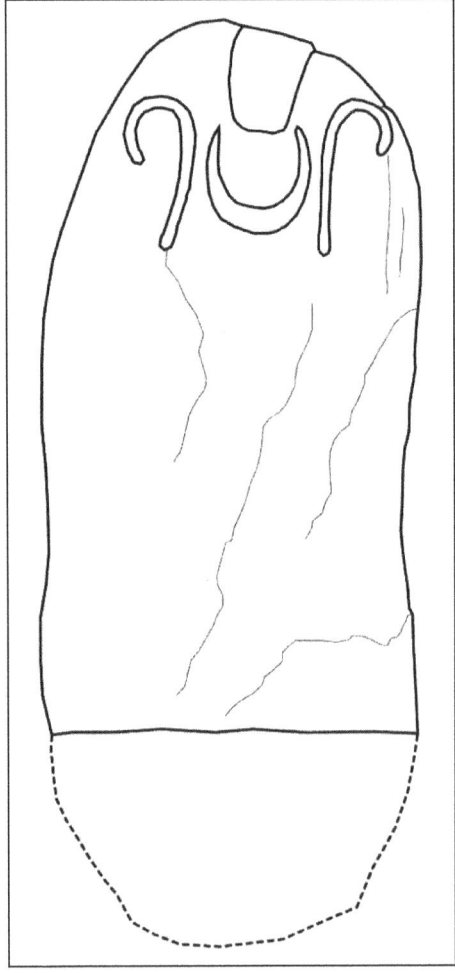

Figure 7 – Menhir with crescent moon.
(Drawing by Calado & Rocha, 2010)

These two factors of geographical orientation and iconography, together with symbolic artefacts found in archeological contexts, 'make the megalithic monuments the first durable materialization of this relationship between the Moon, the landscape, and the ritual calendar' (Oliveira and Silva 2010: 89). Then, according to the same authors (2010), the moon can appear as a symbolic representation of life and its disappearance might have represented death, making the sky dark during its absence.[4]

The idea of a moon calendar can also be applied to a group of paintings from Lapa dos Gaivões, a Copper Age rock shelter in Alentejo, formed by four rows of seven parallel lines 'as if to represent the full cycle of the Moon with its four phases of approximately seven days each' (Oliveira and Silva 2010: 86). The same possibility seems to exist at *Roccia dei alabardieri* (Mount Bego, France), where two anthropomorphic figures, carved during the third or second millennia BC, each hold a long halberd with seven dots in the handle, possibly constituting one phase of the moon.

Regarding ancient sky observation and consequent interpretations about the cognitive and spiritual abilities of our ancestors, the role of archaeoastronomy is becoming more and more useful.

However it must be stressed, as we already have more than once, that in order to avoid subjectivity or even mistakes, research must be done in a cooperative way, involving archeologists and astronomers in the same team (Coimbra 2008a, 2008b, 2010). Some archeologists are still suspicious about archaeoastronomy, but this results from the beginnings of this discipline where, indeed, some researchers were non-scientific, using very ambiguous and subjective approaches (Coimbra 2008b). Today archaeoastronomy is becoming much more considered and accepted in the scientific community. Indeed, archaeoastronomical studies can be extremely useful: In the 1990s, an interdisciplinary team of archeologists and astronomers studied more than 300 dolmen in the Iberian Peninsula, concluding that only 3 per cent were turned to the sunrise at any time of the year (Belmonte 1999). It was the end of the archeological myth that almost all the megalithic monuments from that region were aligned with the sunrise due to funerary rituals (Coimbra 2008a).

It must also be mentioned that the team that has been working on megaliths from central Alentejo and their moon and sun alignments, involves an astronomer[5] and several archeologists.

III – COMETS AND METEORS

Through history, comets and meteors have been seen alternatively as good or bad omens (Sagan and Druyan

---

[4] According to J. Belmonte (1999), the idea of life after death conceived by several people can have its origin on the successive phases of the moon, a cycle of birth, death and resurrection.
[5] This astronomer is Prof. Cândido Marciano da Silva, from New University of Lisbon, who works in central Alentejo since the mid 70's.

1986), but their influence on the minds of the observers is usually very intense.

Although it is not easy to find unambiguous images of comets engraved on rock surfaces, they do occur, some of them having been studied not only by archeologists but also by astronomers.[6] Indeed, it is this cooperation of the two disciplines that can provide trustable examples of comets and meteors depicted in rock art.

This section develops the research for two previous articles (Coimbra 2007, 2010), presenting in the second one, nine case studies of comet depictions in rock art, followed by an interdisciplinary analysis based on astronomical, geological and cultural data (mythology, pre-classical and classical texts).

Although we deal in this article with non-literate societies, it is crucial to be aware of what pre-classical and classical texts say about such astronomical events[7] in order to understand better how prehistoric people looked at them. Let us refer to some examples:

A Babylonian inscription dated from the 12th century BC mentions a shining comet with a tail looking like a scorpion, which was considered a good omen (Sagan and Druyan, 1986).

In classical literature, writers like Pliny the Elder and Seneca, among others,[8] described several cometary phenomena.

According to Pliny, a comet appeared in Rome shortly after the death of Caesar and was interpreted by the population as a sign that his soul had been received by the immortal gods. This comet was considered a good omen and a temple was made for worshipping this astronomical event (Coimbra 2010).

If a comet was worshiped in Rome in the first century BC it seems natural that this kind of astronomical phenomenon received the same reverence in earlier times and so it can have been depicted in rock art as a manifestation of the gods. Indeed, according to Bailey (1995: 663), 'the extreme preoccupation of most early societies with celestial imagery and the making of astronomical observations appear to be part of a world-wide phenomenon during the period leading up to and including the Bronze age'. Bailey also argues that 'comets and comet related phenomena seem to have played an important part in the beliefs and social habits of most known civilizations from the very earliest times' (Bailey *et al.* 1990: 8). Another British researcher mentions that 'traces of this ancient sky should be detectable in the artefacts and belief systems of the earliest cultures' (Napier 1998: 31). In fact, as we mentioned, comets and meteors appear depicted in rock art and also on Celtic and Roman coins. Comets were seen frequently in China, Greece, Egypt and Asia Minor, and were noted by the Chinese as early as the third millennium BC (Hasegawa 1980).

The biggest concentration of cometary phenomena depicted in rock art found so far is among the San people from South Africa. In fact, among the nine case studies that we published previously (Coimbra 2010), three of them are from that region: a fireball[9] from Bethlehem District, a double-headed comet from Fouriesbourg and a comet or meteor also from Fouriesbourg. The first example appears above three anthropomorphic figures, which seem to have feathers on their arms and from their attitude they look as if they are flying, probably a ritual scene (Coimbra 2008a: Fig. 5.2). The second one can be seen on a painting, depicting a sacrifice to a rain snake with a double-headed comet appearing on top of the image, over the characters (Coimbra 2010: Fig. 1). According to B. Woodhouse (1986), it may be a depiction of the comet Biela in 1846 and 1852. The third is associated with human figures depicting San medicine-men holding sticks and other characters in the attitude of clapping hands (Figure 8). J.F. Thackeray argues that 'comets and meteors were conceptually associated with trance among at least some population groups in Southern Africa' and that the example depicted in the Fouriesbourg painting, 'juxtaposed with human figures using sticks in the manner adopted by San medicine-men and Nguni diviners in trance, could reflect conceptual associations with trance experience' (Thackeray 1988: 51).

In Bahia (Brazil), there is a cave known as the Toca do Cosmos (Cave of the Cosmos), where the rock art themes are celestial bodies such as sun images and stars. In this astronomical 'environment' there is an image of what seems to be a comet, consisting of a circle with four long tails, revealing a typology that is very similar to an example that appears on the famous Comet Atlas from Mawangdui (China), which has the same kind of circle and four tails bending to the left (Coimbra 2010: Fig. 3, Fig. 4).

As for cometary phenomena, some myths from different cultures seem to have their origin in these astronomical events. For example, in Hindu mythology, Garuda is a divine cosmic bird, which, according to the Mahabharata, was as bright as the sun, could change its shape at his will, destroy other divinities through launching fire, and provoke red dust storms that obscured the sun and the moon (Kobres 1992). All these characteristics – brightness, changing shape, launching fire and provoking red dust storms in order to obscure other celestial bodies – are related to comets and meteors. The Chumash Indians from California believed that a meteor was a

---

[6] For a list of case studies see Coimbra, 2010.
[7] According to Bailey *et alli* (1990: 7), "cuneiform literature contains a wealth of detailed information on a variety of astronomical topics, including the observation of comets, meteors and meteorites."
[8] The Greek scholars Ephorus of Cyme, Epigenes, Apollonius of Myndus, Posidonius and Aristotle (Yeomans, 1991), among other examples.

[9] A fireball is a meteor with a luminescence equivalent to Venus, which leave a tail visible for some minutes. The astral body that appears in this example was identified as a fireball by Tim Cooper, Director of the Comet and Meteor Section of the Astronomical Society of Southern Africa (Ouzman, 2006).

Figure 8 – Comet or meteor, being observed by a San group. (Drawing by Woodhouse, 1986)

person's soul on its way to the afterlife (Whipple 1985), but other Native Americans, like the Blackfeet of Montana, feared these astronomical events. They believed that a meteor was a sign that sickness would come to the tribe in the coming winter, or that a great chief had just died (Coimbra 2010), considering these events as bad omens.

The cultural anthropologist Pascal Boyer (1993) argues that some aspects of religious traditions may be explained by intellectual factors, mainly the cognitive need of explaining and controlling natural phenomena. Indeed, the observation of comets and meteors must have created the necessity for an explanation among non-literate people. According to Boyer, the 'meanings' that are present in cultural phenomena are 'the consequence and manifestation of physical phenomena' (Boyer 1993: 8). Thus, a comet or a meteor (physical phenomena) creates the need for explanation, which produces spiritual or mythological thought (cultural phenomena).

According to Eliade (1975), among Indo-European cultures the sky itself was associated with the supreme god. Thus, unusual happenings such as cometary phenomena could have been interpreted as divine manifestations.

FINAL STATEMENTS

The astronomical representations in rock art that exist all over the world reveal a preoccupation of non-literate people with celestial events, registering those happenings in the sky probably for future generations. The ancient sky observation results, thus, in cognitive and spiritual processes, as this article has tried to illustrate. For example, if cometary phenomena have deeply impressed the minds of the observers, through time and space, it is not difficult to admit that these events could have been interpreted by early societies as manifestations of the gods and thus were carved or painted on rock surfaces in order to be worshipped.

After the analysis of several megalithic enclosures from Alentejo with respect to moon observation, the 'Equinox appears to be related to the Spring Full Moon, and this seems to be well supported by the orientation of funerary megaliths, as symbolic representations of resurrection, rebirth, or new life at the onset of Spring' (Oliveira and Silva 2010: 89).

These ideas become more plausible when connected to the depiction of crescent moons on some megaliths of the same region and with artefacts found in funerary contexts, such as votive limestone crescent moons and fertility symbols (hares, rabbits) made in bone (Oliveira and Silva 2010). And they fit with what E. Anati wrote some years before, that 'the illustration of myths and beliefs outlines essential aspects of our intellectual roots and displays the existential relationship between Man, Nature, and the Supernatural' (Anati 2004: 6).[10]

The sun images studied in this article focused only on rayed circle motives, with or without 'body', because the circle by itself can represent other subjects, as mentioned before.

---

[10] The number of the page in this Anati's article concerns the online version.

The examples analysed regarding the sun and the moon took into consideration that the art of sedentary populations 'with diversified economies, including farming activities, is characterized by mythological scenes, representation of human-like divinities or spirits, and repetitive schematic groupings of signs' (Anati 2004: 12). In fact, the sun depictions from Saimaly-Tash with a human body seem to fit perfectly with this classification.

Finally, we want to stress the preliminary character of this article, with reference to sun and moon depictions, since it is one of our aims to promote discussion among colleagues interested in this theme, in order to contribute to the development of research.

Acknowledgments

The presentation of this article in the XVI UISPP Congress at Florianopolis (Brazil) was supported by the Portuguese Republic, through FCT – Fundação para a Ciência e a Tecnologia, regarding the project PEst-OE/CTE/UI0073/2011.

Bibliography

ABELANET, J. 1990 Les roches gravées nord catalanes. *Terra Nostra*, no. 5, pp. 101–209. Centre d'Etudes Préhistoriques Catalanes. Université de Perpignan, Prada.

ALVIM, P. 2005 Megalithic enclosures of the region of the Monfurado hills and the 'hillocks of the mid-world'. www.crookscape.org

ANATI, E. 1994 Il linguaggio delle pietre. *Studi Camuni, XIII*, pp. 101–40. Centro Camuno di Studi Preistorici, Capo di Ponte.

ANATI, E. 2004 Introducing the World Archives of Rock Art (WARA): 50,000 years of visual arts. In *New discoveries, new interpretations, new research methods*, Proceedings of XXI Valcamonica Symposium. Edizioni del Centro, Capo di Ponte (online version), pp. 1–22. www.ccsp.it/ANATI WARA rev PRE.htm

BAILEY, M.E. 1995 Recent results in cometary astronomy: Implications for the Ancient Sky. *Vistas in Astronomy*, 39, pp. 647–71. Pergamon Press, Oxford.

BAILEY, M.E., CLUBE, S.V.M.; NAPIER, W.M. 1990 The origin of comets, pp. 1–39. Pergamon Press, Oxford,

BAPTISTA, A.M. 1981 A Rocha F-155 e a origem da arte do Vale do Tejo, pp. 9–83. GEAP, Porto.

BARALE, P. 2003 Il Cielo del popolo del Faggio: Sole, Luna e Stelle dei Ligures Bagienni, pp. 62, 122–34. Associazione Turistica Pro Loco, Pollenzo.

BELMONTE AVILES, J.A. 1999 As Leis do Céu. Astronomia e Civilizações Antigas, pp. 11–134, 169–287. Mareantes Editores, Lisboa.

BOYER, P. 1993 Cognitive aspects of religious symbolism, pp. 4–47. Cambridge University Press, Cambridge.

CALADO, M. 2004 Menires do Alentejo Central. Génese e Evolução da Paisagem Megalítica Regional. PhD thesis presented to the University of Lisbon (online version). www.crookscape.org

CALADO, M.; ROCHA, L. 2010 Megaliths as rock art in Alentejo, Southern Portugal. In D. Calado; M. Baldia; M. Boulanger (eds), *Monumental Questions: Prehistoric Megaliths, Mounds, and Enclosures*, Proceedings of the XV IUPPS Congress, pp. 25–31. BAR Publishing, Oxford.

COIMBRA, F.A. 2007 Comets and meteors in rock art: evidences and possibilities. 13th SEAC Conference Proceedings, Isili, pp. 250–6.

COIMBRA, F.A. 2008a Cognitive archeology, rock art and archaeoastronomy. In F. Coimbra; G. Dimitriadis (eds), *Cognitive archeology as symbolic archeology*, Proceedings of the XV IUPPS Congress, pp. 35–40. BAR Publishing, Oxford.

COIMBRA, F.A. 2008b Algumas considerações teóricas sobre Arqueoastronomia. *Revista de Portugal, Nova Série*, no. 5. Solar Condes de Resende, V.N. de Gaia, pp. 7–15.

COIMBRA, F.A. 2009 When open air carved rocks become sanctuaries: methodological criteria for a classification. In F. Djindjian; L. Oosterbeek (eds), *Symbolic Spaces in Prehistoric Art – Territories, travels and site locations*, Proceedings of XV IUPPS Congress, pp. 99–104. BAR Publishing, Oxford.

COIMBRA, F.A. 2010 The sky on the rocks: cometary images in rock art. *Fumdhamentos* IX. Proceedings of the Global Rock Art International Congress, Serra da Capivara, Brasil. Fumdham, São Raimundo Nonato. DVD.

DAVIS-KIMBALL, J.; MARTYNOV, A. 1993 Solar rock art and cultures of Central Asia. In *The Sun, symbol of power and life*, pp. 208–21. Harry N. Abrams, Paris.

ELIADE, M. 1975 História das ideias e crenças religiosas, pp. 173–80. Rés Editora, Porto.

GREEN, M. 1991 The Sun-Gods of Ancient Europe, pp. 11–60, 137–8. B.T. Batsford, London.

HASEGAWA, I. 1980 Catalogue of ancient and naked-eye comets. *Vistas in Astronomy, 24*, pp. 59–65, 102. Pergamon Press, Oxford.

KOBRES, B. 1992 Comets and the Bronze Age Collapse. http://abob.libs.uga.edu/bobk/bronze.html

MARTYNOV, A. 1999 Rock images of the ancient sanctuary Saimaly-Tach. CD-ROM. Pinerolo: CeSMAP. NEWS-95 International Rock Art Congress Proceedings.

MARTYNOV, A.; MARIACHEV, A.; ABETEKOV, A.K. 1992 *Gravures Rupestres de Saimaly-Tach*, pp. 3–57. Alma-Ata: Ministére de l'Instruction Publique de la République du Kazakhstan.

NAPIER, W.M. 1998 Cometary catastrophes, cosmic dust and ecological disasters in historical times: the astronomical framework. In B.J. Peiser; T. Palmer; M.E. Bailey (eds), Natural catastrophes during Bronze Age civilisations: archeological, geological, astronomical and cultural perspectives, *BAR International Series, 728*, pp. 21–32. Oxford.

OLIVEIRA, C.; SILVA, C.M. 2010 Moon, Spring and Large Stones. Landscape and ritual calendar perception and symbolization. In D. Calado; M. Baldia; M. Boulanger (eds), *Monumental Questions: Prehistoric Megaliths, Mounds, and Enclosures*, Proceedings of XV IUPPS Congress, pp. 83–90. BAR Publishing, Oxford.

OUZMAN, S. 2006 Flashes of brilliance: San rock paintings of Heaven's Things. In Lewis-Williams meeting book.

PLINY, C. 1951 *Plini Secundi – Naturalis Historiae, Liber II*. Translated by Jean Beaujeu, pp. 38–45. Société d'édition Les Belles Lettres, Paris.

RUGGLES, C.L.N.; BURL, H.A.W. 1995 Astronomical influences on prehistoric ritual architecture in North-Western Europe: the case of the stone rows. *Vistas in Astronomy, 39*, p. 517. Pergamon Press, Oxford.

SAGAN, C.; DRUYAN, A. 1986 Cometa, pp. 25–45, 159–71. Editora Gradiva, Lisboa.

SILVA, C.M. 2000 Sobre o possível significado astronómico do cromlech dos Almendres. *A Cidade de Évora, II / 4*, pp. 109–27. Évora.

SILVA, C.M.; CALADO, M. 2003 New Astronomically Significant Directions of Megalithic Monuments in the Central Alentejo. *Journal of Iberian Archaeology, 5*, pp. 67–88. ADECAP, Porto.

TAÇON, P.; CHIPPINDALE, C. 1998 An archeology of rock-art through informed methods and formal methods. In The Archeology of Rock Art, pp. 1–10. Cambridge University Press, Cambridge.

THACKERAY, J.F. 1988 Comets, meteors and trance: were these conceptually associated in southern African prehistory?. *Monthly Notes of the Astronomical Society of Southern Africa, 47*, pp. 49–52.

VIANA, A. 1950 Arqueologia dos arredores de Elvas. *Trabalhos de Antropologiae Etnologia, XII*, pp. 293, 304–6, 315–22. SPAE, Porto.

YEOMANS, D.K. 1991 Comets. A Chronological History of Observation, Science, Myth and Folklore, pp. 1–17, 42–50. Wiley and Sons, New York.

WHIPPLE, F. 1985 The Mystery of Comets, pp. 1-9. Cambridge University Press, Cambridge.

WOODHOUSE, B. 1986 Bushman paintings of comets?, *Monthly Notes from the Astronomical Society of South Africa*, 45, pp. 33–5.

ANCIENT MYTHS AND SCIENTIFIC FICTION: THE REPRESENTATION OF THE BIG HEAD IN PREHISTORIC ART AND ITS RECREATION IN WESTERN CULTURE

Santiago Wolnei Ferreira GUIMARÃES

Museu de Arte Pré-Histórica e do Sagrado no Vale do Tejo Largo, Mação, Portugal

Abstract: *In the history of social anthropology, the discussion concerning the creation of myth has been associated with the development of cultures. From this perspective, the mythological worldview of societies considered as primitive was, on the one hand, seen as a necessary factor for their existence as a group and, on the other hand, as an element of comparison between traditional and scientific knowledge. To know some of the similarities and differences of both worlds is important in order to better evaluate how the phenomenon of the creation of mythological knowledge should be understood. In this paper, we discuss this perspective using examples of figures that show anthropomorphic beings with a disproportionately large head compared with the rest of the body, both in prehistoric rock art and in images of contemporary society.*

THE PRE-CONTACT PUEBLO KACHINA IN THE AMERICAN SOUTHWEST: ITS ICONOGRAPHY, FIRST APPEARANCES, AND CONTEXTS OF SYMBOLIC MEANINGS

Jessica Joyce CHRISTIE

East Carolina University, USA

In this essay, I consider the forms and origin of the Pueblo Kachina (Katsina, pl. Katsiman in the Hopi language) and then discuss its multilayered meanings in pre-contact societies in the American Southwest. Methodologies of analysing Katsiman will be critically evaluated and questioned. The Katsina is internationally known in its form of carved and brightly painted wooden dolls which have become an icon of the Southwest (Figure 1). These Katsina dolls, *tihu* sgl., *tithu* pl. in the Hopi language, are derivatives of the wooden dolls the Hopi used to give to children in order to teach them the diagnostic features of their supernaturals. This example illustrates that the Katsina is not a figure of the remote past but well and alive among 21st-century Pueblo societies and in a global market. In order to explore the pre-contact meanings of the Pueblo Katsina, we have to strip away contemporary layers and concentrate on archeological materials and early appearances of Katsina features in rock art, on pottery sherds, as well as in *kiva* murals (kivas are semi-subterranean chambers reserved for religious performances). The pre-contact era in the Southwest came to an end in 1540 when a Spanish expedition led by Francisco Vasquez de Coronado reached the Zuni villages. Ethnographic analogy will be used as a vital methodology to illuminate cultural context since ancestral Pueblo societies did not leave any written records. Such an approach, of course, relies on strong cultural continuities between the pre-contact period and the decades before and after 1900, during which time most ethnographic reports were composed.

Who are Katsiman? Katsiman are powerful supernaturals in the American Southwest related to clouds, rain and agricultural fertility, to the dead and the ancestors. They manifest themselves in their costumes and ritual paraphernalia, in particular specific masks, as ritual impersonators of the deities and in the form of carved Katsina dolls in their likeness. Katsina iconography has been documented at pre-contact ancestral Pueblo sites and they continue to perform in contemporary Pueblo and related Hopi and Zuni villages, all situated in the larger area of the Four Corners region (the point where the state lines of New Mexico, Arizona, Colorado and Utah meet at 90 degree angles) in the southwestern United States (Figure 2). Katsiman continue to visit the Hopi villages according to the ritual calendar: they arrive around the time of the winter solstice in the middle of winter and stay through the planting and growing season. At harvest

Figure 1 – Katsina doll representing Talava (Morning Singer). Adapted from Pearlstone 2001a: Fig. II.1

time at midsummer, they return to their homes in the San Francisco mountains.

Katsiman are identified by their masks. Although they wear a full body costume, it is the mask which defines their individual identity. In Hopi villages, Katsina masks are powerful ritual objects which are kept wrapped and

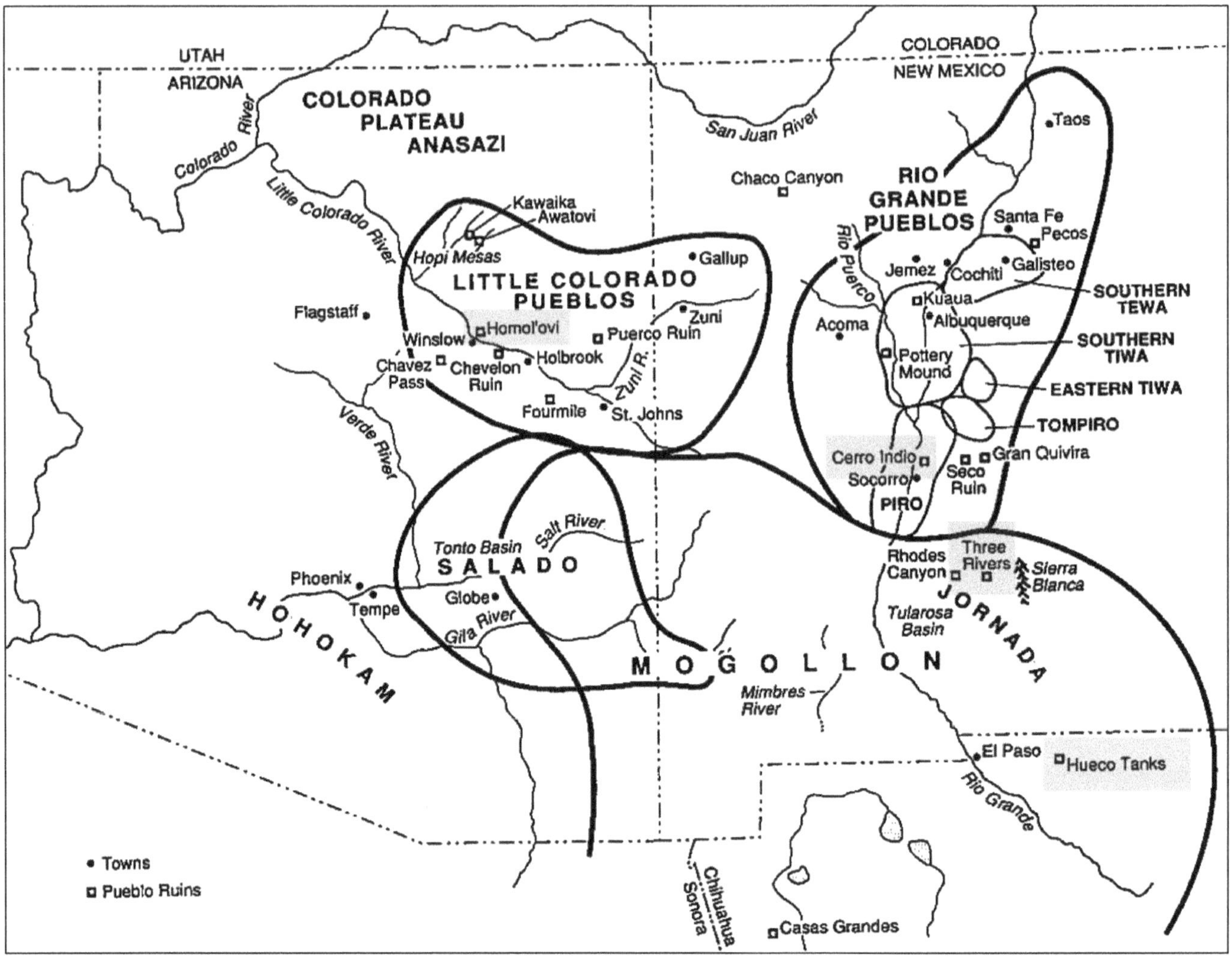

Figure 2 – Map of Ancestral Pueblo sites, contemporary Pueblos, and Pueblo-related cultures. Sites mentioned in the text are shaded. Adapted from Adams 1994: Fig. 5.1

stored away and only taken out for use in performances. Armin Geertz (1986: 45) reports about the mask:

> Every boy who is initiated into the Katsina Cult has the right to own a mask. A mask is made of leather but it is believed to be alive. Therefore it must be kept fed and hidden when stored, just like other animate ritual objects. The term for the mask is tuviku, but this term is seldom used, since the uninitiated children would learn that the Katsinas are not gods but their uncles, fathers and brothers in masks and costumes. Thus the masks are always called kwaatsi, 'friend'.

Thus the potency of the mask is of beneficial nature to the Hopi people and must be carefully guarded and protected. Louis Hieb (1994: 28–30) reports specific meanings of the mask belonging to the Ma 'lo Katsina (Figure 3): the mask is formed of a leather casing painted red and blue (or green) and has a tubular mouth. At the left side of this mask, there is a squash blossom and at the right side two tall feathers with a tuft of red hair. The mask rests on a wreath of Douglas fir. All the elements of the mask hold specific meanings which local consultants identify: the colours of the Katsina, yellow, blue, red, and white, are related to the four cardinal directions (Hieb 1994: 29).

Figure 3 – Drawing of Ma 'lo Katsina mask. Adapted from Hieb 1994: Fig. 4.4a

Alexander Stephen (1936: 215–16) explains that the eye of the Katsina is the seed of all plants and vice versa, the seed of any plant is its eye (*poosi*). It follows that the eyebrow becomes a cloud over the seed ready to release rain and start germination. The two black tipped feathers represent the Above and the feather spray on top of the mask represents the Below (Hieb 1994: 29). Stephen (1936: 216) further elaborates that the mouth is an ear of corn with open slits through which the impersonator emits his song-prayer. The Hopi usually depict the corn ear in a realistic manner but here it is only shown in a cylinder form to indicate its prototype. The reason for this is that 'through the mouth come prayers, not only for corn, but for all other essentials, hence the corn ear should not be too specifically manifest' (Stephen 1936: 216). In these ways, the Katsina mask communicates on multiple levels, setting up Hopi moral space and cosmology as well as the place of humans within it to those literate in the traditional iconography.

FIRST APPEARANCES OF KATSIMAN

Researchers agree that Katsina cults have pre-contact origins (Adams 1994: 37–9; Schaafsma 1994; Hays 1994; and many others). Spanish documents dating as early as 1582 report on Katsina ceremonies and depictions of Katsina figures in murals on the walls of rooms (for example, White 1932). Two-dimensional images of Katsina masks abound in rock art and ceramics dated approximately to between the late 1200s and 1450 (Adams 1994; Schaafsma 1994, 1999) and are common in kiva murals and on painted stone slabs.

THE KATSINA MASK IN ROCK ART

The earliest evidence of images in the form of abstract masked faces comes from the Zuni-Cibola and Quemado regions and has been assigned dates prior to AD 400 based upon close stylistic similarities with Basketmaker II designs in the surrounding areas (Young 1988: 65–8) (Figure 4). Polly Schaafsma, together with her husband Curtis, has devoted a lifetime to the investigation of rock art in the Southwest and has accumulated vast amounts of data. Many of Polly Schaafsma's publications concentrate on the eastern or Rio Grande Pueblos (Figure 2). Concerning the origins of Katsina imagery, she offers a compelling model developed from rock art (Schaafsma 1994). According to her (1994: 64–5,78–9), images of Katsina masks abound in Jornada Mogollon and Rio Grande rock art in the 14th century. Jornada Mogollon sites are situated in the lower regions of the Rio Grande River, corresponding to southern New Mexico, and have been dated between 1000 and 1450 CE. Rio Grande Pueblo sites are located along the contiguous upper sections of the Rio Grande and date slightly later with a temporal overlap between about 1300 and 1400 CE. Katsina-style imagery in the form of mask depictions spread from the Mogollon to the Pueblo areas and is visible in possibly a thousand petroglyphs portraying Katsina-like masks. The petroglyphs were created by scratching and pecking dark patina from rock surfaces to expose the lighter-coloured rock underneath. The lighter colour makes up the lines and solid areas which compose the images.

Three Rivers is a Jornada Mogollon site located in southern New Mexico to the east of the Rio Grande River (Figure 2). Its dates range broadly from about 1050 and 1450 CE. Three Rivers exhibits the foundations and walls of a Pueblo-style settlement. Further uphill, dark boulders are scattered along a ridge line, which displays hundreds of petroglyphs. Many of these petroglyphs are figurative and include images of masks (Figure 5). Schaafsma (1994: 66–7) explains the Jornada-style masks as links between the earlier human and animal figures on Classic Mimbres funerary ceramics (c. 1050–1150 CE) and later Rio Grande Pueblo IV Katsina imagery. Cerro Indio (Figure 2) is a 14th-century Piro site belonging to Rio

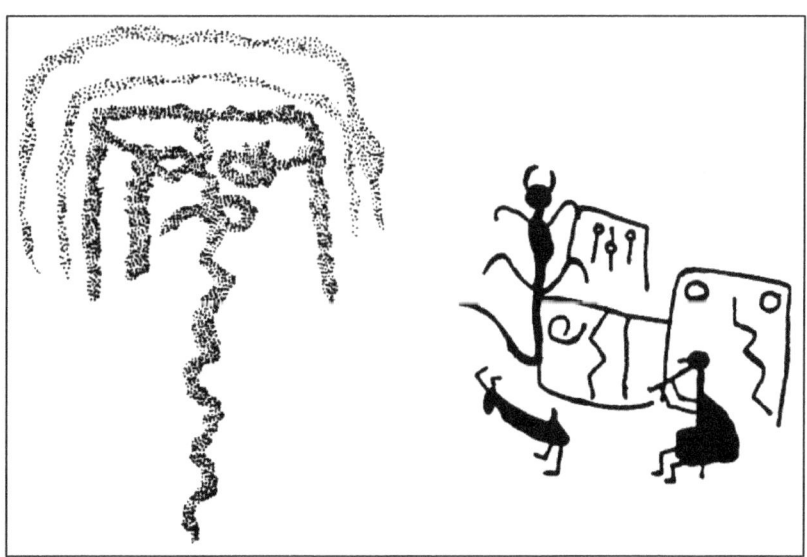

Figure 4 – Early pecked and abstracted masks possibly executed before A.D. 400.
Adapted from Young 1988: Figure 25

Figure 5 – Three Rivers, petroglyph portraying Katsina-style mask. Adapted from www.coxontool.com/index.php/Travels/20090520

Figures 6 – Cerro Indio, petroglyph of Katsina-style mask. Note the stepped motif referencing clouds. Photograph by the author

Figure 7 – Petroglyphs of Koyemsi Katsina near Homol'ovi II on the Little Colorado River, Arizona, and post-contact Koyemsi or Mudhead mask. Adapted and combined from Adams 1994: Fig. 5.2 and Hieb 1994: Fig. 4.4b

Grande Pueblo IV and is situated north of the city of Socorro in central New Mexico, a short distance east of the Rio Grande. The site layout is similar to that of Three Rivers: on a hillside, near the ruins of a settlement, dark-coloured boulders exhibit hundreds of petroglyphs, a majority of which represent masks (Figure 6). Sally Cole (1990: 148–50) documented Katsina imagery in rock art of the Little Colorado River Basin west of the Rio Grande (Figure 2) and has assigned dates of 1250–1300 CE based upon their association with radiocarbon dated pueblos (Figure 7).

In her survey of rock art in the Zuni-Cibola region, Jane Young (1988: 139–45, 245–6) recorded numerous Katsina images. Most notable are long panels of colorful painted masks and figures at her site 1, the area surrounding a large ancestral Pueblo living complex known as the Village of the Great Kivas and dating to the early part of the 11th century. Numerous petroglyphs and pictographs were documented and some of them are probably contemporary with the ruin. Young's Zuni consultants have identified most of the masks with Katsiman they are familiar with (Figure 8). She (1988: 139, 157–8) dates these paintings between AD 1325 and the late 1800s, including the possibility that some were executed as recently as in the last 50 years. The latter possibility is confirmed by the fact that a new mask of a mountain sheep or wild ram was added during the time of the survey between 1980 and 1981 (Young 1988: 245–6, Figures 75, 76). Other deeply incised figures of Katsiman and masks have been documented at site 2 and roughly dated to the late seventh-century period of occupation of an associated village (Young 1988: 246, Figures 14, 26b, 26c, 26e).

Why were these petroglyphs and pictographs created and how would they have been used? In the absence of archeological material directly associated with the boulders or ethnographic accounts which would describe pre-contact visits of the petroglyphs by local people, I take the approach of analysing their spatial setting. Physical space surrounding most petroglyph boulders as well as in rock shelters is limited, precarious and does not accommodate large audiences. This would suggest that the mask petroglyphs were created for personal and individual encounters with Katsiman or visions thereof, as opposed to Katsina performances in Pueblo plazas

Figure 8 – Section of a panel of painted Katsina masks and figures from the Village of the Great Kivas site, Zuni-Cibola region; dated post-1325 to present. Adapted from Young 1988: Figures 69, 73-76

organized for the entire village. Although Adams (1994: 42–4) argues that Katsina iconography appeared in conjunction with enclosed plaza-type Pueblo communities, Katsiman seem to have communicated in multiple settings in pre-contact times: public appearances in Pueblo plazas, more private performances inside kivas, and individual interactions at rock art panels as well as between dancer and mask, if we project current practices back into the past (see above).

THE KATSINA MASK IN CERAMICS

Depictions of masked human-like faces on Pueblo pottery have been documented as early as the late 1200s and became widespread by the mid-1300s (Hays 1989, 1994). Katsina-style masks are shown on different pottery types from the southern areas of the Four Corner region (Hays 1994: 48–9, Table 6.1) (Figure 9). Kelly Hays (1989) analysed the ceramics from six related Ancestral Pueblo sites near Winslow, Arizona, which are collectively known as Homol'ovi and have been dated to the earlier Pueblo IV period, approximately AD 1275–1400. The 14th century was a time of growth in the Homol'ovi settlements, and Hays (1989: 305–7) suggests that the emerging Katsina cult as documented in ceramics could have served as a social mechanism to integrate and hold together the growing communities. Her argument is based upon ethnographic analogy: Pueblo societies have traditionally had many war, healing, and rainmaking sodalities which initiated selected individuals shaping a religious hierarchy. The Katsina cult, on the other hand and especially at Hopi, is open to all community members and would have propagated a message of social unity and cooperation. Such a context is further reinforced by the archeological provenance of most of the ceramics bearing Katsina depictions: the majority was found in domestic and refuse deposits and in burials as opposed to kivas. If Katsina iconography had been concentrated in kivas, it would speak for exclusive elite rites. Further, certain vessels with Katsina imagery, from all kinds of deposits, show some use wear (Hays 1989:

Figure 9 – Sherd from a Talpa Black-on-white pot and rockart images with horned Katsina masks, origin of ceramic sherd: Pot Creek Pueblo, Rio Grande; origin of rockart from the Little Colorado River. Adapted and combined from Hays 1994: Fig. 6.8 and Adams 1994: Fig. 5.2

306). The archeological evidence therefore suggests that Katsina masks on pots did not originate in any restricted elite social or ritual context.

THE KATSINA MASK IN KIVA MURALS AND ON PAINTED SLABS

Katsina-related imagery has further been documented in kiva murals dated between 1400 and 1600, for example at Kuaua in the Rio Grande Valley and at Pottery Mound. At Kuaua, some 600 rooms were unearthed including multiple kivas. One kiva had been replastered at least 87 times and 25 of these 87 thin plaster layers held murals. The murals were executed when Kuaua society prospered, approximately between 1450 and the early 16th century. Although fragmentary, many murals display ceremonial figures with mask-like features and holding Katsina-related paraphernalia. Bertha Dutton (1963) investigated the meaning of these murals, enlisting the help of Native North American consultants. A Zuni consultant, Zna'ote, identified a masked figure on Layer N-41 as Paiyatuma (Dutton 1963: 56–8) (Figure 10).

Paiyatuma appears to have been a powerful supernatural with multiple aspects, all of which were beneficial to humankind. In oral traditions, he is linked with the sky and rainbow, agricultural fertility, the hunt, the sun as well as with music (Dutton 1963: 57–8, 75–6, 110–11). Hays and Gilpin (1999: 19–20) offer the interesting suggestion that he personifies one of the cases in which female progenitive power as represented in Flower World imagery coalesces with male ritual activity. Parsons

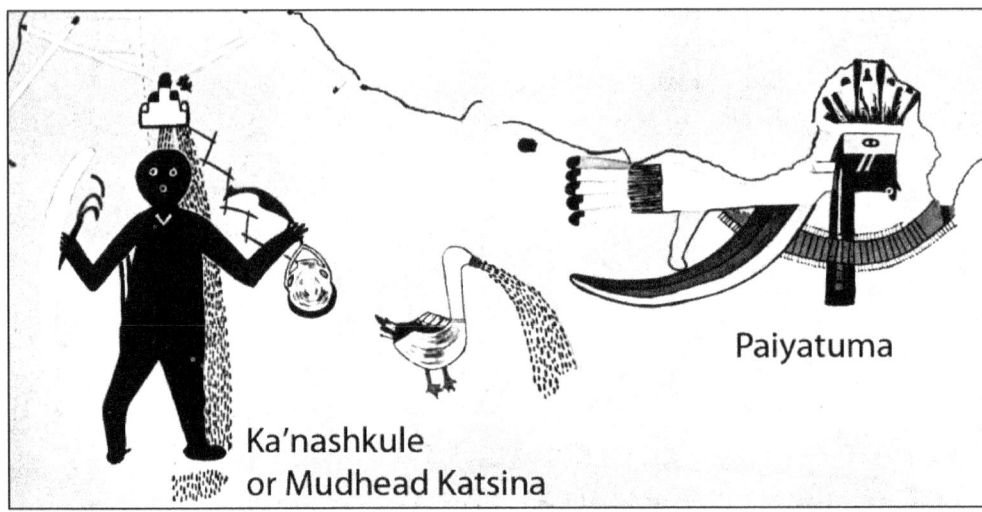

Figure 10 – Paiyatuma and Ka'nashkule in Layer N-41 of the Kuaua murals, Coronado State Monument, New Mexico. Adapted from Dutton 1963: Figures 93, 95, Plate X

(1920: 91) notes that at Laguna, Paiyatuma was impersonated among the Katsiman and appeared in the mixed Katsina dances. Continuing on Layer N-41, the next ceremonial figure to the right of Paiyatuma exhibits a dark body and eyes and mouth formed by white circles. This outfit is characteristic of the well-known contemporary Mudhead Katsina, who performs in many pueblos as a general clown. Zna'ote identified him as K'a'nashkule, a leader who procures food for his people, as a rain cloud altar hovers above his head (Dutton 1963: 58). Dutton (1963: Figure 95) explains Ka'nashkule as a priest-clown-medicine man. I count the Paiyatuma and Ka'nashkule figures among the strongest cases of documented pre-contact Katsina images within a partially reconstructable context of meaning.

As a more general observation, kiva iconography seems to concentrate on narrative scenes involving multiple ritual impersonators, while a majority of examples in rock art and on ceramics display masked heads cropped from their full bodies. The spatial context infers that kiva murals explained Katsiman performances inside kivas, whereas petroglyph masks documented individual encounters with Katsiman.

Pre-contact Katsina depictions have also been attested on painted stone slabs (Hays 1989: 307). Scholars think that such slabs originally functioned as altar paraphernalia, since similar objects formed parts of altars, according to ethnographic reports.

MEANINGS OF KATSIMAN

Katsiman are the main supernaturals of the Pueblo people whose economy used to be based primarily on agriculture, and consequently their meaning centred on plant fertility. More specifically, Katsiman are related to rain, clouds, the dead and ancestors. As we explore these meanings further, we must keep in mind that the Pueblo people were and are composed of many different subgroups who even speak different languages. Given the scope of this short essay and by employing ethnographic analogy, we are by necessity suppressing such differences and emphasizing strong cultural linkages among social groups and over time.

First and foremost, the meaning of Katsiman is deeply embedded in the southwestern landscape and seasonal cycles. In Puebloan thought, mountains are the homes of the Katsiman: they visit human villages during the growing season and return to their mountain homes after the harvest. For example, the Hopi identify the San Francisco Peaks as Katsiman homes and the Acoma Mount Taylor (Schaafsma and Taube 2006: 238; Schaafsma 1999: 173). These same mountains attract clouds, collect water and dispense rain. Zuni narratives further describe Katsiman homes as a Katsiman village situated in a lake inside a mountain. There are references which liken some masks of the Katsiman to clouds (Stevenson 1894: 315; Schaafsma and Taube 2006: 239; Schaafsma 1999: 173–4). In Zia oral narratives, clouds are explained as masks of the rainmakers (Stevenson 1894: 38). Clouds are typically represented as a terraced stepped form and this cloud terrace constitutes a multivalent symbol in the Southwest, which may also recall mountains and the rain-bringing spirits of the dead (Schaafsma and Taube 2006: 239). Cloud terraces frequently appear in Katsina-related imagery, for example the pre- and post-contact *tablita* headdresses (Figure 11). Potent examples which coalesce multiple references to the rain cult are petroglyphs portraying Katsina masks with cloud terrace designs and assuming the shape of a bowl referring to a container of the desired liquid (Figure 12).

References to clouds link Katsiman with selected dead and the ancestors; for instance, the Hopi placed cloud masks of cotton over the faces of their deceased. At several pueblos, the dead were prepared for burial by painting part of the body white. At Zuni, ownership of a Katsina mask guaranteed that the deceased would be

Figure 11 – Tablita with Qa'otiyo (Corn Boy) Katsina which combines a tablita headdress with a Katsina mask. Adapted from Pearlstone 2001b: Fig. 3.59

Figure 12 – Early Pueblo IV petroglyph mask in the form of a bowl with cloud symbolism. Adapted from Schaafsma 1999: Fig. 12.20

admitted to Katsina Lake and become a Katsina who would return to his village bringing rain for the living (Schaafsma and Taube 2006: 261). Thus Katsiman are instrumental in regenerating the cycle of life from death to ascending to the cloud spirits and producing rain to fertilize the earth and engender new life. In this sense, they may be seen as the personifications par excellence of the life forces in the arid environment of the southwest.

The stepped motifs of the cloud terraces often appear in sets of four recalling the four world mountains as well as the four colours of the cardinal directions. For example, the Museum of Indian Arts and Culture in Santa Fe, New Mexico, owns an El Paso Polychrome bowl dated approximately AD 1200–1425 which exhibits four cloud terraces along its rim decorated with rainbows (Schaafsma and Taube 2006: Figure 7; Young 1988: Figures 49.50). Dutton (1963: 110–11) cites a beautiful scene of a band of aged finely dressed flute players seated around a great world bowl. Paiyatuma introduced the ghost-like sisters of the seven earthly corn maidens, each

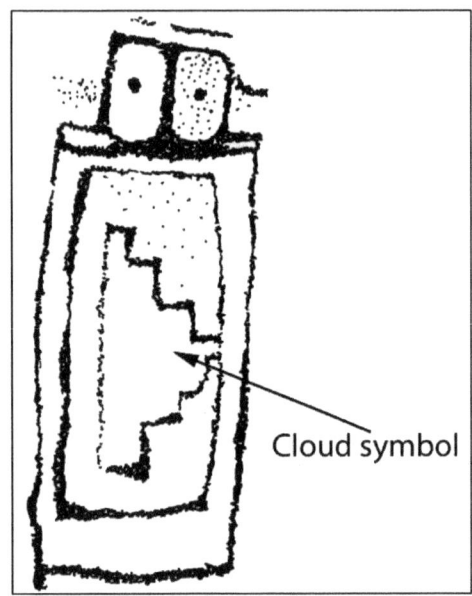

Figure 13 – Tlaloc figure with stepped cloud motif, from Three Rivers, New Mexico. Adapted from Schaafsma 1999: Fig. 12.11

holding wands of cottonwood from which rose tiny clouds. 'White mists floated up from the wands of the maidens and mingled with the breath of the flutes over the terraced world-bowl, above which sported the butterflies of Summerland, about the dress of the Rainbow in the strange blue light of the night' (Dutton 1963: 111). Katsina masks and costumes are always painted in unmixed colours of normal value and full intensity, often referencing the four world colours (see the Ma 'lo Katsina mask above). It therefore appears that the Katsina figure also condenses the four horizontal cardinal directions. We may conclude that the pre-contact Katsina represented the centre of the Pueblo cosmogram and world order by personifying the vertical divisions of the cosmos from the watery underworld to the cloud spirits of the sky as well as its quadripartite horizontal extension.

As a geographic extension, scholars have noted similarities in Mesoamerican and Southwest iconographies. One figure who is closely related to the Katsina cult is the Mesoamerican Tlaloc (Schaafsma 1999). Tlaloc is a highly complex deity with various associations which range from rain and agricultural fertility to warfare. He may appear in multiple disguises, but one of his persistent identifying features are circular goggle eyes (Figure 13). In the Southwest, masks with goggle eyes begin to appear on a Mimbres black-on-white bowl between AD 1000 and 1150 and continue to be portrayed in Jornada Mogollon and Rio Grande Pueblo-style rock art (Schaafsma 1999: 175–84). Although the southwestern Tlaloc figure does not seem to carry all the dimensions of his Mesoamerican counterpart, the Mogollon and Pueblo people clearly adopted him as a rain-bringer. The evidence is twofold: first, many of the Tlaloc representations show stepped fret and terrace motifs, all cloud symbols, decorating their torsos. Second, the site of Hueco Tanks located outside El Paso, Texas, boasts at least 17 Tlaloc paintings linked to its function as a rest stop with water in the Chihuahuan desert. Hueco Tanks consists of three rock outcrops rising above the flat surrounding desert landscape. These outcrops are filled with caves and rock overhangs, passageways and small stone reservoirs where water collects. Numerous Tlaloc faces and other masks have been documented in recesses containing water (Schaafsma 1999: 179, Figure 12.7). The parallels with Tlaloc expand the meanings of the pre-contact Katsina to Mesoamerican rain and fertility cults and worldviews.

CONCLUDING REMARKS

While this essay considers the meanings of the pre-contact Katsina, we cannot lose sight of the fact that Katsiman continue to be living and active beings in contemporary Pueblo societies. They still visit the Hopi according to the traditional calendar, but indigenous Southwest cultures have undergone remarkable changes. Most Pueblo people no longer live off the land but have city jobs and return to their communities on days of ritual and celebration. Thus individuals have distanced themselves from the seasonal agricultural cycles. Nevertheless, most Zuni subscribe to what Young (1988: 172) calls an 'aesthetic of accumulation'. What she means is that Katsina appearances and calendar rituals are not limited to the goal of soliciting rain but that they encompass a general concept of increase and multiplicity of all aspects of wellbeing. This was observed by Barbara Tedlock (cited in Young 1988: 172) during the summer rain dances. Traditionally, performers have carried fruits and seeds of important crops in their belts to empower their requests. Accompanying the economic shift at Zuni from farming to the tourist market, many dancers now carry chunks of turquoise instead of agricultural products in their belts. Although the song texts have not changed, the performance of visual culture alludes to prosperity in terms of increased sales of jewellery. Katsiman play roles of differing importance in individual families; for example, carvers live from the sale of their Katsina dolls whereas traditionalists oppose such proliferation of Katsina iconography (Kuwanwisiwma 2001). The Katsina has taken on a public and even global identity as a result of the tourism industry (Pearlstone 2001), yet at the same time it has maintained a private face and acquired contexts of meanings that we, as cultural outsiders, are not privileged to share. From this perspective, the Katsina remains the personification of the Pueblo worldview in the 21st century and demands our respect. We should further project the multiplicity of roles for Katsiman in contemporary Pueblo societies back to pre-contact times and emphasize that Katsiman have always been living dynamic entities who evolve and adjust to specific historical circumstances, whose meanings are never static and defy simple explanations. Such processes can be condensed under Young's (1988: 158–9) concepts of ambiguity and permeability. Pre-contact images of Katsiman may be ambiguous in their power to evoke multiple narratives of myth time and at the same time specific in their ability to manifest living supernatural beings. The boundaries between past and present are fluid and the past permeates the present.

References

ADAMS, C. 1994 The Katsina Cult: A Western Pueblo Perspective. In Kachinas in the Pueblo World, edited by Polly Schaafsma, pp. 35–46. University of New Mexico Press, Albuquerque.

COLE, S. 1990 Legacy in Stone. Johnson Books, Boulder CO.

DUTTON, B. 1963 Sun Father's Way. The Kiva Murals of Kuaua. The University of New Mexico Press, Albuquerque.

GEERTZ, A. 1986 A Typology of Hopi Indian Ritual. Temenos 22: pp. 41–56.

HAYS, K. 1989 Katsina Depictions on Homol'ovi Ceramics: Toward a Fourteenth-Century Pueblo Iconography. Kiva, Vol. 54, No. 3, pp. 297–311. The Homol'ovi Research Program: Investigations into the Prehistory of the Middle Little Colorado River Valley. Published by Arizona Archeological and Historical Society.

HAYS, K. 1994 Kachina Depictions on Prehistoric Pueblo Pottery. In Kachinas in the Pueblo World, edited by Polly Schaafsma, pp. 47–62. University of New Mexico Press, Albuquerque.

HAYS-GILPIN, Kelley and HILL, Jane H. 1999 The Flower World in Material Culture: An Iconographic Complex in the Southwest and Mesoamerica. Journal of Anthropological Research, Vol. 55, No. 1, pp. 1–37. Published by University of New Mexico.

HIEB, L. 1994 The Meaning of Katsina: Toward a Cultural Definition of 'Person' in Hopi Religion. In Kachinas in the Pueblo World, edited by Polly Schaafsma, pp. 23–33. University of New Mexico Press, Albuquerque.

KUWANWISIWMA, L. 2001 Introduction: From the Sacred to the Cash Register – Problems Encountered in Protecting the Hopi Cultural Patrimony. In Katsina Commodified and Appropriated Images of Hopi Supernaturals, edited by Zena Pearlstone, pp. 16–21. UCLA Fowler Museum of Cultural History, Los Angeles.

PEARLSTONE, Zena (editor) 2001a Katsina Commodified and Appropriated Images of Hopi Supernaturals. UCLA Fowler Museum of Cultural History, Los Angeles.

PEARLSTONE, Zena (editor) 2001b The Contemporary Katsina. In Katsina Commodified and Appropriated Images of Hopi Supernaturals, edited by Zena Pearlstone, pp. 38–127. UCLA Fowler Museum of Cultural History, Los Angeles.

SCHAAFSMA, P. 1994 The Prehistoric Kachina Cult and Its Origins as Suggested by Southwestern Rock Art. In Kachinas in the Pueblo World, edited by Polly Schaafsma, pp. 63–79. University of New Mexico Press, Albuquerque.

SCHAAFSMA, P. 1999 Tlalocs, Kachinas, Sacred Bundles, and Related Symbolism in the Southwest and Mesoamerica. In The Casas Grandes World, edited by Curtis F. Schaafsma and Carroll L. Riley, pp. 164–92. The University of Utah Press, Salt Lake City.

SCHAAFSMA, P. and TAUBE, K. 2006 Bringing the Rain: An Ideology of Rain Making in the Pueblo Southwest and Mesoamerica. In *A Pre-Columbian World*, edited by Jeffrey Quilter and Mary Miller. Dumbarton Oaks Research Library and Collection, Dumbarton Oaks, Washington, D.C.

STEPHEN, A. 1936 Hopi Journal of Alexander M. Stephen. Edited by E.C. Parsons, Columbia University Contributions to Anthropology 23 (2 vols). Columbia University Press, New York.

WHITE, L. 1932 The Acoma Indians. Forty-Seventh Annual Report of the Bureau of American Ethnology, 1929–1930, pp. 17–192.

YOUNG, J. 1988 Signs from the Ancestors. University of New Mexico Press, Albuquerque.

DEER REPRESENTATION IN SERRA DA CAPIVARA NATIONAL PARK: MORPHOLOGY, SYNTAX AND ARCHEOLOGICAL CONTEXTS. A VISUAL ANALYSIS

Elaine IGNACIO, Portugal

Abstract: *If we try to articulate these different themes, we understand that they rely on a detailed comprehension of the deer's behaviour in their relationship with humans; in other words, the different themes illustrate the essential moments of the relationship that we may call symbiotic: the deer are the sustenance and identity component of humans and the humans are the guarantee of the deer's preservation. The anthropomorphic figure carrying the deer is an element that crowns this relationship.*

The morphological analysis of the deer paintings facilitated the identification of a restricted set of themes. The syntax of these themes suggested the organization of the themes in two main sets: the scenes with human presence and the ones without it.

In the first group, it is possible to identify three themes: the isolated deer (the theme of identity of the base), the deer in double representation (that illustrates three basic units of the deer's behaviour, the conjugation of both sexes, the maternal relationship and the two males, which may be seen as a confrontation between them) and the deer in a group (representation of the social unity of the deer).

In the second group, it is possible to identify two hunting-related themes: the hunt (the group of humans in relation with the group of deer) and the anthropomorphic figure carrying a deer (a prime symbiotic image).

INDIGENOUS DOLLS AND FIGURINES: WHERE SACRED AND SOCIAL WORLDS MERGE

Sharon K. MOSES, Philadelphia, USA

Abstract: Archeologists are often confronted with figurines or miniature objects that replicate human beings, human-hybrid forms, or zoomorphic images. These artefacts frequently turn up in or around middens, courtyards and outlying places, and as a consequence are often given the designation of child's toy. Conversely, when they are found in a collective niche or special deposit, they are designated as cult objects. This dichotomy gives two very different trajectories of investigation and attention to the artefact. If the label is 'toy' its implied associations with children will likely place it in an uninterpretable category because it is viewed as an expression of children's play or discard and therefore, an arbitrary deposit. In addition, children's activities have been historically viewed as less pertinent than adult activities when archeologists search for patterned behaviours that are expected to answer larger social, economic, or religious questions.

This paper will argue that these dichotomies reflect a Western bias about material culture, and by interpreting dolls or figurines from non-ritual contexts in such a dichotomized way, archeologists miss opportunities to allow artefacts to inform on the social and religious complexity of non-literate peoples. Dolls and figurines are frequently imbued with multiple meanings, both sacred and secular, in oral tradition societies. They are simultaneously expressions of art, the supernatural and social learning artefacts, and when allowed to 'speak', give insights into those communities. This paper will posit different ways to view these artefacts and enrich archeological interpretation rather than limit it according to Western paradigms.

INTRODUCTION

The problem

Figurines and other items of material culture that fall into the category of children's playthings tend to be disregarded by archeologists and viewed as less serious objects of study. Unfortunately, archeologists from Western cultures tend to follow interpretative assumptions about the role of children in any given society and by caveat, any objects believed accessible to or used by children. Children are often assumed to have limited agency, hold minor roles in society and are primarily located at the periphery of larger social issues in an adult world. Although the archeological literature over the last two decades concedes that children are affected by and also affect social matters, the view persists that children act and contribute to the archeological record primarily under adult rules and supervision and therefore their behaviour patterns and material culture are sources of secondary importance, if at all. According to the defining points of that paradigm, children's behaviour outside adult supervision, such as their use and effect on the deposition of artefacts, is seen as arbitrary and without rational interpretative value. Children's independent activities and resultant artefact distribution have historically been perceived in archeology as an interference in interpretation rather than a meaningful addition to it (David and Kramer 2001:14–16; Hammond and Hammond 1981).

Furthermore, children's social value is often summed up in terms of their contribution as a labor source in societies where the household is the core economic unit and their value based upon production or as actors in supporting roles (Deevey 1968; Hassan 1980; McDowell 1981; Sussman 1972; White 1975). Therefore, it is the adult agenda, adult behaviours and adult material culture associated with adult agency that is primarily imbued with legitimacy and it is this data set that archeologists focus upon to inform on larger social issues. In recent years some have expressed concern about overcoming these self-limiting and outdated paradigms (Baxter 2005; Handel 1988; Lillehammer 1989; Sofaer Derevenski 1994).

Matters such as economics, trade, power relations, religion, technology, and production, to name a few, dictate the direction of many research questions away from what is considered the child's purview. It seems only when questions are directed toward socialization and related issues that children and their material culture come to the fore as a primary interest. Over time, this dichotomous approach driven by Western cultural assumptions and social values has led to an entrenched research approach based largely upon perceptions about adult or sub-adult roles and agency in society. Ironically, I argue it is this very factor that limits archeologists as they strive to understand preliterate cultures and reconstruct the daily lives of ancient populations.

Contrary to this entrenched view, there is an abundant ethnographic corpus about pre- and non-literate cultures that demonstrate that material culture often represents multivariant, utilitarian and sacred uses and meanings simultaneously. These meanings frequently overlap and pose implications for larger social issues. These artefacts may function as art, ritual object(s), or children's toys or socialization devices (Child and Child 1993; Gill 1983; Lee 1999; McQuiston 1995; Park 1998; Underhill 1953, 1965; Zedeño 2008).

It would seem archeologists must first come to an agreement in terms or at the very least, identify the core of the problem with the categories we use: what are we labelling dolls, toys, figurines, or cult or ritual objects? To begin with, the word 'doll' in the Western lexicon conjures up ideas regarding purpose and design. A standard dictionary definition generally identifies a 'doll' as a miniature or anthropomorphic replica resembling a human being, normally intended as a child's plaything. This definition follows a Western perspective and attached to it is Western cultural baggage that may be inappropriate for non-Western cultural interpretations. The definition of toy also sets up a delineation of value: a plaything has less value than a utilitarian or necessary object.

Besides amusement, toys in a Western view may be teaching or communicative aides and most obviously play a role in socialization: proper behaviours connected to gender, age, class or other aspects of social identity. Toys may also reflection cultural trends. Ultimately, however, a toy holds little significance beyond the child's social and cultural world. Once removed from the child's world and associated with adult deposits and uses, however, the category of doll disappears and the literature reflects this shift. These artefacts are referred to as figurines, statuettes, miniatures or cult objects.

Archeologically, context determines the range of interpretative value. Simultaneous or multivariant meaning that relates equal social importance is practically non-existent in a Western interpretation. Value is prescribed according to who possessed the artefact last based upon its contextual disposition. Context might suggest a shaman, an artist, or a merchant and so on.

The concept of necessity also seems intertwined with the concept of value in the Western mind; this attribution should be avoided in assessing the material culture of non-literate societies. Some studies suggest that artistic examples of self-expression, the sacred and identity came first in utilizing new and experimental technologies in non-literate societies. It was after technologies used in creative expression were established that they were directed toward generating utilitarian objects (Hosler 1995; Vandiver et al. 1989).

The wheel in pre-Classic and Classic Mesoamerica for instance, was a component of a number of discovered toys and figurines. At the same time, the wheel was not used for transport on adult-use conveyances. Also, metals and metalworking were little exploited, although resources (copper) were available. Metalworking for ceremonial or decorative items such as copper bells seems to have been the exception (Hosler 1995). While it can be argued that the wheel was known but not utilized due to lack of beasts of burden and the rough geographic terrain in regions of Central America, Mesoamerican civilizations were adept at creating complex city landscapes and roadways. One would assume that if not practical for overland transport, the wheel could have served in urban landscapes had they been inclined. It was not until the post-Classic period in Mesoamerica that metal working of utilitarian items such as weaponry or tools (axes) are found.

Another example from the Upper Paleolithic and the Early Neolithic period of the Near East is the absence of fired pottery or ceramics. Despite the fact that much of human society had become sedentary and had developed domestic plants and/or animals, firing and partial firing of clay first makes an appearance with figurines and beads. The Neolithic Revolution, a phrase coined by V. Gordon Childe (1936), designated a period of new social organization and lifestyle. Neolithic phases were part of a progression, spreading across western Asia, the Mediterranean and eventually Europe. Aceramic culture is a signature characteristic of the Early Neolithic of the Near East. These aceramic periods have been labelled the Pre-Pottery Neolithic (PPN) phases and are further broken down according to region and period.

Ceramics as part of household utilitarian material culture do not appear until after the technology was established with figurines and small objects (Vandiver et al. 1989). While many figurines were sun-dried, some reveal different degrees of firing: some accidental, some apparently experimental and others purposeful. The technology for firing to alter and enhance the longevity of clay objects was known for hundreds of years before the knowledge was used to produce pottery.

Figurines often appear to be stylized anthropomorphic representations. What or whom they symbolize has been the topic of ongoing debate (Bailey 2005; Talalay 1993). Throughout much of the PPN in western Asia, anthropomorphic and zoomorphic clay figurines seem ubiquitous. The scope and length of this paper is too limited to engage in an in-depth discussion of figurines and the vast typological categories that have been applied to them over the past several decades or the differences in theory that guide the choice and method of classification. Suffice it to say that figurines have held varied roles in society and all too often, they have been labelled with an 'either–or' approach. They have been classified as goddess or cultic representation, toy, teaching aide, wish vehicle or magic device, but rarely as multivariant and multi-interpretative objects with equal cross-categorical significance.

The point of this argument is not just to suggest that artistic and ritual expressions inspired new technologies, which then existed long before they were used to produce utilitarian material culture. More importantly, I argue that the Western propensity for joining function and necessity to value does not always do justice to interpretations of non-Western, non-literate societies. It cannot be overstated that objects also functioned as symbols in prehistoric society and communicated multiple concepts for hundreds of years before and after the same technologies were used to create necessary items. I now focus on value as applied in equal measure to child and adult material culture represented by the same objects.

PATTERNS OF CREATION: EVIDENCE OF ORAL TRADITION IN FIGURINE CONSTRUCTION

Clay figurine construction offers an opportunity for teaching sacred narratives in many non-literate societies. Children usually learn traditional knowledge through activities connected to the home and shared by elders. Figurines reflect production techniques that are highly repetitive in prehistory. The simplicity and consistency over generations suggest a method of teaching linked with oral traditions.

In some indigenous communities, children are taught stories and shown drawings, figurines and so forth in order to teach them important mythologies about ancestors and creator spirits, or life lessons. Telling or showing a spirit animal or ancestor's story invokes its spirit once the image is completed, song sung, or prayer recited (Haley 1997; Underhill 1965:130–1,147). This reminds the child that the entity may be watching or listening, adding importance to recalling the story or lesson correctly. That is to say, crafting the figurine challenges the listener as well as the teller or teacher to be respectful of the image as a thing that possesses power; it is not merely an image or inanimate object.

Often when myths are retold there is an aspect of performance that goes along with the story, requiring the teller to create a material object while he or she tells the myth. In the performance, parts of the figurine serve as mnemonic devices that mark important points in the story so that each part is crafted in proper manner and the sequence is enhanced (Gill 1983: 43–59).

Denise Schmandt-Besserat (1997: 51) discovered a sequence of zoomorphic figurine production in an assemblage from prehistoric 'Ain Ghazal. These figurines (cattle or bulls) closely resemble other assemblages found across the Near East and Anatolia. She believed these were indicative of a prescribed style and configuration for these kinds of figurines. Schmandt-Besserat identified the following steps for the order and manner of figurine making that reflect an almost institutionalized approach.

1) First the neck and head of the animal were made from coiled clay and smoothed over.

2) The back side was pressed against a hard surface in order to give it flat hindquarters.

3) Truncated legs and tail were pinched on.

4) Finally, horns were moulded separately and added on last.

This approach to creating figurines in a non-specialist production environment like the household would be consistent with the oral tradition story-telling linked with performance. At each step of manufacture, a story coincides with adding on or shaping each piece as a mnemonic device to ensure future attempts will be executed in exactly the same way. If figurines were made from household to household in an unguided, individualistic way one would expect to see more individuality among the samples, particularly over long periods of time. Yet, configurations and execution style suggest creation by learned instruction and by rote.

DOLLS AND FIGURINES IN INDIGENOUS SOCIETIES: MULTIPLICITY OF MEANING

Archeologists expect to encounter certain kinds of objects within certain contexts. For example, one expects to find toys in houses or perhaps as grave deposits among children's burials. In addition, archeologists tend to think of toys and teaching aides as material culture crafted by women or children. Gendered presumptions of production, place and function suggest that when figurines are absent from expected locations like a house, for example, there were the following possibilities:

1) that toys were organic and left no archeological record;

2) that children did not have toys as their time was allocated to adult-oriented tasks;

3) there must not have been children present;

4) that figurines, when found at the site but absent in homes, were not toys but ritual objects, particularly when they were deposited together.

The first two arguments are conceivable and even probable in many cases, given that prehistoric and/or non-literate peoples' resources were primarily organic and likely would not survive in the archeological record. Children play in all cultures as part of the social and psychological maturation process, but that play may be defined and expressed in different ways and not necessarily with dolls. The Western concept of childhood as a leisure time set aside for a specific age set is a relatively modern one, appearing within the last century and a half. In the prehistoric and historic past, evidence and textual sources indicate that many children were expected to work and contribute to household needs in ways appropriate to physical and mental capability as well as the adults (Airies 1960). Having said that, alternatively, indigenous cultures have long considered dolls and figurines as items necessary to performing sacred rituals and narratives as well as for the socialization processes. The locus of these principles is not atypically found embodied in the same artefact.

Ethnographic accounts of indigenous groups tell us that it is an erroneous assumption to think of doll and figurine production as belonging only to the realm of women and children. A significant number of Arctic and Native North American dolls were originally crafted by men rather than women, particularly dolls that were meant to represent males or that were initially used for ceremonies (Kennedy 2002). Katsina (kachina) dolls of the American southwest, for example, were created for rituals, and originally all of these were made by men (Kennedy 2002). Katsina dolls are now produced by women as well as an economic resource, sold commercially to tourists and collectors.

Indigenous cultures frequently define toys as playthings and as sacred objects simultaneously, imbued with agency of their own in the correct circumstances. Because of this, it is it not unusual to find various restrictions on dolls, depending on the culture, over where they are kept (the house) or how they are handled. Spirits perceived as dwelling within dolls and figurines may be credited with the ability to cause harm or otherwise affect an individual or population if not properly cared for.

For example, Bering Straits indigenous traditions prohibit children from sleeping with dolls during the night because dolls are believed to have the power of animation at that time of day. At night, a doll may move freely in the house if it chooses and cause mischief, harm or other problems for the family (Fair 1982).

In southern regions of Alaska, traditional indigenous beliefs about dolls include the view that they are seasonal playthings. Dolls are usually constructed from plant and other organic materials, much of which are mainly available in the summer. They are appropriate, therefore, for summer play, and are designed from nature and so should be stored outdoors. Tradition dictates that if the doll were kept inside the house during the winter rather than the summer months, it could potentially bring bad luck upon the entire family or village (Fair 1982). A doll, once brought into existence, was resistant to being kept against its will in an unnatural environment and would wreak vengeance based upon the actions of a careless child. These traditions communicated lessons to children designed to cultivate respect for nature and proper behaviour, and to ingrain a sense of identity and responsibility in the family and the clan or group at large, since careless behaviour could result in harm for everyone. The doll, having a spirit of nature within it, was not to be taken lightly even if it was primarily constructed for the enjoyment and use of a child.

Native North American Indians frequently used dolls as catalysts for healing ceremonies and protection, to affect the environment (helpful rains and so forth) by appealing to specific entities represented by the doll and to invite benevolent spirits that may assist an individual through life. The life cycle of figurines or dolls often followed a natural progression that once they fulfilled their ritual purpose they were likely to be given to a child as a toy. In turn, the figurine or doll continued to function as a socialization and learning device to teach traditions and incorporate a sense of identity through play (Lenz 1986: 39). Dolls and figurines are found in nearly every indigenous culture with a wide variety of uses, symbolic meanings and purposes.

An exception worth noting is that of the American southwest's Navajo Indians. This indigenous group is one of the minority populations that did not make dolls for children before European contact. Navajo cosmology limited the representation of the human form except for religious reasons. After European contact, dolls became an economic item to sell to tourists. Although in modern times it is not unusual to see Navajo children playing with commercially created dolls as with any other child population, there are still those who subscribe to a cautious view about the supernatural potential of a human figure: 'a crew of Navajo workmen refused to continue working at an archeological site because of the wooden figures that were found there. Even when children are allowed to play with dolls, there is a strong feeling that a doll should not be mistreated or broken, although as one Navajo man said, "If you handle it nicely, it probably won't hurt you."' (Lenz 1986: 37).

Cuna shamans of Panama carved wooden dolls for curing ceremonies, to protect against malevolent spirits that cause illness, or to recover an individual's soul that has left the body, also causing illness (Lenz 1986: 45). Caduveo Indians of Brazil considered it appropriate for children to play with sacred dolls that represented saints. Sometimes referred to as 'little old man', the doll represented a character from a sacred myth. In the myth a saint came to earth but was captured by men and imprisoned until a storm destroyed the village and inadvertently set him free. Modern Caduveo Indians still observe this tradition of sacred narrative, the doll in performance and the doll as plaything, although now the doll is identified with Christian saints. These Caduveo dolls continue to embody both sacred and secular meaning for adults and children.

Gitxsan people of Canada from the Skeena River area created wooden dolls to be used in the performance of sacred dances; the dolls were dressed in bald eagle skin, cedar bark and sometimes painted. Afterwards, the dolls could be given to children. Today, the sacred dances are still performed as a way to pass on traditions to children and to tell Gitxsan-origin stories at feasting events (Smithsonian Museum 2011).

Dolls and figurines have also been used as memorial items for the dead. Yahua and Witoto Indians from the Amazon River area created wooden dolls, painted them with plant-derived dyes and used them to commemorate deceased loved ones in realistic ways (Smithsonian Museum 2011). In other cultures, dolls meant to represent the dead are purposefully made with less human characteristics as a safety precaution, not wanting the spirit of the deceased to be too attracted to its own likeness and stay, instead of moving on in the afterlife.

The Ojibwa made dolls out of feathers to represent an infant or very young child who had died. The grieving mother would 'care' for the substitute child until she perceived her child was able to take care of itself in the spirit world. Effigies made of a simple post dressed in a deceased child's clothing was called a 'ghost pole' and kept in the home of some grieving Sioux families for up to a year (Lenz 1986: 53).

Memorial dolls can also be found in a modern context as a survival and modification of a much older tradition.

Before the second world war, Japanese traditions dictated that spirit spouses for individuals who died in childhood or before marriage could be arranged with living partners for a limited period of time in order to keep the spirit of the prematurely dead happy. Japanese culture is very family centred; the bond of the family with the larger community is a foundation of society. This practice provided grieving families with a way to assuage grief by providing partners for their deceased loved ones so that they could fulfil a life not lived spiritually. In Buddhist tradition these spirits could then eventually move on and join a collective spirit (Schattschneider 2001).

Male or female living partners were paid by the family of the deceased to be their loved ones' spouses for a specific period of time. However, the fear that the deceased would possibly want the living spouse to join them in the spirit world (and thus bring about untimely death) led to the use of dolls during the second world war period, when large numbers of young men were killed in the line of duty. The practice of marrying spirits to dolls became known as 'bride-doll marriage' for deceased soldiers who had not had the opportunity to marry and have a family. The family purchased commercially made 'bride dolls' which were ceremonially married to the spirit of the deceased. The bride dolls were kept in glass cases, sometimes in special shrines, visited by family members, and were maintained and received gifts from them for up to 30 years. At the end of that period, the dolls were disposed of by 'ritual fire or floated out to sea' (Schattschneider 2001: 855). Though these dolls were not used as playthings by children, they also functioned as memorial art. Glass cases over time incorporated gifts, including photographs, toys (to symbolically represent cars and other activities for the spirit couple to engage in) and personal items. These cases can be thought of as time capsules and culturally communicative. They contain items of remembrance and function as social statements with 30 years' worth of symbolic reflection on Japanese spiritual and secular values.

All of these ethnographic examples demonstrate that it was typical for indigenous traditions to blur the delineations between sacred and secular, plaything and ritual object, art and social statement. Therefore, this paper advocates a new approach for anthropologists and archeologists towards understanding and interpreting oral tradition societies from their artefacts, such as dolls and figurines.

A NON-WESTERN APPROACH TO THE INTERPRETATION OF DOLLS AND FIGURINES

Ethnoarcheological, ethnographical and sociological studies have detected patterns in children's play activities and areas that suggest certain child behaviours transcend cultural and temporal lines (Bonnichsen 1973; Deal 1985; Hammond and Hammond 1981; Sobel 1990: 10; Trimble 1994: 27). Simply put, children from prehistory to modern times consistently seek to play away from adult supervision, away from culturally structured spaces where prescribed social behaviour will not be enforced.

These places are usually on the periphery of lived spaces: vacant, unused, seldom used or abandoned structures; in and around animal pens; garbage areas; courtyards; and natural and undeveloped landscapes, like forests and so forth.

Children who are assigned tasks helping in crop fields, hunting and gathering, animal pasturing, etc will also find ways to play and engage in games simultaneously in these places when possible. Archeologists often find figurines in various stages of wear in these areas, but dismiss them as uninterpretable and evidence of random discard. Rather than dismissing these, documenting and compiling the number and kinds of figurines from these contexts may indicate children's collective activity areas around a site. I propose that a compilation of object contexts that appear random when compared and contrasted with those from structured contexts of the same object or very similar objects will suggest their multi-vocal nature in a non-literate, oral tradition culture. Methodological strategies may include:

1) identifying potential areas of children's play and discard around a site, based upon sociological, ethnoarcheological and ethnographical accounts;

2) identifying the types of figurines, statuettes, 'dolls' and other artefacts that may be considered a 'toy' in one context and 'cult object' in another;

3) compiling the incidence rate of same or similar figurines found in different kinds of locations at a site;

4) identifying the types of figurines, statuettes, 'dolls' and other artefacts that are found exclusively in culturally structured or enclosed spaces (houses, special purpose spaces that may indicate ritual use, burials, etc) and in considered special deposits, possibly of a ritual nature;

5) identifying performance areas (public communal cooking and gathering areas as well as areas of a house) where feasting, socializing, and/or ritual events may have occurred;

6) comparing and contrasting figurines and their scope of contexts to compile a possible life cycle for certain artefacts.

A picture should emerge of the multivariant meanings certain items in material culture share. By cross-comparing the find spots and the kinds of figurines that occur in them (or are excluded), these can inform on the multivariant symbolism and use of an object in a non-literate society. This approach, I posit, will garner a fuller and much more balanced interpretation than the 'either-or' approach that one finds in the majority of literature when figurines are designated as dolls rather than as ritual objects.

CONCLUSION

Sacred figurines, statuettes and similar cult objects in Western culture are typically limited access items; these

Figure 1 – Author's photograph of Bering Strait traditional dolls and figurines – ivory, mammoth tusk, seal fur and leather materials

objects are rarely considered appropriate in the hands of a child. Exceptions may include a ritual event or context wherein religious observances are prescribed. Sacred objects fulfil an ideological and/or cosmological purpose, neither of which is considered a common part of the child's world in Western traditions.

However, rigid typological categories that separate toy, figurine, ritual object and utilitarian material culture are counterproductive when attempting an interpretation of non-Western cultures from the past. These categories are often blurred or do not exist in non-literate, oral tradition societies. Ethnographic and historic accounts of children's behaviour demonstrate that children usually find isolated or unstructured areas for play where they can avoid adult supervision. Children frequently fashion playthings from readily available or recycled materials. These playthings fulfil an important role in the socialization process on several levels and may be indicative of an artefact with a longer life cycle that began before the object was a child's toy (Baxter 2005; Daiken 1965; Lee 1999; Sutton-Smith 1986). The reconfiguration of sacred object to child's toy is not an alien concept but a very common one in many indigenous cultures. The sacred and secular often overlap or are indistinguishable from one another in daily life.

Figurines created for or by children often reflect a standardized method of construction. Some of these are consistent with oral traditions and stories told while youths are given instruction while at the same time being enculturated with traditional myths and sacred narratives. Once completed, artefacts like figurines are meant for children to play with and relive the myths and their importance through play.

A burial deposit, a house, a midden, an open courtyard or a special niche deposit all suggest different meanings. The goal of this paper is not to object to contextual assessments for interpretations. Rather, the purpose is to widen contextual considerations and encourage comparison to allow for multi-vocal meanings. In a ritual context, dolls and figurines may act as supernatural catalysts, protective or healing devices, a component of a sacred performance that facilitates communication with the other world; they can be artistic interpretations of sacred narratives or memorial or remembrance objects for the dead. I propose that the wide array of categories attribute meaning but that these are not always mutually exclusive. Therefore, archeologists should strive to determine how many categories in the lifecycle of figurines or dolls may be indicated in order to give a more balanced interpretation of non-literate societies.

References

ARIÈS, P. 1960 Centuries of Childhood: a Social History of Family Life. Vintage Books, New York.

BAILEY, Douglass W. 2005 Prehistoric Figurines: Representation and Corporeality in the Neolithic. Routledge, New York and London.

BAXTER, J.E. 2005 The Archeology of Childhood: Children, Gender and Material Culture. AltaMira Press, Walnut Creek, CA.

BONNICHSEN, Robson 1973 Millie's Camp: An Experiment in Archeology. World Archeology, 4, pp. 277–91.

CHILD, A.B.; CHILD, I.L. 1993. Religion and Magic in the Life of Traditional Peoples. Prentice Hall, Englewood Cliffs, NJ.

CHILDE, G.V. 1936 Man Makes Himself. Oxford University Press, Oxford.

DAVID, N.; KRAMER, C. 2001 Ethnoarchaeology in Action. Cambridge University Press, Cambridge.

DEAL, M. 1985 Household Pottery Dispersal in the Maya Highlands: An Ethnoarchaeological Interpretation. Journal of Anthropological Archeology, 4, pp. 243–91.

DEEVEY, E. 1968 Pleistocene Family Planning. In R.B. Lee and I. DeVore (eds), Man the Hunter. Aldine, Chicago.

FAIR, Susan W. 1982. Eskimo Dolls. Suzi Jones (ed.). Alaska State Council on the Arts, Anchorage.

GILL, Sam D. 1983 Native American Traditions. The religious life of man series. Wadsworth, Belmont, CA.

HALEY, J.L. 1997 Apaches: a History and Culture Portrait. University of Oklahoma Press.

HAMMOND, G.; HAMMOND, N. 1981 Child's Play: A Disturbance Factor in Archeological Deposition. American Antiquity, 46, pp. 634–6.

HANDEL, G. 1988 Socialization and the Social Self. In G. Handel (ed.), Childhood Socialization, pp. 11–19. Aldine de Gruyter, New York.

HASSAN, F.A. 1980 The Growth and Regulation of Human Population in Prehistoric Times. In. M.W. Cohen *et al.*, (eds), Biosocial Mechanisms of Population Regulation. Yale University Press, New Haven, CT.

HOSLER, D. 1995 The Sounds and Colors of Power: the Sacred Metallurgical Technology of Ancient West Mexico. MIT Press, Cambridge, MA.

KENNEDY, R. 2002 Astor Collection Katsina Dolls as Art and Commodity. Charlottesville, University of Virginia.

LEE, M. (ed.) 1999 Not Just a Pretty Face: Dolls and Human Figurines in Alaska Native Cultures. University of Alaska Museum, Fairbanks.

LENZ, M.J. 1986 The Stuff of Dreams: Native American Dolls. Museum of the American Indian, New York.

LILLEHAMMER, G. 1989 A Child is Born: the Child's World in an Archeological Perspective. Norwegian Archeological Review, 22(2), pp. 89–105.

McDOWELL, N. 1981 Reproductive Decision Making and the Value of Children in Rural Papua New Guinea. Institute of Applied Social and Economic Research, Papua New Guinea.

McQUISTON, D. 1995 Dolls and Toys of Native America: A Journey Through Childhood. Chronicle Books, San Francisco, CA.

PARK, R. 1998 Size Counts: The Miniature Archeology of Childhood in Inuit Societies. Antiquity, 72, pp. 269–81.

SCHATTSCHNEIDER, E. 2001 'Buy me a bride': death and exchange in northern Japanese bride-doll marriage. American Ethnologist, 28(4), pp. 854–80.

SCHMANDT-BESSERAT, D. 1997 Animal Symbols at 'Ain Ghazal. Expedition, 39(1), pp. 48–58.

Smithsonian Museum of the American Indian 2011. Gitxsan Catalog Collections.

SOBEL, D. 1990 A Place in the World: Adults' Memories of Childhood's Special Places. Children's Environments Quarterly, 7(4), pp. 5–12.

SOFAER DEREVENSKI, J. 1994 Where are the Children? Accessing Children in the Past. Archeological Review from Cambridge: Perspectives on Children and Childhood, 13(2).

SUSSMAN, R. 1972 'Child Transport, Family Size, and Increase in Human Population during the Neolithic. Current Anthropology, 13, pp. 258–69.

TALALAY, L.E. 1993 Deities, Dolls, and Devices: Neolithic Figurines from Franchthi Cave, Greece. Indiana University Press, Bloomington and Indianapolis.

TRIMBLE, S. 1994 The Scripture of Maps, the Names of Trees. In Gary Nabhan and Stephen Trimble (eds), Why Children Need Wild Places, pp. 15–31. Beacon Press, Boston, MA.

UNDERHILL, R.M. 1953 Indians of the Pacific Northwest (Indian Life and Customs). Branch of Education. Bureau of Indian Affairs.

UNDERHILL, R.M. 1965 Red Man's Religion. University of Chicago Press, Chicago.

VANDIVER, P.B.; SOFFER, O.; KLIMA, B. 1989 The Origins of Ceramic Technology at Dolni Vestonice, Czechoslovakia. Science, 246, pp. 1002–8.

WHITE, B. 1975 The Economic Importance of Children in a Javanese Village. In M. Nag (ed.), Population and Social Organization. Mouton, The Hague.

WHITE, R. 1989 Production complexity and standardization in Early Aurignacian bead and pendant manufacture: evolutionary implications. In The Human Revolution, Paul Mellars and Chris Stringer (eds), pp. 366–90. Edinburgh University Press, Edinburgh.

ZEDEÑO, M.N. 2008 Bundled Worlds: The Roles and Interactions of Complex Objects from the North American Plains. Journal of Archeological Method and Theory, 15, pp. 362–78.

CONVEYING AN UNDERSTANDING OF THE LANDSCAPE: THE ROCK ART OF THE TAGUS AND THE GUADIANA VALLEYS

Luiz OOSTERBEEK

Pró-Presidente, Relações Internacionais, Instituto Politécnico de Tomar, Portugal
Secretary-General, UISPP, Tomar, Portugal

Abstract: The dawn of pastoral agriculturalism in southwest Iberia is closely related to the Guadalquivir–Guadiana-Tagus fluvial system, with which are associated important rock art clusters. Two main technocomplexes have been identified in this process: one paying tribute to the cardial coastal dispersal (with no association with the rock art) and another composed of a mosaic of groups with different but converging strategies, that seem to privilege the inland routes (these being the putative authors of the rock art major clusters). Despite many stylistic differences, some common trends may be recognized: the visual dominance of deer and anthropomorphs, the widespread occurrence of circles and spirals, the abundance of ideomorphs, the apparently chaotic character of the panels, the not so abundant superimpositions, the divergence between an easily spotted carved art (at the bottom of valleys) and a restricted painted art in the often hardly reachable rock shelters. These rock art clusters offer a cohesion to the region, and it is by no accident that it coincides with the main passageways through which the new technologies and ideologies were conveyed, building new landscapes between the seventh and the third millennia BC. Areas like São Simão, in the Tagus, or Cheles, in the Guadiana, are associated with shallower passages across the big rivers, in scenarios that would potentially generate dilemmas for these earlier communities: it was in times of environmental lesser productivity, due to the scarcity of water, that the river became a crossable path and no longer a dangerous boundary. Despite the fact that the strict meaning of the art panels is beyond our access, one should consider two elements, one related to knowledge and the other to behaviour. Knowledge in non-literate societies needs to be strictly codified and transmitted (often through mnemonics and associated songs), since it is the basis for human survival. (Where to go? What to eat? What to run from or after? How does the environment change through time in short or even longer cycles? How to differentiate us from others? How to identify sources of knowledge and power?) Learning is far more consolidated when it is embedded in multi-sensorial experiences, and it is likely that, besides mnemonic texts (with rhythms) and music (to listen to and make), people could profit from moments of recording ideas (touching, seeing), thus widening the scope of used senses. This could occur in limited (for initiation?) spaces (paintings) or in wider ceremonial collective events (regularly, or associated with specific moments like equinoxes?). For sure, different sites would have had different purposes, and not all are as imposing as Fratel (Tagus) or Cheles. This also suggests a specific management of the landscape that goes beyond the mere attempt to mark the territory, possibly with connections with the economic strategies of the human groups and their specific relation to the surrounding environment and beyond.

Southwest Iberia is a complex of lowlands dominated by hercinic old rocks (namely slate, occasionally granite as well), with a series of limestone meso-cenozoic massifs, both cut by several river beds filled in with detritus deposits. The three main valleys are, from the east to the west, the Guadalquivir, the Guadiana and the Tagus. In their lower itineraries, the territories in between them never exceed 500 metres asl, and are often lower than 200 metres asl, forming extensive plateaux that are easily crossed by people and animals.

The dawn of pastoral agriculturalism in southwest Iberia is closely related to the Guadalquivir-Guadiana-Tagus fluvial system, with which are associated important rock art clusters. The spread of farming technologies follows mainly a coastal path until reaching southeast Iberia, and this is evidenced by the early Neolithic sites dated from the sixth millennium BC in Catalunya, Valencia and Andalusia. Moving westwards, the steep slopes that lead to the central massifs give way to lower gradients, and this enabled a faster spread of the new technologies using inland routes: the valleys and the hills across.

Two main technocomplexes have been identified in this process: one paying tribute to the cardial coastal dispersal (with no association to the rock art) and another composed of a mosaic of groups with different but converging strategies, that seem to privilege the inland routes (these being the putative authors of the rock art major clusters). From a strict technological perspective, these two technocomplexes differ: the coastal one is very close to the Mediterranean 'Neolithic package', with cardial impressed ware, seashell beads, occasional bracelets, polished stone, etc, whereas the inland one is less impressive in terms of pottery decoration and fabrics, is still dominated by heavy stone artefacts (including choppers and chopping tools), alongside polished stone tools and scarce bladelets and leptolithic materials. Looking in depth into these assemblages, one can perceive a close relation to the Mediterranean Neolithic trends, though: intensive gathering and likely occasional horticulture (although farming has not yet been demonstrated for the early stages of the Neolithic in these areas), having a close relation with some hunted and later domesticated animals: deer, but also cattle and goat.

Moving across the land and crossing major river beds with animals must have imposed a different approach to the landscape and hence a different understanding of the cosmos for these people. Even if one must accept that the Neolithic spread is much more a spread of novelties embedded in a network of established people in the region (the Epipalaeolithic and Mesolithic occupations are not substantially discontinued by these new strategies), and not a heavy migration of alien groups, it remains that coastal people would need to master the tide cycles, the winds along the coast, the nature of light but less productive soils and a more maquis-type vegetation cover. Inlanders needed to focus on forest diversity, on a different biological set, on animals' migration routes and on more fertile but often too heavy soils. Husbandry became more relevant for the latter, and one may imagine that whereas sea, sun and crops impressed the coastal groups (even before farming), the forest, the animals and the river would tend to be dominant concerns inland. The sense of space also had to differ, since in the coast the great landscape dichotomy would tend to be land and sea, and inland it would rather be based on topography, geology or any other physiographic criteria. Mobility would play a greater role inland, due to the need to master greater levels of physiographic diversity, whereas the coast, often contained by the limestone chains, would also offer a more stable food staple, namely in the estuaries.

One should not understand these two clusters as completely segregated. Indeed, Iberia was a mosaic of interconnected groups from the later Upper Paleolithic, with limited changes in the transition to the Holocene (as Nuno Bicho first demonstrated in the Rio Maior region). These groups occupied several niches and had seasonal patterns of mobility. There is no evidence to suggest that people from the coast and people from inland did not meet or prevented themselves from accessing the other ecozones. Some evidence, namely the circulation of some important local raw materials (like flint or some green stones for polishing), demonstrates this. This economic interaction also justified the early models of seasonality with which scholars in the 1970s and 1980s tried to explain the differences of occupation in the two clusters. Significant symbolic differences, and also economic ones now recognized due to new archeobotanical and zooarcheological studies, persuade us to understand the record as not a result of seasonality but of distinct clusters of groups.

The most important distinction relates to carved rock art, indeed: present in the Tagus, in the Guadiana and occasionally in the Guadalquivir valleys, it is almost absent on the coast, where the symbolic decorative motifs are to be mainly found on ceramics.

Despite many stylistic differences, five major common traits may be recognized in the rock art of the Tagus and the Guadiana, the two best studied valleys.

First is the visual dominance of deer and anthropomorphs. Although other zoomorphs also occur, deer and anthrpomorphs are the dominating figurines. The latter have been related, in some cases, to anthropomorphic praying characters that may also be recognized in cardial pottery decorations, but this should not be considered as any sort of direct evidence, since the motive is widespread. The deer representation, sometimes evidencing a butchering approach (x-ray representations), but mainly depicted through very schematic and somewhat fantastic traits (an oblong ellipse or circle, with some appendixes standing for the feet and head), meets the zooarcheological evidence that deer were present and hunted at the time, being probably the most impressive beast with which humans could interact (taming attempts have been documented in various contexts on the planet). The deer and the human seem to share a similar territory and a similar pathway, a relation that cannot be identified in the coastal areas. Like the humans, deer occupy vast territories and need to protect themselves from predators. The cyclic fall of antlers offers a time-cycle basis, most useful for humans. The finding of deer bones in some burials in the Alto Ribatejo (Tagus basin) supports this symbolic relation, which would be based on a symbiotic relation.

Second is widespread occurrence of the circles and spirals matrix, which is also a common motif in other cultural contexts, but forming in this case the matrix of the art itself, and even some figurines, namely the hollow fantastic deer. This dominance of circles, that was recently suggested by Mila S. Abreu to stand for possible indicators of foot passages across the river, also facilitates the building of an equivocal dimension of the representations: most being very similar, even when they stand for animals (deer or other), or for possible maps or ideal plans of villages (as in Gardete 11), they are hardly naturalistic representations and they seem to stand for ideas and concepts, and not as directly observed individuals or scenes. In fact, they convey a second key understanding of the landscape: that it is made of a series of units, as a discontinuous and hierarchic space, each unit being similar and interchangeable with the others. This converges with the observed nature of the settlement patterns: a mosaic of short-lived dwellings, within a still not fully stable scenario.

Third are the scenes within the matrix. The abundance of ideomorphs, the global schematic nature of the art and the apparently chaotic resemblance of the panels (reinforced by the dots and circles) should hence stand for the representation of tales rooted in the interpretation of the territory (one may vaguely recognize recurring themes, like the anthropomorph by the big spirals, the hunting scenes, the anthropomorph carrying a deer, or the running deer, but mostly we cannot perceive the meaning). But in global terms, this art relates a matrix of basic subgeometric units (circles and ellipses) from which emerge scenes, both in close relation to the river crossing, since these carvings are made mainly at the bottom of the river, as in Frate-Tejo or in Molino Manzanez-Guadiana, on surfaces only accessible in the dry season, precisely when crossing the river would be possible, generating contradictory feelings (the positive accessibility to extra territories versus the shortage of water and food resources due to drought).

Fourth is the relevance of the river and not the exact place. The quite uncommon superimpositions, in contrast to earlier and later artistic cycles (Upper Paleolithic and Iron Age), is also very relevant, and suggests the tributary dimension of these carvings, a sort of toll when going across the river, and not so much a performing ritual dependent on the place. It seems that it was not the place where the carvings were made, but the action of carving in the river bed without damaging previous similar actions that was significant. This has a direct relation with the nature of human mobility across these rivers and pastoral herding, and it also explains why these big rock art clusters are more important in the southwest, and become minor to the point of being absent in the Douro/Côa rock art cluster: the reason is that the model of Neolithic inland pastoralism spread across the lowlands is restricted to the southwest, and hence generated a specific type of ideological expression. This also explains why the cluster of the Tagus seems bigger than the Guadiana one, which is bigger than the Guadalquivir: the more to the west the smoother is the topography and the more active the human groups' mobility would be. Elsewhere, one will find echoes of sacred mountain art (like most of the schematic painted art) or later arrivals of the coastal cluster (dominated by decoration on pottery and portable art, like in the Douro/Côa region).

Fifth is the dichotomy of the collective path and the sacred mountain. The divergence between a carved art to be easily spotted (in the bottom of valleys) and a restricted painted art in the often hardly reachable rock shelters is another common trait, the latter being much more widespread, but referring to the three big river basins. We have shown in a previous paper on the art of the Ocreza valley (a tributary of the Tagus) that while the bottom of the valley carvings are carefully placed in order to be observed along the foot path, the paintings in the hardly accessible rock shelters, besides the formal differences (of techniques and motifs), are in fact hidden art. Whereas the carvings were made to be seen collectively, the paintings remaining on the rock slope shelters to see the humans down in the valley can only be observed by very restricted numbers of people at a time and were possibly made as part of initiation rituals or related processes. But it is this painted art that enables us to link the carved territories with the remaining ones with schematic art across southern Iberia.

These five traits illustrate the cosmovision and intellectual operational notions of the first pastoralist farmers of southwest Iberia: a discontinuous space made of interchangeable units, structured horizontally by human activities and carvings and structured vertically by hilltop paintings, where mobility along given itineraries was fundamental (for economic and possibly ideological reasons), requiring some performances that would include carvings when going across the big river in the dry season, possibly focused on a sort of a central sacred figure (anthropomorph, deer or both).

The rock art clusters (Molino Manzanez or Retorta in the Guadiana, Fratel or Ocreza in the Tagus) offer a cohesion to the region, and it is by no accident that they coincide with the main passages across the valleys through which the new technologies and ideologies were conveyed, building new landscapes between the seventh and the third millennia BC. Areas like São Simão, in the Tagus, or Cheles, in the Guadiana, are associated with shallower crossings across the big rivers, in scenarios that would potentially generate dilemmas to these earlier communities: it was in times of environmental lesser productivity, due to the scarcity of water, that the river became a crossable path and no longer a dangerous boundary.

Despite the fact that the strict meaning of the art panels is beyond our access, one should consider two elements, one related to knowledge and the other to behaviour. Knowledge in non-literate societies needs to be strictly codified and transmitted (often through mnemonics and associated songs), since it stands as the basis for human survival (Where to go? What to eat? What to run from or after? How does the environment change through time in short or even longer cycles? How to differentiate us from others? How to identify sources of knowledge and power?). It is likely that the various groups sharing these territories would have their own mnemonics and would also perform rituals when some of those would be repeated, so that knowledge would not be lost. Various groups sharing similar cultural trends would converge into a cultural nexus. Although maintaining their differences, we can still recognize them in the artistic styles or the technologies of artefact production.

Learning is far more consolidated when it is embedded in multi-sensorial experiences, and it is likely that, besides mnemonic oral texts (repeated with rhythms) and music (to listen and to make), people could profit from moments of recording ideas (touching, seeing), thus widening the scope of used senses. This could occur in limited (initiations?) spaces (e.g. where we find painted motifs) or in wider ceremonial collective events (regularly or associated with specific moments like equinoxes?). Rituals not necessarily associated with rock art (but possibly with art expression on organic materials, including body art) were performed from the earliest stages in association with the building of megalithic monuments. One function of all these features (carvings, paintings, megaliths, settlements and other unmoveable artefacts) was not only to mark the territory but to disseminate within it a series of material mnemonics.

For sure, different sites would have had different purposes, and not all are as imposing as Fratel (Tagus) or Cheles. This also suggests a specific management of the landscape that goes beyond the mere attempt to mark the territory, possibly with a relation to the economic strategies of the human groups and their specific relation to the surrounding environment and beyond.

THE DEER FIGURE IN TAGUS ROCK ART

Sara GARCÊS

Museu de Arte Pré-Histórica e do Sagrado do Vale do Tejo, Mação, Portugal. Instituto Terra e Memória
Grupo Quaternário e Pré-História do Centro de Geociências (u. ID73 – FCT) Bolseira FCT (SFRH/BD/69625/2010)
Ph.D Candidate in Quaternary, Materials and Cultures (Universidade de Trás-os-Montes e Alto Douro – Portugal)
This work was supported by the Portuguese State through FCT – Fundação para a Ciência e Tecnologia within the project (SFRH/BD/69625/2010)

Abstract: This monographic study on the figures of deer and of their associations reveals the special role played by this animal in the conceptual world of the prehistoric makers of the rock art in the Tagus Valley.

HISTORICAL BACKGROUND AND LOCATION

The Tagus Valley Rock Art Complex has been the target of repeated attempts at interpretation since its submergence in the 1970s, when the Fratel dam was built causing the loss of about 90% of the rock art that was in schist rocks on both sides of the Portuguese High Tagus River, over 40 km. This complex is roughly located in a territory between the Cedillho dam (which marks the border with Spain) and the Ocreza river mouth (a tributary river on the right bank of the Tagus River) (Figure 1).

BIBLIOGRAPHICAL BACKGROUND

Over time, some literature contributions on the interpretation of this rock art complex have been made, mostly of a general nature, focusing on the chronological question, although some monographs have proposed specific models of interpretation. Recently, a dissertation entitled 'The Deer on the Tagus Valley Rock Art: contribution to the study of the recent prehistory (Garcês 2009) has highlighted the importance of the figure of the deer, especially in the symbolic realm of the prehistoric

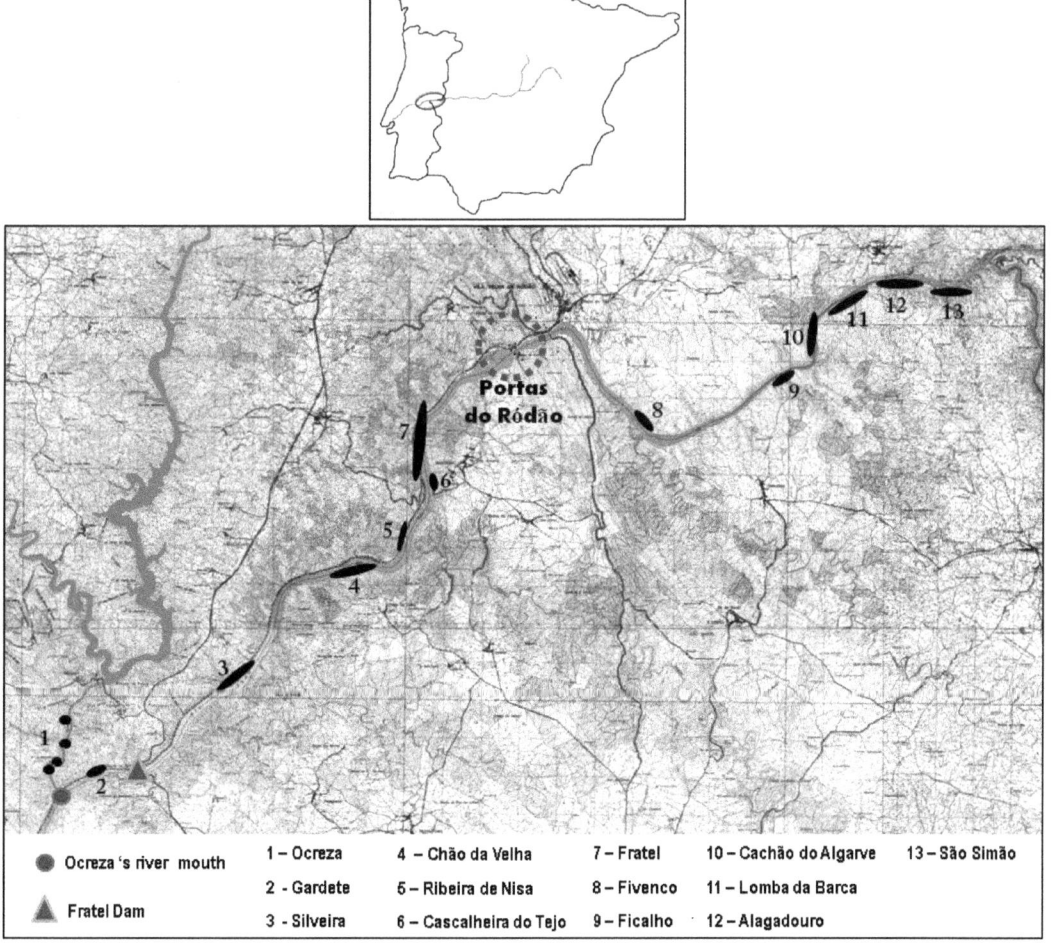

Figure 1 – Map of the Tagus Valley Rock Art Complex rock art sites (according to Serrão, 1978, 1981).
Adapted from the Portuguese Military Chart numbers 313, 314, 315, 323 & 324

communities of the Tagus River. The deer figure has particular associations with a wide-range figurative, in particular, human figures and animals, and is believed to arise in different chronological periods. Mário Varela Gomes has recently presented his doctoral dissertation on the rock art of the Tagus Valley in which he proposes a global reading of this rock art complex. The Prehistoric Rock Art and the Sacred Tagus Valley Museum has begun a programme of systematic review of the surface moulds of the engraved rocks that were made in the 1970s under the rock art project, at the same time that the Fratel dam was being built. These moulds are now the object of an intensive research methodology, photography and registration, in order to be able to collect all possible information on this type of material, which is rare, but which maintains the traces of this magnificent rock art site. This work aims to contribute to the organization of the corpus of representations of the complex and its detailed study. The purpose of developing a work focusing on the figure of the deer was varied: the deer is one of the best represented mammals in Paleolithic and post-Paleolithic art in the Iberian Peninsula and its importance is not just the facts that arise in the rock art of the Tagus but because it is a prime factor in the economy of the prehistoric societies of the transition to agro-pastoralism. In Portugal, the deer even has had a relevant function since ancient chronological periods, such as those depictions in the Côa Valley from the end of the Pleistocene until the mid-Holocene.

There have been records of 'written stones' on the Tagus River since 1946. The ethnographer Paulo Caratão Soromenho, who knew the region very well, followed some of the Group for the Study of the Portuguese Paleolithic in the first day of the discovery of the engravings of the Tagus. These are, in general, obtained by pecking on the flat schist platforms, often arranged horizontally. It is believed that the large amount of quartz and quartzite pebbles that abound in the region may have been used as raw material for the incisors. These rocks, arranged on both banks of the Tagus River, suffered the effects of erosion of the river for thousands of years, a fact which made them so conducive to engraving. However, resistance is also one of their characteristics; hence it was possible to reach up to today well preserved (Àrca *et al.* 2001; Baptista 1986; undated; Farinha 2005; Oosterbeek 2008; Santos 1985; Silva and Alves 2005).

The motifs are primarily of abstract symbolic character and the circle and circular and geometric combinations are the most dominant themes. Other characteristic motifs are zoomorphic figures including deer (predominant) and also goats, horses, dogs, snakes, a bear and a bird (the range of animals represented may increase with continued research in the moulds of the rocks). Some of these motifs are related to each other or to geometric figures, schematic and even stylized, associated with other figures, or not, usually the circles and spirals. Other relevant artefacts also arise in the Tagus Valley Rock Art Complex, called idols stele, human footprints, cup-marks and some rare tools, and some authors defend the existence of weapons (although this is difficult to interpret). Schematic, abstract and symbolic are predominant (Baptista 1986; Santos 1985).

CHRONOLOGICAL BACKGROUND

Early theories about the chronology of the engravings were conceived. The first, advocated by Octavio da Veiga Ferreira, raised serious doubts about the antiquity of the engravings (Ferreira 1973), but Emmanuel Anati, inspired by his periodization of the Galician-Portuguese group, argued on behalf of the first theory about the chronological Tagus. The theory was based on two cycles separated by an occupational gap, according to general climatic factors, which, according to Anati, had conditioned the volume of the river and therefore the temporary immersion of the river bank on which the engravings were made, and he proposed two very distinct phases. The first corresponded to a time evolved from the Boreal (6500–5500 BC), that would be called Epipaleolithic, and the second phase of the Sub-Boreal (3000–2000 BC) that belonged to the Late Neolithic (Baptista 1986; Caninas e Henriques 1985; Henriques et al. undated; Jorge, 1983, 1987; Oosterbeek 2008; Serrão 1978). According to Anati, these are the stages when the river had its lowest flow rate, resulting in a drier climate, and such changes in the water level would make man give a great importance and consequent worship by engraving (Anati 1975).

Later, Eduardo da Cunha Serrão, the team leader that was supervising the work of moulding the rocks of the Tagus, argued that 'The prehistoric temple is sketched, took a long time, probably since the Neolithic, the Bronze Age or even later' (Serrão 1978: 5). The first start in the Neolithic period (5500 BC) finished in the Bronze Age (1750 BC). The second period had its peak in about 700 BC or the Iron Age (Caninas and Henriques 1985; Henriques et al. undated). Later, António Martinho Baptista, Eduardo da Cunha Serrão and Manuela Martins, in the São Simão study, proposed a new periodization divided into three phases: a pre-megalithic style with a subdued naturalism and chronologically framed possibly in the first half of the fifth millennium BC. The second and third phase, described as the richest in motifs, are dated to the fourth and third millennium BC during the development of the megalithic peninsular culture (Baptista *et al.* 1978a; Caninas and Henrique, 1985; Henriques et al. undated; Jorge 1983, 1987; Oosterbeek 2008). According to A.M. Baptista, 'One cannot infer that Tagus art goes beyond the Early Neolithic', and refers to the emergence of geometric figures in the early art of the Tagus River, demonstrating the antiquity of certain figures usually attributed to later periods of prehistory. The discovery in 2000 in the Ocreza River, by the same author, of a picture of a horse, engraved by pecking and dated to the Gravettian style, draws parallels between this and similar pictures of the old phase of Pleistocene art of the Côa Valley, that is, more than 22,000 years BP. With the re-timing of the chronology on the Tagus, the author argues that there are four major

Figure 2 – Rock number 60 of Alagadouro. Possible hunting scene (?) involving an anthropomorphic presence of a different artistic style (Gomes, 1989, 1990a, 1990b, 2000a; 2001, 2002)

phases (Paleolithic, Neolithic, Bronze Age and historical – a few of this last one), without a connection between the Ocreza Paleolithic art and the next phases of the Tagus rock art (Baptista 2001).

In 1980, a new theory was presented by Gomes and Pinho Monteiro of a long cycle of artistic development covering six different phases (Baptista 1986; Caninas and Henriques 1985; Henriques *et al.* undated; Gomes 1980, 1987, 1989, 2001, 2002; Jorge 1983, 1987; Monteiro and Gomes, 1980). Period I was 'subnaturalism': hunter-gatherers in post-glacial times who prolonged a Paleolithic traditional economy and figurative design marked by large animals, almost all deer, segmented bodies, elegant and precise profiles, with well reproduced details. These engravings would date from the sixth millennium BC and would note the concern of man in joining a world where survival depended on the precise knowledge of the natural rhythms of the animals. Period II was 'static-stylized': a process of increasing stylization, with representation of deer and goats, sometimes with the interior of the body divided by the lifeline, by parallel lines horizontally striped or filled by pecking. Period III was 'dynamic-styled': anthropomorphic figures with different dimensions and participating in scenes from nature accompanied by hunting dogs and varied and small fauna with rounded bodies. There are perspective, oblique direction and vitality. The author also defends the existence of religious behaviour. Period IV was 'meridional', acknowledging an iconographic renewal by societies of the late Neolithic and Chalcolithic, and the anthropomorphic and zoomorphic forms are reduced to their essential and adopt a geometric symbology; there are rare footage, rare artefacts and pairs of sun-shaped figures. Period V is 'Atlantic', with strong symbolic representations of spirals, concentric circles, meander forms, mazes, shield figures and schematic anthropomorphism. Period VI is 'circles and lines', characterized by a large amount of very simple idiomorphic figures, associations with pictures of the previous periods, representations of weapons with shields, swords and fantastic animals, as well as snakes (Baptista 1986, Caninas and Henriques 1985; Henriques *et al.* undated; Gomes 1980, 1987, 1989, 2001, 2002; Jorge 1983, 1987; Monteiro and Gomes 1980).

There are 14 rock art sites that are directly part of the Tagus Valley Rock Art Complex (Portuguese side): São Simão, Alagadouro, Lomba da Barca, Cachão do Algarve, Ficalho, Fivenco, Fratel, Cascalheira do Tejo, Foz da Ribeira de Nisa, Chão da Velha, Silveira, Gardete, Figueiró and the Ocreza River. However, considering the state of research on the figure of the deer in the rock art of the Tagus, not all these places have been looked at, though there is information about some of these sites since the rock moulds and bibliography present us with some data. According to the authors who have dedicated themselves over the last years to writing about the Tagus rock art, the deer is the most represented animal in this complex. However, it is a figure that raises many questions since it is represented in various ways and styles. Different chronological periods? Different symbolic moments? Different groups?

ALAGADOURO

The core of the Alagadouro rock art is located on the left bank of the Tagus River, about 3 km downstream of the Cedilho dam, in Vila Velha de Ródão. It is one of rock art sites of the Tagus Valley which is currently submerged. In this nucleus is one of the most curious figures known in the Tagus, and its interpretation is very controversial. The scene presented exhibits a characteristic to be taken into account. The deer are stylistically different from the anthropomorphic figure that accompanies them. Can we certainly infer that these are different chronological periods? If we consider the chronological hypothesis that some authors have raised for the Tagus, is it likely that the anthropomorphic figure is later than the deer? This is a scene that can be interpreted as a hunting scene, but it can only be understood in this way after the addition of the anthropomorphic figure of the scene.

On the vertical rock, rock number 60, of Alagadouro we observed near one of the ends, a couple of large deer, showing well-detailed heads and frames (Figure 2). The anatomical features of each deer allow the finding that this are female, with less developed antlers, the body much wider, perhaps representing a pregnancy, and different hair. On the opposite side, about 0.5 m away and on the edge of the support, it is possible to identify an anthropomorphic figure, standing with arms half-raised and, it seems, wearing a skirt. It is possibly a hunter who stalks his prey, covered by a dense set of vertical cracks (Gomes 1989, 2001). In contrast to this position, A.M. Baptista (1981), describing the rock of Fratel number 155, stresses a lack of hunting scenes or scenes of everyday life in the art of the Tagus. The circles, spirals, meanders, lines and geometric figures would become inexplicable.

CACHÃO DO ALGARVE

Cachão do Algarve is located on the right bank of the Tagus River, almost opposite the Lomba da Barca nucleus. This is the second rock art site of the Tagus that presents the largest number of zoomorphic figures that embrace both the subnatural style (Epipaleolithic) and the stylized-static (Early Neolithic) (Gomes 2007). According to Serrão (1978), this set contains about 2,140 rock art engravings. One of the most enigmatic figures of deer in the Tagus rock art is located on rock number 59, a huge deer with the head and body in perspective, superimposed by several other geometric figures. Gomes (1987, 1989, 2007) puts this deer chronologically in the Epipaleolithic (period I) by assigning it a subnatural style. In contrast, Baptista (1981) states that this figure belongs to the second phase (Late Neolithic) and proves that the spiral is older than we think, since this figure is superimposed by the deer. In fact, this theory was likely to prove the detailed study of the moulds of the rocks of the Tagus, which confirm that the antlers of this deer effectively override a spiral.

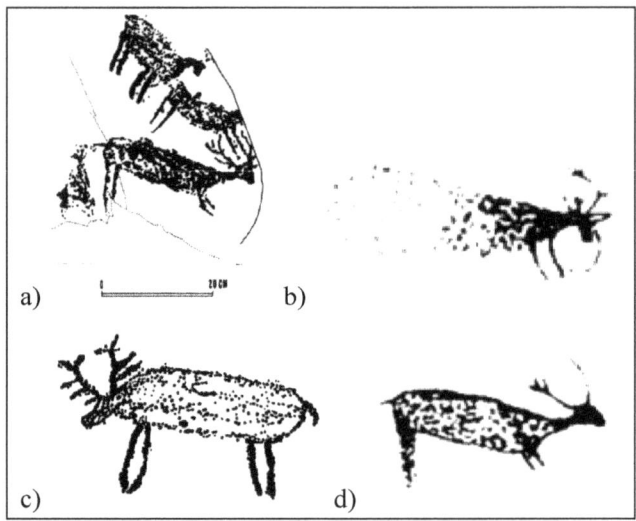

Figure 3 – Deer figures from Chão da Velha rock art site. a) (Gomes, 2001). b) (Baptista *et al.* 1974; Querol *et al.* 1975; Serrão, 1978). c) (Gomes, 2007). d) (Baptista *et al.* 1974; Querol *et al.* 1975; Serrão, 1978)

CHÃO DA VELHA

The Chão da Velha rock art site is located on the left bank of the Tagus River, south of Fratel, near the dam that submerged it. One of the four known deer figures of this site (Figure 3) presents itself associated with another zoomorphic figure which Gomes said belonged to a 'hunting-related myth' belonging to the dynamic-styled period (Full Neolithic).

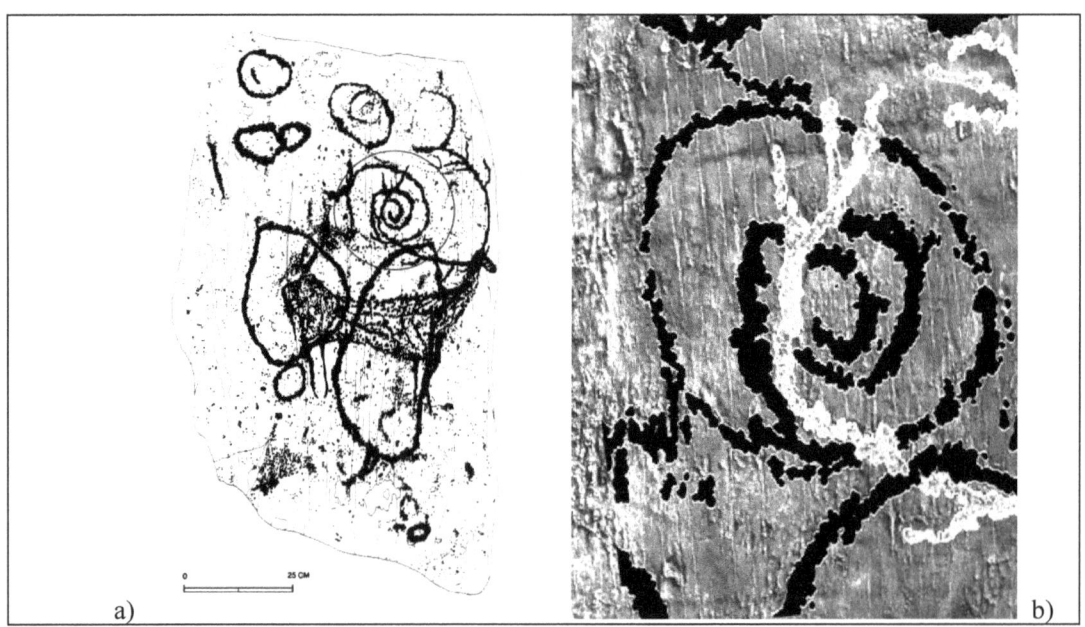

Figure 4 – a: Rock number 59 from Cachão do Algarve (Gomes, 2007) b: Details of rock number 59 from Cachão do Algarve – tracing of the mould. Source: Instituto Terra e Memória

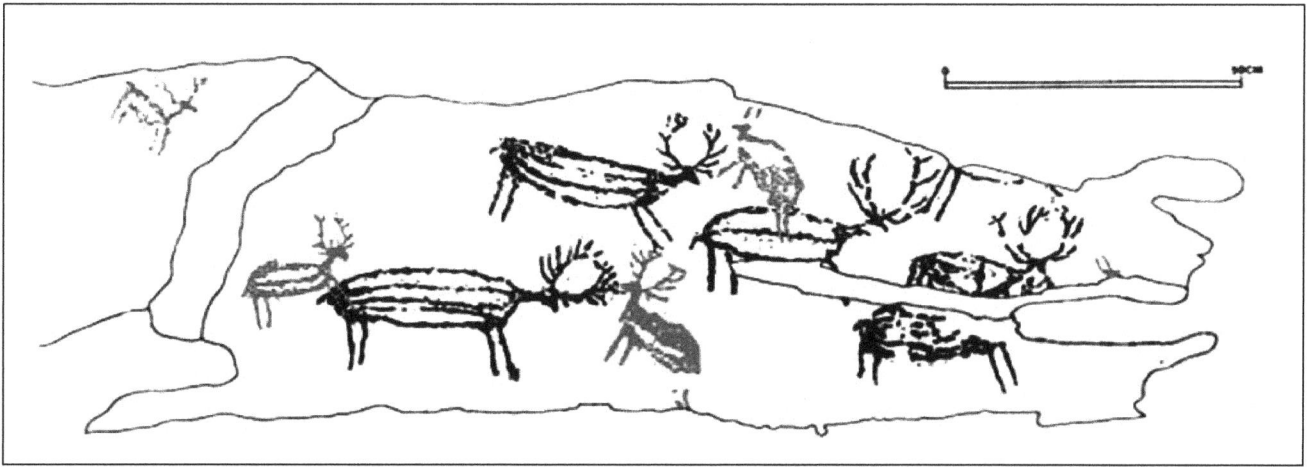

Figure 5 – Rock number 49 from Fratel. The black colour deer of the first group (Full Neolithic) and gray colour deer in the second group (Late Neolithic) (Gomes, 1990a; 2007)

FRATEL

The Fratel nucleus has one of the largest concentrations of rock engravings of the Tagus Valley, consisting mainly of deer, extending for about 1.5 km on the right bank of the Tagus River. It is also the first group of prints located downstream of the monumental natural geological phenomena Portas do Ródão, a narrow gorge of massive quartzite that the river has created over time (Gomes 2007). In this nucleus there are two of the most famous rocks of the entire complex. These are the most studied and quoted rocks in publications in Tagus rock art and the most important for representations of deer both in quantity and in quality. For the research so far undertaken in this site, there are 29 figures of deer, 11 of them belonging to rock 49 (Figure 5).

The rock in question is located in a section of the right edge of the middle Tagus River, near the Portas do Ródão. According to Gomes (2007), the deer in this rock are presented according to two distinct groups. In the first group they are stylistically similar, sharing certain characteristics which refer to the same chronological period of engraving (Early Neolithic). The second group of deer, some of which overlap those of the first group, present some different characteristics from the first one. They have smaller dimensions and, according to the author, are chronologically later. He infers that they belong to the Full Neolithic, in which there are myths about hunting activities involving figures such as deer, dogs, a very varied fauna, scenes of mating pairs of deer and representations of flocks.

Gomes (1990a) attempted to pre-empt a possible interpretation of the rock described based on the idea of building religious systems according to the importance that hunting, for sure, would have for communities, following the laws of shamanism. Religious practices would include the engraving of the animal which might be hunted, if the animal were found in nature and the hunt was consummated again and again (Gomes 1990a).

Fratel is considered to be the most important rock art site of the Tagus complex, both by extension, density and diversity of the pictures contained therein, as for being seen as vital in defining the early stages of the art (Baptista 1981).

This site includes another rock which is extremely important in the rock art of Tagus. Rock 155 (Figure 6) is considered one of the most notable engraved rocks in Tagus and is vital for understanding the religious and ideological motivations of the art of the Tagus. Erosion and oxidation of the ferrous elements shale skated a lot and gave it a colour between dark blue and red-brown rust. According to the author, there are about 104 figures on this rock (nine of them are deer). Although the two authors who have dedicated themselves to studying the rock art of Tagus disagree on the chronology, they have a point in common: the rock of Fratel 155 is indeed an important milestone in the perception of the more remote engravings of the Tagus.

One of the most important details about this rock is the overlap and associations between spirals and zoomorphic figures or circles. According to Baptista (1981), an analysis of the most significant overlaps shows that the spirals are always on the bottom of the stratigraphy and above those are the zoomorphic figures in naturalistic style (the oldest ones). This conclusion is supported, according to the author, by the patine 'which also show a great antiquity for the most anthropomorphic figures, but here is one to take into account certain technical variety among the figures'.

SÃO SIMÃO

The São Simão rock art site is one of the three remaining sites where it is possible, even today, to have access to the rocks at certain times of year. It is considered one of the sites with the greatest concentration of rock art of the Tagus, along with Fratel and Cachão do Algarve. The deer known to belong to this site are not many, but of the

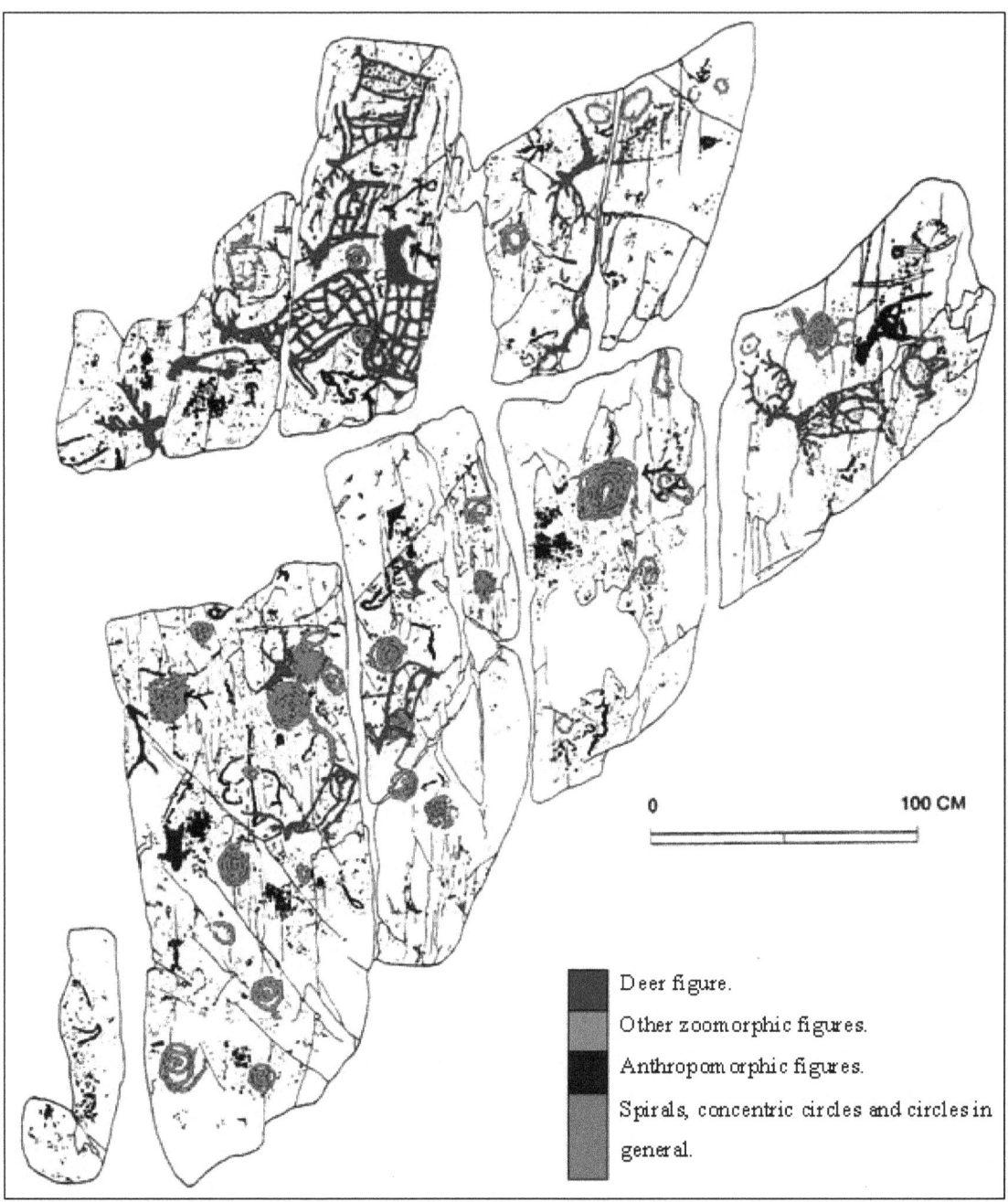

Figure 6 – Rock number 155 from Fratel. This reproduction attempts to demonstrate the level of possible associations between deer and zoomorphic figures in general with this type of motif. The representation of the rock is based only on a personal interpretation of the figures that exist within it (because it was impossible so far to make the tracing of the rock mould). However, Baptista (1981) argues that deer figure belongs to the period Classic Subnaturalism or Evolved including spirals that seem to be associated to them

existing six, three of them fall into very interesting contexts. In particular, the famous rock of São Simão that presents a phallic anthropomorphic figure with a deer on his back, interpreted as a 'dead animal hanging in the air' or an 'anthropomorphic representation of sustaining a dead deer' (Gomes 1983, 1987, 1989, 1990a, 2001; Serrão 1981; Baptista 1986; Jorge 1991). This is quite an amazing figure given that is associated with two more deer, an animal not yet identified and what looks like the antlers of one another. In the Tagus rock art we can find parallels to these engravings in other rocks, but with the dead deer replaced by figures of the sun.

OCREZA RIVER

In the 1970s, in the Ocreza River (Tagus River mainstream) some panels containing similar engravings were identified in the surveys which were made along with the construction of the dam that wiped out most of the art of the Tagus River. Thus was identified the maximum size of the Tagus Valley Rock Art Complex. In the Valley of Rovinhosa, there are five deer, three on a rock called the Rock of the Deer, R2 (Figure 7), while the other two are located on Rock Two Deer, R3. R2 is considered one of the most interesting surfaces of rock art

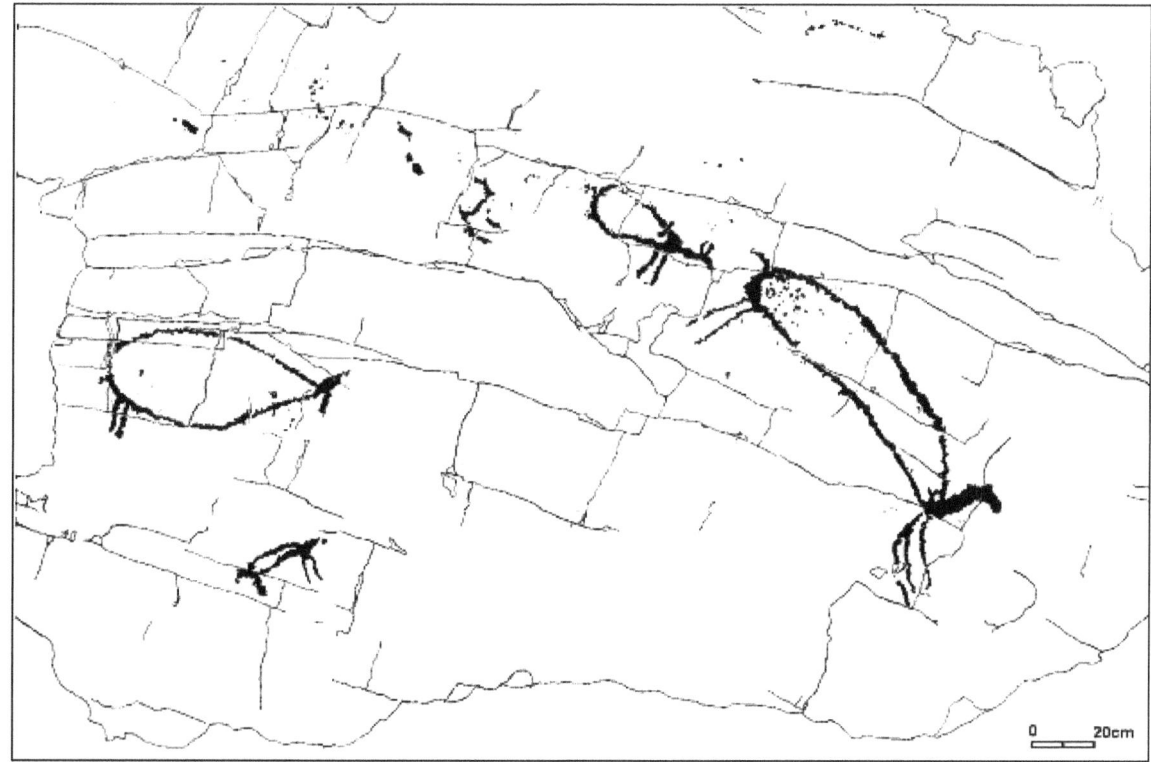

Figure 7 – Rock of the Deer – Rovinhosa Valley, Ocreza River. Source: Instituto Terra e Memória, Portugal

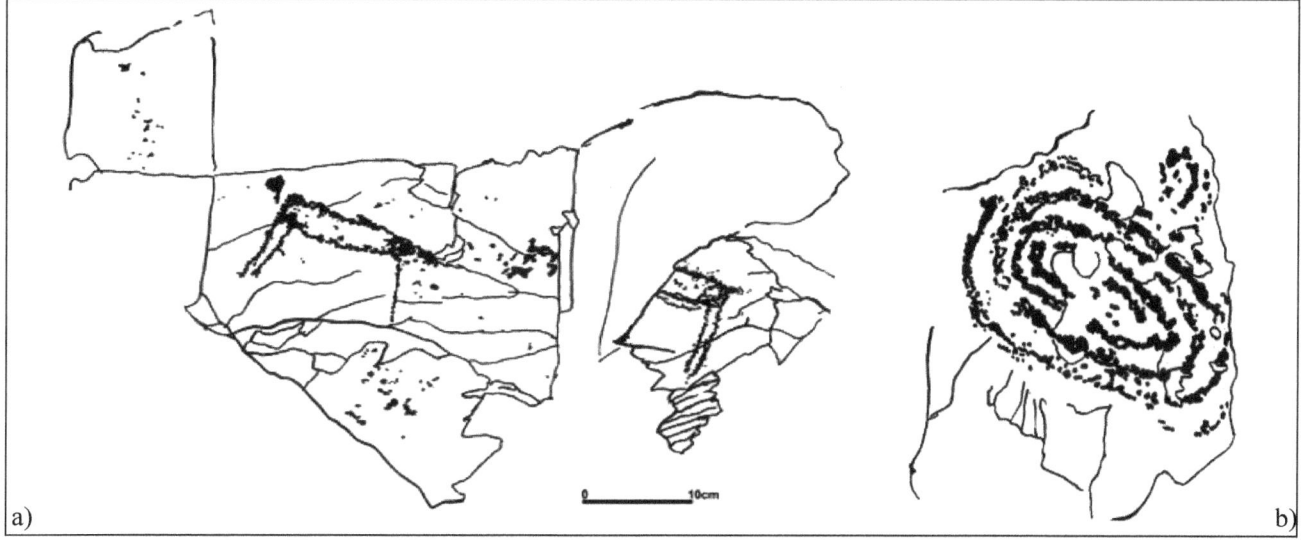

Figure 8 – a) Panel 1 from Two Deer Rock – Rovinhosa Valley, Ocreza River. Source: Instituto Terra e Memória, Portugal. b) Panel 2 – Rovinhosa Valley, Ocreza River. Source: Instituto Terra e Memória, Portugal

in the Ocreza Valley, despite the support being already in an advanced state of erosion, making it difficult to interpret the engravings. However, it is possible to identify in one of the deer (which is on the right edge of the rock) the typical representation of the full pecked neck and head, characteristic of deer in Tagus rock art. R3 is divided into two panels. On the first one, there is a pair of zoomorphic figures identified as deer, which represent only the hind legs and one front leg and a series of perforations which appear to be the neck. The head is missing but it is possible to see clearly a part of the back, a double line of the belly (common in Tagus deer) and the hind legs (Figure 8). The second panel consists of a series of concentric lines (spiral?), a popular motif in Tagus rock art. Is it feasible to suggest a possible association between these two deer and a spiral or concentric circle?

It is interesting to understand the predilection for engraving the deer figure regularly at a particular time of the year. Most deer are engraved with great and branched antlers, and if we take into account the annual cycle of life of this animal, one can conclude that most of the

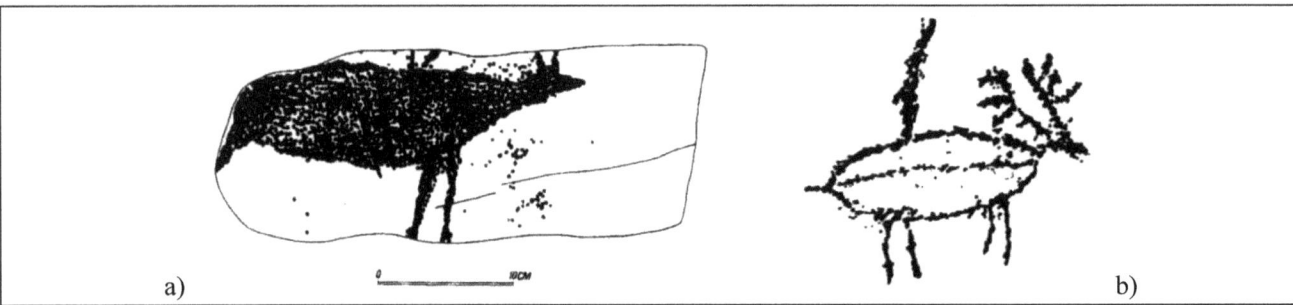

Figure 9 – Representations of deer pierced with weapons. a) Rock number 45 from Fratel (Gomes, 1989). b) Rock number 56 from Cachão do Algarve (Gomes, 1990a, 2007)

engravings were probably made in late summer, early autumn, the peak of growth for antlers, which are used at this time of year to impress the females, fight rivals and mark its territory in the bush. In addition to the previously presented figures of deer, there are some representations in the Tagus that have been interpreted as mating, hunting, religious rituals, the presence of weapons associated with deer, etc. According to data collected so far, the presence of weapons in Tagus rock art is extremely rare and precise interpretation of the type of weapon is still very difficult. This kind of picture makes visible the direct presence of man in rock art. Gomes (2001) states that 'human presence is reflected in the iconography of earlier periods, not only through the behaviour of certain animals in a state of alert, possibly due to the approaching hunters, but also because are observed throwing weapons, spears or darts, fixed on the back of at least two images of deer (rocks number 56 from Cachão do Algarve and 45 from Fratel)' (Figure 9).

The scene represented in Figure 10 is very interesting and one of the possible interpretations is that it is a mating scene between two deer. According to Gomes (2007), associations of sexual themes found in various pieces of rock art of the Tagus reflect the learning of natural cycles and the mythical aspects of fertility connected with sympathetic magic or shamanic rituals. According to the same author, the art of the last hunter-gatherers consists of more careful figuration, and more elegant and more detailed anatomical features, especially in the head. Here are presented mainly representations of deer in the so-called subnaturalist style. However, the author argues that the existence of zoomorphic figures fits in the same chronological period, but they have some different anatomical features. So, despite being integrated in the same phase above, these are considered to be a little later, in the words of the author, described as figures more than shafts, less elegant, oversized, with traces or stains inside the body and antlers in perspective. The subnaturalist art belongs to communities of hunter-gatherers prolonged into post-glacial times, with an economy, figurative design and cognitive Paleolithic origin. The absence of anthropomorphic figures in more remote periods can then be explained by a concern for nature inherent in the anatomy and natural rhythms of the animals, which had a vital importance for the survival of man and thus are the only representations of that period, since on this knowledge would depend their survival (Gomes 2007).

Figure 10 – Possible mating in rock number 155 from Fratel. According to M.V. Gomes (1987, 1990a; 2000b) associated with the female to a male of the archaic period of phase I (subnaturalistic)

Another author (Baptista, 1981) argues, likewise, that this type of zoomorphic figure and typical representations of hunting societies has a Neolithic chronology (Gomes claims they are typical representations of Epipaleolithic, also covering part of the Full Neolithic) and says that the various spirals can be interpreted as associations with animals, for example, the rock of Fratel number 155. However, he also states that despite these possible associations, the spotlight continues to be the zoomorphic figure itself, which in the example of rock 155 seems to be an adult male, soon to be represented at the centre of the activity represented on the rock. Similarly, the author attributes this kind of representation of hunter communities to a shamanic tradition (….) because the shaman hunter besides engraving or painting the hunted animal usually split its trunk, in their attempt to fix the vital parts of the skeleton, knowing that the non-destruction and subsequent jointing of the bones of the slaughtered animal are vital to his resurrection. This engraving of the internal parts of the animal (sometimes also of vital organs) may be a simple lifeline, which sometimes represents itself in meander spirals, more common in Siberian and Arctic art. The act of re-

Figure 11 – a) Rock number 60 from Alagadouro. Couple of deer and possible hunter (?) (Gomes, 1989, 1990a, 1990b, 2000a; 2001, 2002). b) Rock number 174-175 from Fratel. Possible hunting scene involving anthropomorphic figures, one (or more) possible dog and deer (the zoomorphic which is in the middle of the scene could possibly be interpreted as a deer?)

engraving an animal previously prepared and used in any type of ritual ceremony may be sufficient to make it reborn – hence, perhaps, the fact that they processed the remakes always and only in animals and never on the geometric symbols (spirals) that may accompany them. In this way ... not only the sub naturalistic style but also by the type of representation, the main motifs of the rock number 155 are the expression of the ideology of a society in which hunting was one of the main economic activities, and are the main features pointed out, which have initially attached to such shamanic rituals. Tradition does not disappear at all, as proved by rock 56 from Cachão do Algarve.

This figure has an amazing parallel in the quite similar figure, also interpreted as a scene of mating in the northwestern Peninsula, the Laxe das Lebres em Poio (Anati 1968; Gomes 2007).

Rock 56 from Cachão the Algarve (Figure 9) is described by Baptista (1981) as a remarkable composition of Tagus rock art, featuring a circle and inside a schematic deer with a throwing weapon stuck in the back. The existence of the weapon is considered to be a rare fact in Tagus schist and the author attributes the deer to Phase III (which includes all the Bronze Age), trying to show that that other authors think the deer is a different date from the circle. This must be revised since, according to the author, style should not dictate chronological periods and the associations to spirals in later chronological periods proves that this kind of sub naturalist association was kept for a long time (Figure 12). Gomes (1990a, 2007) states that this type of figure is one of the oldest testimonies directly related to hunting. The same author argues that deer figures like the ones in rock numbers 59 and 61 from Cachão do Algarve, rock number 155 from Fratel and rock numbers 43 and 119a from São Simão, in spite of being chronologically different, are in some way overlapped by circles, concentric circles and/or spirals, but they are much later, belonging to the period of circles and lines, period VI of the Late Bronze Age or Early Iron Age.

As mentioned earlier, some authors argue that the first chronological periods of the Tagus rock art do not include anthropomorphic figures since man's entire existence was based on the capacity for subsistence, and this depended on wisdom in relation to nature and the elements that composed it. 'Most of the engravings were performed by the first farmers still heavily dependent on hunting and gathering. It is therefore natural that their representations also denote the great proximity and knowledge they had acquired in the representation of animals – horses and deer – during the Upper Paleolithic' (Farinha, 2005). If we consider that rock art is the expression of social, economic and ideological or religious communities, it is apparent why in the most remote chronological periods human beings focused their attention on what really mattered: the animals, their primary livelihood. According to the same authors, it is in the Late Neolithic that anthropomorphic figures emerge in Tagus rock art, however, also associated with the mentality of the early hunters' timelines. Rock number 158/241 from São Simão has one of the most beautiful and famous scenes from the Tagus rock art: a phallic anthropomorphic sustains his arms raised in a dead deer. Eduardo da Cunha Serrão (1981) considers this rock as one of the rare scenes of the river Tagus that contributes to the symbolic nature of this complex and, according to the author, corresponded to the fulfillment of a ritual gesture, the river being the main hub of all the important ceremonies in the communities.

It was also assigned a first moment of dynamism by Baptista (1986); however, the author claims that it belongs to the Final Neolithic in contrast to Gomes (1983), who argues that this rock belongs to the Full Neolithic and continues to express the myths of hunting. However, this author also thinks that this scene is one of the most important in Tagus rock art for understanding

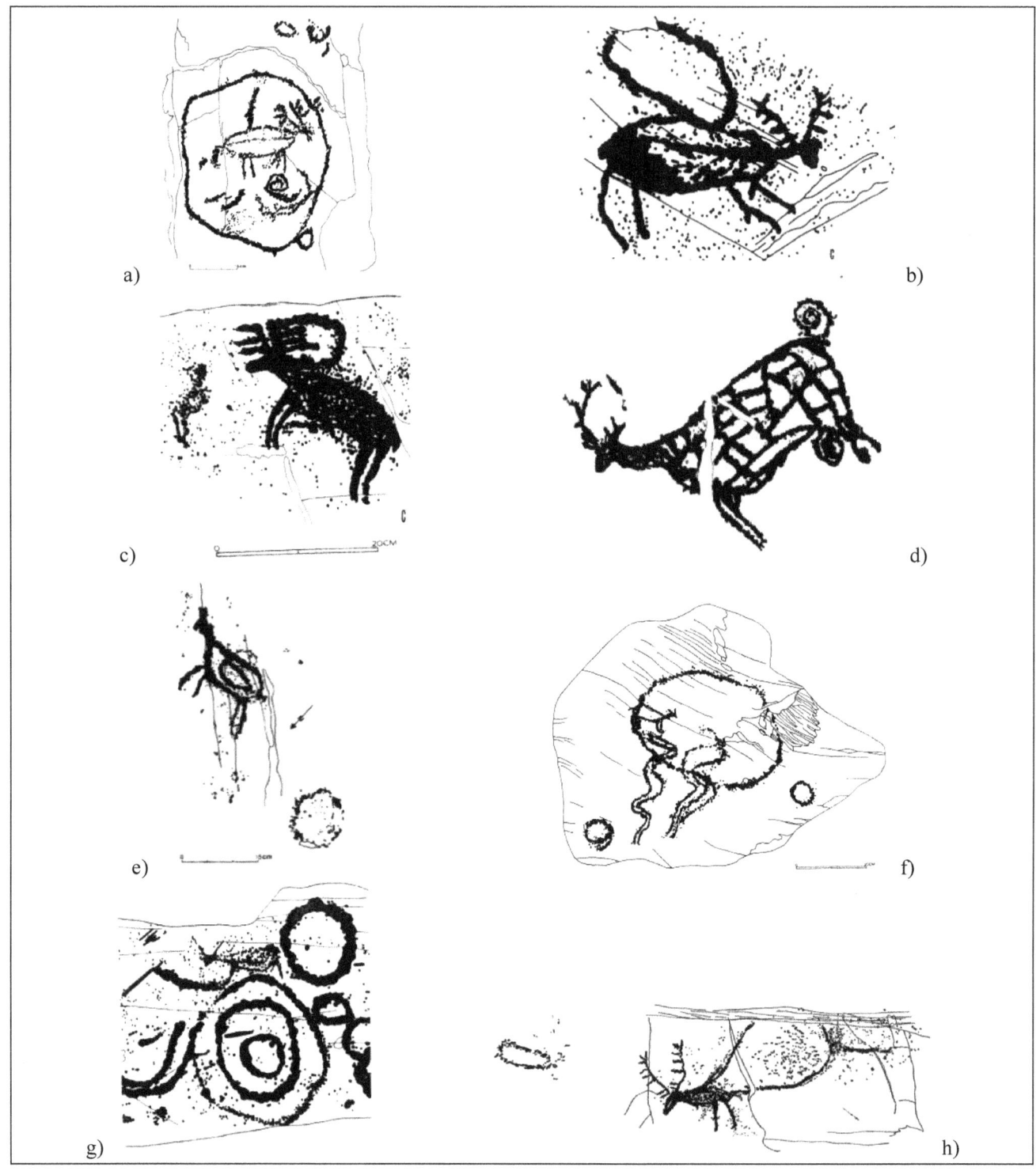

Figure 12 – Example of deer/ circles and spirals association. a) Rock number 56 from Cachão do Algarve (Baptista, 1981). b) Rock number 61 from Cachão do Algarve. c) Rock number 111 from Fratel d) Rock number 155 from Fratel. e) Rock number 211[a] from Fratel. f) Rock number 43 from São Simão g) Rock number 119[a] from São Simão. h) Rock number 386 from São Simão

this complex as a place of religious manifestations. At first it might be possible to interpret the scene as a likely situation of hunting and the symbolism of the consequent conquest, or as a possible initiation ritual by a young hunter, a trial of strength and power by an important member of the community. The chances are negligible in the field of interpretation and all could be considered valid until we have a better sense of Tagus rock art. It is not because of any of these situations, because it is possible to find similar figures, according to some authors, a little schematic, but in the same attitude, sustaining not a deer or zoomorphic, but solar symbols (Gomes, 1983).

The deer is now replaced by the solar symbol, leading to an interpretation that goes through the evolution of

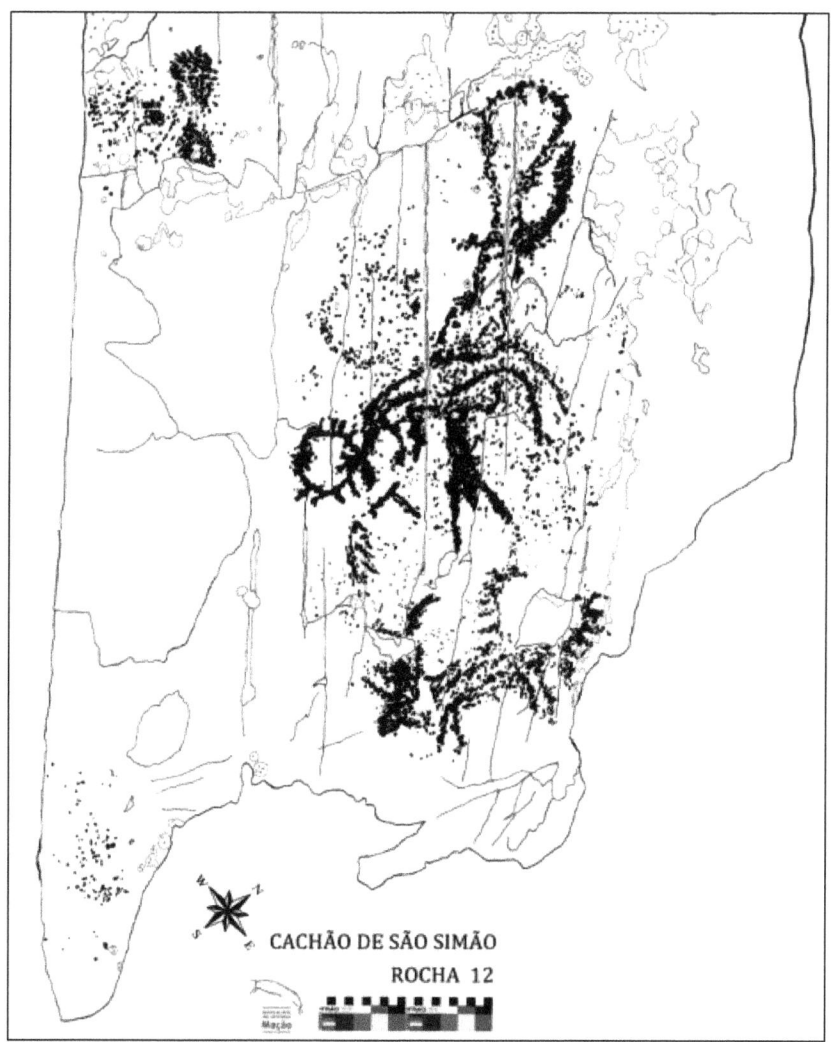

Figure 13 – Phallic anthropomorphic sustaining a dead deer in his arms. Rock number 12 from São Simão.[1] Interesting to consider the possibility of the antlers of the deer have been made in a later phase than the deer itself. The part that joins the two points appears to be different than the rest of the antlers. Coincidence or not, the antlers appears to have had an ultimate goal solar representation

behaviour, mentality, from time. According to Farinha (2005), 'in the early Neolithic period ... when hunting was still an essential element of survival, animals appear small profiles, dynamic, suggesting a hunting scene in which you can see hunters, dogs and wildlife hunting. By the end of the Neolithic, hunting scenes are replaced by astral elements – especially the Sun, suggesting an element of mystification of the creator element and fortified crops and life. Finally, with the first metallurgists, there are schematic and symbolic ways, typical of the Chalcolithic culture of the southern peninsula.' Also according to Gomes (1983), that is when the human being begins to have a greater sense of self, an awareness of who and what he does, giving yourself the same importance so far only intended for animals.

CONCLUSION

After this short analysis of deer of the Tagus, and bearing in mind that research is ongoing and in a very early stage, some considerations can be made more precise. The most important refers to an important fact about the deer presented. Most zoomorphic figures present highly developed antlers and hence we can reach some interesting conclusions. Taking into account the type of deer presented this is probably the *cervus elaphus*, the most common deer in the Peninsular Holocene (Baptista 1981), which makes us believe that most are male, young

---

[1] The Rock Art Laboratory of the Museum of Prehistoric Art of Mação, Portugal, has carried out a thorough study of the Tagus Valley Rock Art Complex. The project "Ruptejo" (co-ordinated by Luiz Oosterbeek) involves the detailed work both in the rock art sites still out of water and the tracing of the Tagus engraved rocks in the Rock Art Laboratory. Recently (2011), field work at the rock art site of São Simão (coordinated by Mila Simões de Abreu) enabled the evaluation in situ of some of the engraved rocks which were accessed already in the lab through the moulds of the Tagus. São Simão is one of the few rock art nucleuses that are still visitable because some engraved rocks remain out of water.

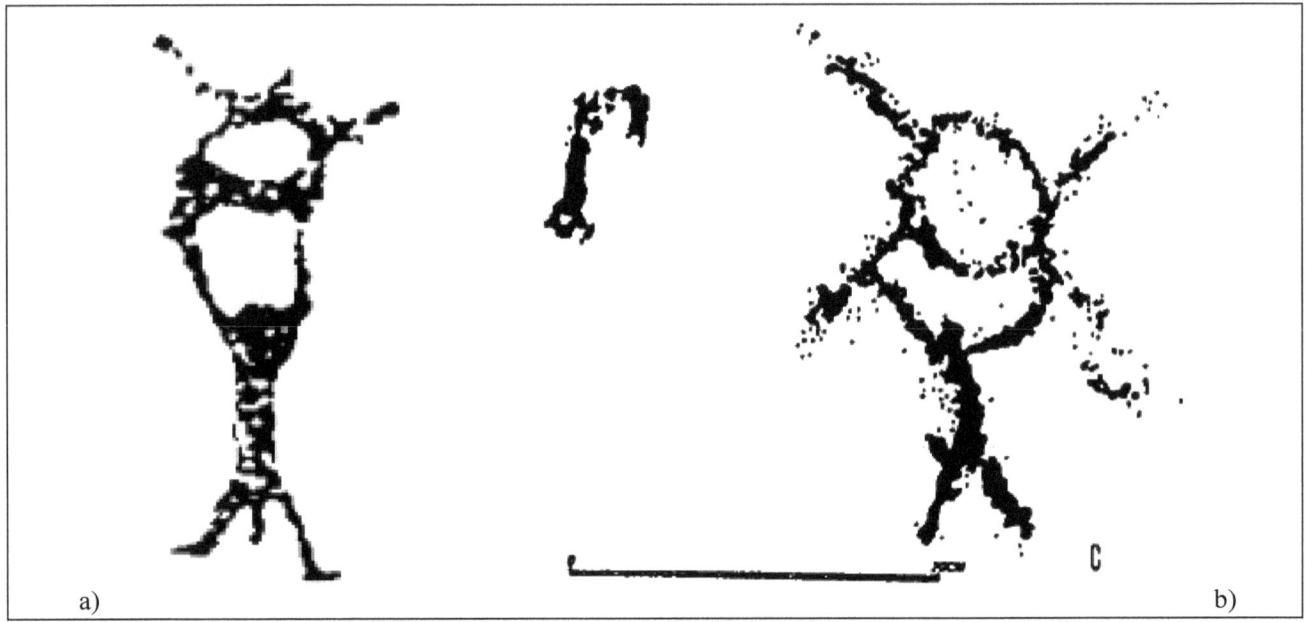

Figure 14 – Anthropomorphic figurations sustaining solar figures in the air. Rock number 126 from Fratel (Baptista *et al.*, 1974; Gomes, 1983, 1987, 1989, 2001; Querol *et al.*, 1975; Serrão, 1978; Gonçalves, 2004) and rock number 12 from Ficalho (Baptista, 1989; Gomes, 1983, 1989, 2001; Jorge e Jorge, 1991)

or adult males, but not old. The rise and fall of the antlers are connected with the activity of the sexual organs and affect their characteristic shape around seven or eight years old. The antler loss typically occurs between February and April and its next development lasts about four months, so that with high probability, most of these zoomorphic representations have been made in late summer or early autumn, when the antlers are at the peak of their development and are used as a weapon against other males at the time of heat, and as a marker of territory (by odorous signals).

Understanding the dynamics of relationships between humans and deer is a task that can be looked at gradually. The deer is the animal most represented in the rock art of the Tagus and becomes associated with the anthropomorphic figures, geometric figures, weapons, and other zoomorphics. It is definitely an animal that shows the importance it holds in the imagination of the first agro-pastoral society, and the Tagus River itself seems to have a pivotal role in this relationship.

This is part of a research programme in the Alto Ribatejo region on fauna, the paleo-environmental and the paleo-climate (Almeida 2010; Ferreira 2010; Campos 2009) and occupancy territory, as part of anthropological, material and symbolic research (Nobre 2006, Tomé 2011; Cruz 2011), and these are the sets of data that it is believed will support the continuation of research on deer in the Tagus Valley Rock Art Complex.

References

ALMEIDA, N. 2010 A Constituição das Primeiras Economias Agro-Pastoris, Paradigmas em Debate. O Contributo da Zooarqueologia e Tafonomia para o Alto Ribatejo. Dissertação de Mestrado em Arqueologia Pré-Histórica e Arte Rupestre (policopiado). Instituto Politécnico de Tomar/Universidade de Trás-os-Montes e Alto Douro.

ANATI, E. 1968 Arte Rupestre nelle Regioni occidentali della Penisola Iberica, Archivi di Arte Preihistorica 2. Edizioni del Centro. Centro Camuno di Studi Preistorici, Brescia.

ANATI, E. 1975 Incisioni rupestri nell'alto valle del Fiume Tago, Portogallo. Bollettino del Centro Camuno di Studi Preistorici, 12, pp. 156–60.

ARCÀ, A.; BEDNARIK, R.G.; FOSSATI, A.; JAFFE, L. e ABREU, M.S. 2001 Damned dams again: the plight of Portuguese rock art. Rock Art Research, 18(1), pp. I–IV.

BAPTISTA, A.M. 1986 A arte rupestre pós-glaciária. Esquematismo e abstracção. História da Arte em Portugal. Do Paleolítico à Arte Visigótica, pp. 30-55. Publicações Alfa, Lisboa.

BAPTISTA, A.M. 1986a Arte Rupestre do Vale do Tejo: a arte dos Povos Neolíticos do Vale do Tejo. CIART: Centro de Interpretação de Arte Rupestre do Vale do Tejo. (Vila Velha de Ródão).

BAPTISTA, A.M. 2001 Ocreza (Envendos, Mação, Portugal central): um novo sítio com arte paleolítica de ar livre. In Ana Rosa Cruz e Luiz Oosterbeek (coord.), Territórios, mobilidade e povoamento no Alto-Ribatejo. II: Santa Cita e o quaternário da região, Tomar. Arkeos: perspectivas em diálogo, 11, pp. 163–92. Tomar: CEIPHAR – Centro Europeu de Investigação da Pré-História do Alto Ribatejo.

BAPTISTA, A.M.; GOMES, M.V.; LEMOS, F.S.; MARTINS, T.; MONTEIRO J.P., RAPOSO L.;

SERRÃO V.M.; SILVA, A.C. da.; QUEROL, M. de los A.; SERRÃO, E. da C. 1974 O Complexo de Arte Rupestre do Tejo. Processos de Levantamento. Actas do III Congresso Nacional de Arqueologia, 1, pp. 293–324. IV ests. Ministério da Educação Nacional, Porto.

BAPTISTA, A.M.; SERRÃO, E. da C.; MARTINS, M.M. 1978 Arte Rupestre do Vale do Tejo. Exposição. 6p. Museu de Arqueologia e Etnografia da Junta Distrital de Setúbal, Setúbal.

CANINAS, J.; HENRIQUES F. 1985 Testemunhos do Neolítico e Calcolítico no Concelho de Nisa. Actas das 1ªs Jornadas de Arqueologia do Nordeste Alentejano, pp. 69–82.

CAMPOS, L. 2009 Dinâmicas Climáticas e Comportamento Humano na Península Ibérica de 14 a 4 mil cal.BP. Dissertação de Mestrado IPT/UTAD. (texto não publicado)].

CRUZ, A.R. 2011 A Pré-História Recente do vale do Baixo Zêzere. Dissertação de Doutoramento (policopiado)]. Universidade de Trás-os-Montes e Alto Douro. 3 vols.

GARCÊS, S. 2009 Cervídeos na Arte Rupestre do Vale do Tejo: contributo para o estudo da Pré-História Recente. Dissertação de Mestrado em Arqueologia Pré-Histórica e Arte Rupestre (policopiado)]. Instituto Politécnico de Tomar/Universidade de Trás-os-Montes e Alto Douro.

GOMES, M.V. 1980 Arte do Tejo. Enciclopédia Verbo de Cultura 20, pp. 1300–4. Editorial Verbo, Lisboa.

GOMES, M.V. 1983 Arte esquemática do Vale do Tejo. Zephyrus 36, pp. 277–85. Salamanca.

GOMES, M.V. 1987 Arte Rupestre do Vale do Tejo. Arqueologia no Vale do Tejo, pp. 26–43. IPPC – Instituto Português do Património Cultural, Lisboa.

GOMES, M.V. 1989 Arte Rupestre do Vale do Tejo – um santuário pré-histórico. 'Encuentro sobre el Tajo: El agua y los asentamientos humanos'. Cuadernos de San Benito 2, pp. 49–75. Fundacion San Benito de Alcantara.

GOMES, M.V. 1990a A rocha 49 de Fratel e os períodos estilizado-estático e estilizado-dinâmico da arte do Vale do Tejo, Homenagem ao Professor Santos Júnior I, pp. 151–77. Instituto Português de Investigação Científica, Lisboa.

GOMES, M.V. 1990b A Importância dos Elementos Naturais e do Ambiente na Arte Rupestre. Jornadas sobre Parques com Arte Rupestre, pp. 123–48. Zaragoza.

GOMES, M.V. 2000a A rocha 175 de Fratel – Iconografia e interpretação. Estudos Pré-Históricos, 8, pp. 81–112.

GOMES, M.V. 2000b Arte Preistorica del Portogallo, 40000 Anni di Arte Contemporanea, L'Art Preistorica d'Europa, pp. 23–41. Centro Camuno di Studi Preistorici, Capo di Ponte.

GOMES, M.V. 2001 Arte rupestre do Vale do Tejo (Portugal) – Antropomorfos (estilos, comportamentos, cronologia e interpretações), Série Arqueológica – Semiótica del Arte Rupestre, pp. 53–88. Academia De Cultura Valenciana, Sección De Prehistoria Y Arqueología. Valência: Diputación Provincial de Valência.

GOMES, M.V. 2002 Arte Rupestre em Portugal – perspectiva sobre o último século. In José Morais Arnaud, Arqueologia 2000: Balanço de um Século de Investigação Arqueológica em Portugal. Arqueologia e História – Revista da Associação dos Arqueólogos Portugueses, 54, pp. 139–96.

GOMES, M.V. 2007 Os períodos iniciais da arte do Vale do Tejo (Paleolítico e Epipaleolítico). Cuadernos de Arte Rupestre, 4, pp. 81–116.

GONÇALVES, V.S. 2004 Portugal na Pré-história. In João Medina(Dir) História de Portugal. Portugal na Pré-história, 1 607pp. (173–82, 329, 449). Edita Ediclube, Alfragide.

FARINHA, L. 2005 Uma janela sobre o Ródão. História, 80, pp. 56–59.

FERREIRA, O.V. 1973 Acerca das chamadas 'gravuras rupestres' de Fratel (Portas de Ródão). Dólmen, 1, pp. 15–16. Lisboa.

FERREIRA, C. 2010 Contribuição para o Estudo das Transformações Ambientais na Transição para o Agro-Pastoralismo no Alto Ribatejo. Dissertação de Mestrado em Arqueologia Pré-Histórica e Arte Rupestre [policopiado]. Instituto Politécnico de Tomar/Universidade de Trás-os-Montes e Alto Douro.

HENRIQUES, F.; CANINAS, J.; GOUVEIA, J. 2010 Arte Rupestre do Vale do Tejo. Itinerários por Terras de Açafa. Vila Velha de Ródão. Associação de Estudos do Alto Tejo: Câmara Municipal de Vila Velha de Ródão.

JORGE, V.O. 1983 Gravuras Portuguesas. Zephyrus, 36, pp. 53–61. Salamanca.

JORGE, V.O. 1987 Gravuras Portuguesas. In Projectar o Passado. Ensaios sobre Arqueologia e Pré-história, pp. 263–77. Lisboa.

JORGE, V.O.; JORGE, S.O. 1991 Figurations humaines prehistoriques du Portugal: Dolmens órnes, abris peints, rochers graves, statues-menhirs. Colloque le Monte Bego. Une Montagne Sacrée de l'Âge du Bronze, (pré-actas) 1, pp. 391–433. Tende.

NOBRE, L. 2006 Arte Rupestre Pré-Histórica da Margem Esquerda do rio Erges. Dissertação de Mestrado. [policopiado]. Instituto Politécnico de Tomar/ Universidade de Trás-os-Montes e Alto Douro.

MONTEIRO, J.P.; GOMES, M.V. 1980 Arte Rupestre do Vale do Tejo – evolução estilística cronológica e cultural. Resumos do IV Congresso Nacional de Arqueologia, Volume I, pp. 19–23. Faro.

QUEROL, M.A.; LEMOS, F.S.; MONTEIRO, J.P.; GOMES, M.V. 1975 El complejo de Arte rupestre del Tajo (Portugal). Crónica del XIII Congresso Arqueólogico Nacional (Hueva, 1973), pp. 237–44. Seminário de Arqueologia. Zaragoza.

OOSTERBEEK, L. 2008 El Arte del Tejo (Portugal) en el marco de los studios de Arte Rupestre en Portugal. Arte Rupestre do Vale do Tejo e outros Estudos de Arte Pré-Histórica. In L. Oosterbeek e C. Buco (coord.), Arkeos: perspectivas em diálogo, 24, pp. 11–30. Centro Europeu de Investigação da Pré-Histórica do Alto do Ribatejo (CEIPHAR). Tomar.

SANTOS, M.F. 1985 Pré-História de Portugal. Biblioteca das Civilizações Primitivas. 3a Edição. 214pp. Editorial Verbo, Lisboa.

SILVA, A.M.S.P.; ALVES, L.B. 2005 Roteiro de Arte Rupestre do Noroeste de Portugal. Arte Rupestre Prehistórica do Eixo Atlántico. pp. 189–219. Porto, Vigo. Eixo Atlântico.

SANTOS, M.F. 1985 Pré-História de Portugal. Biblioteca das Civilizações Primitivas. 3a Edição. 214pp. Editorial Verbo, Lisboa.

SERRÃO, E.C. 1978 A arte rupestre do Vale do Tejo. Aspectos e métodos da Pré-História. Trabalhos do Grupo de Estudos Arqueológicos do Porto, 1, pp. 5–14. Porto.

SERRÃO, E.C. 1981 As estações de arte rupestre do Vale do Tejo. Arqueologia, 3, pp. 121–2.

TOMÉ, T. 2011 Até que a morte nos reúna. Transição para o agro-pastoralismo na Bacia do Tejo e Sudoeste peninsular. Dissertação de Doutoramento (policopiado). 343 pp. Universidade de Trás-os-Montes e Alto Douro.

THE GEOMETRIC ART OF THE IBERIAN SCHIST PLAQUES

Cristina LOPES, Portugal

Abstract: The alentejan *schist plaques show a very strong personality in terms of graphic language. Their geometric art allows us to re-evaluate the more usual interpretative approaches, and shows us something distinctive about the identity of the dead.*

The possible inspiration for the aesthetic style of the schematic plaques and their anthropomorphic character are considered. The rules of the graphic presentation show motives, shapes and different types of drawing.

Since the 19th century, archeologists have been discovering engraved stone plaques in Neolithic graves in southern Portugal and Spain. These plaques, about the size of one's palm, usually made of slate, and incised with geometric or more rarely zoomorphic or anthropomorphic designs, will be addressed in their various components.

The geometric art of the Iberian schist plaques can be approached in iconographic and aesthetic terms. The possible relationships between schematic art and the patrons are kept in the memory and identity of Iberian schist plaques.

INTRODUCTION

Of the various artefacts we find in megalithic art, the engraved schist plaques are those that immediately present a striking character in their symbolism. It is acknowledged that 'there was a grammar for decorative engraved schist plaques' (Gonçalves 2006: 46), which can be divided into several analyses as syntheses of geometric motifs that allow us to establish an identity for these votive artefacts. The plaques have been found especially among the dead buried in Iberian megalithic tombs, like dolmens or tumuli, but also in tholoi, funerary monuments of later date.

The material is a piece of schist, cut into varying lengths, usually 8–25 cm, mainly dark blue (with different nuances) or sometimes green (serpentine). It is generally trapezoidal in shape, sometimes roughly triangular or quadrangular, rarely in another format.

Its geometric art is quite informative of a phase in which the group developed a social organization and a more complex economy with a synthetic geometric art. The angular motifs are rare in the European Paleolithic art, which is mostly figurative rather than geometric; these patterns appear, especially in the Neolithic, and remain until the end of the Bronze Age.

The rock art in Alentejo occurs mainly on river rocks, and usually rounded motifs predominate. In mobile art, on the contrary, it appears that there is a preference for recurring geometric motifs. In schist plaques, excluding the eye or the sun, round shapes are practically absent.

RULES OF GRAPHIC PRESENTATION: MOTIFS, SHAPES AND DIFFERENT TYPES OF DRAWING

The engraved schist plaques are mostly organized in fields, from top to bottom, the first corresponding to a 'head' separated or not, then a 'body' with elements differentiating the individual, crowned or not, and an area that marks the final end or bottom of the plaque.

Figure 1 shows a drawing of an 'ideal' plaque with most components of the analysis, and the standard nomenclature. On the left, from the top: the head, separator of head and body, the body, the delimiter of the bottom. On the right: the perforation for suspension, the vertical division of the head within the head, sidebands, and the dominant motives, the triangles with vertices at the top of the band.

This image is filled with geometric motifs that are of different types:

1. triangles;

2. zigzag lines;

3. zigzag bands;

4. squares or rectangles;

5. vertical or horizontal bands, straight or curved, usually filled.

Some have an outline in order to underline even more clearly the anthropomorphic character, like the examples of Figures 2 and 3.

The types of drawing are geometric, like in Figure 4. There is a "syndrome of crazy plaques", with the body organized by the central, vertical structuring, as in Figure 5.

INTERPRETATIVE APPROACHES

One of the most common theories suggests that the schist plaques of the gravestones found in several burial structures in Iberia (also found in some sites) are representations of the Mother Goddess (Almagro Gorbea 1973; Gonçalves 1999, 2004a, 2006). This theory has had a great grip. We can realize that the goddess is an iconographic representation of the life force, accompanying the dead. In addition, the first half of the third millennium BC saw a culmination of the worship of the 'sun eye goddess', common in metal societies of the

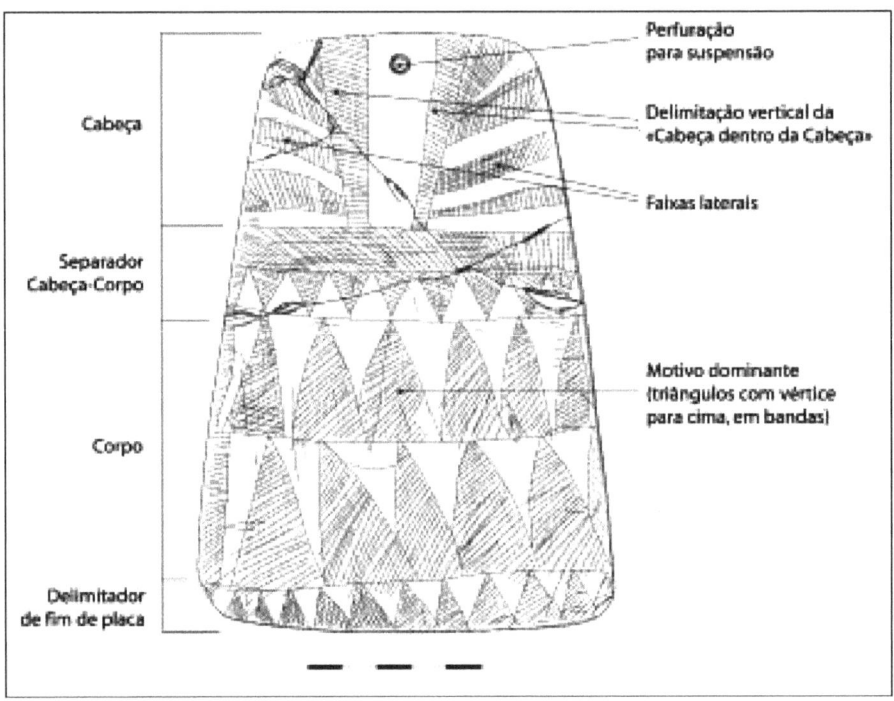

Figure 1 – Standard nomenclature (From Gonçalves, 2004)

Figure 2 – (From Gonçalves, 2004)

Figure 3 – (From Gonçalves, 2004)

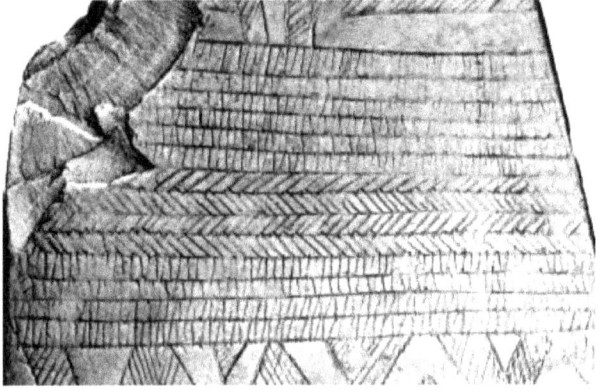

Figure 4 – (From Gonçalves, 2004)

South Iberian Peninsula. These examples of mobiliary art are in pottery or bone; however, in the Alentejo, including the peninsula of Lisbon, south to the Algarve, including the area of Huelva and Badajoz, these symbols of the goddess emerge in association with the geometric art of the schist plaques.

Figure 5 – (From Gonçalves, 2004)

Katina Lillios, after analysing the data on the manufacture and distribution of the plaques, considers that most of the Iberian plaques are genealogical records of the dead that served as durable markers of identity of the local and regional groups. These records were to legitimize and perpetuate an ideology of social difference, in the late Neolithic, in what the author calls 'heraldry for the dead' (today we use a bar code, of course!). These records were made by recording geometric patterns on stones to secure lines of peninsular clans and identify members of their elites, a system of social communication obviously practised long before the introduction of alphabets. The systematic analysis of graphic codes, held in more than 1,100 plaques, collected in South Iberian megalithic tombs, is published online (ESPRIT (Engraved Stone Plaques Registry and Inquiry Tool) http://research2.its.uiowa.edu/iberian/).

According to Manuel Calado (2010), the space issues involved in comparing the geographical distribution of the plaques, their core area of origin and the distribution of rock art in Central Alentejo, including the Alqueva Dam Complex, are of paramount importance. The inspiration of the style of the schist plaques may also be associated with fibre arts, in an ethnographic or anthropological approach, as the anthropomorphic character is suggested. At the site of Águas Frias, Alandroal, the excavation, led by Calado, found all stages of production well represented, and established new perspectives. He advanced the possibility of a single production centre, associated with the rock sanctuary of Alqueva, that could fit an interpretation of the plaques as icons 'including any mother-goddesses, other deities or even ancestors' (Draft, 2010) that worked in parallel with the other idols recognized in the Iberian South (Hurtado 2010). It can be assumed that the designs of the plaques could be decided by customers (based on an established iconographic programme) and were executed by the artists.

DISCUSSION AND CONCLUDING REMARKS

On the late Neolithic pottery, mostly smooth types, we can see that sometimes geometric motifs similar to those of the schist plaques appear. In a later period, the Chalcolithic, the plaques can be considered as one of the inspirations for the symbolic beakers, as well as the ornaments of burnished Final Bronze Age ceramics.

The possibility of the plaques being ethnic markers (Bueno 2010; Hurtado 2010), through the representation of iconographic specialized pantheons, is plausible if we consider the specific entities with specific graphic representations in determined areas. This clearly demonstrates the importance of geometric art that has been preserved in the memory and identity of the Iberian schist plaques.

The interpretative model advanced by Isabel Lisboa and developed by Lillios as heraldic-type records (Lisboa 1985; Lillios 2002, 2003, 2008), is quite interesting; but it sets it apart from the magical-religious approach and the co-relation with other approaches that derive from it.

The Portuguese project 'Placa Nostra' coordinated by Professor Victor Gonçalves has developed the research of these votive artefacts. It has studied, among other things, the phenomenon of reuse of these artefacts in the megalithic monuments in the region of Évora (Gonçalves, 2003), through cutting and polishing. There can be several explanations of why a new record was made. The pragmatic one can be the law of least effort. Or it can be assumed that the symbolism of an original old board could be implemented in a symbolic act again, creating a new magical-religious situation. Another interesting study by this working group is the 'syndrome of mad plaques'. They found out that everything seems to indicate that this syndrome is a result of a degenerative structural concept, of the symmetry in the space filling the support.

It could be observed that in the history of the engraved schist plaques, there was initially a symmetric geometric representation, in the second phase the syncretic fusion with the iconographic and aesthetic associated with the sun eye goddess, and in the third the degeneration of the structural concept as a terminal point of the process.

It seems obvious to me that the diversity of graphic solutions, using the same geometric art, evokes questions concerning the social dimension of the subsystem and the magical-religious agency, among others.

Explanation is never easy. It depends upon the paradigm you follow. For instant, some discuss the advantages that would accrue from aligning archeological explanation to

Marxist theory and in particular the power the Hegelian dialectic can provide. Neo-Darwinists prefer the explanatory power of natural selection, while processual and interpretative approaches favour, respectively, science and social theory. If there is an explanation it is that change is somehow inherent in the system.

Bibliography

ALMAGRO GORBEA, M.J. 1973 Los Idolos del Bronce Hispano.Consejo Superior de Investigaciones Científicas, Madrid. www.crookscape.org/textset2010/textset2010.html

ANATI, E. 1997 I segni della storia, Roma Di Renzo Editore, Roma.

ANATI, E. 1999 Grafismo e semiotica, BCSP n.31-32, Edizioni del Centro, Capo di Ponte.

ANATI, E. 2002 Lo stile come fattore diagnostico nell'arte preistorica. Edizioni del Centro, Capo di Ponte.

ANATI, E. 2007 Capire lárte rupestre. Studi camuni, vol. 26, Edizioni del Centro, Capo di Ponte.

BINFORD, L.R. 1983 In Pursuit of the Past. Thames and Hudson, London.

BUENO RAMIREZ, P. 1992 Les plaques décorées alentéjaines: approche de leur étude et analyse. L'Anthropologie, 96.

CALADO, M. 2004 Menires do Alentejo Central: génese e evolução da paisagem megalítica regional(tese de doutoramento policopiada). FLUL, Lisboa. www.crookscape.org

CALADO, M. 2006 Alentejo. In L. Oosterbeek (dir.), Territórios da Pré – história em, Portugal 8, Arkeos 18.

CALADO, M. 2010 Rock art schist plaques.

CARDOSO, J.L. 2002 Pré-história de Portugal. Ed. Verbo, Lisboa.

GONÇALVES, V.S. 1989 Manifestações do sagrado na Pré-História do Ocidente Peninsular. 1. Deusa(s)-Mãe, placas de xisto e cronologias: uma nota preambular. Almansor. Montemor-o-Novo.

GONÇALVES, V.S. 1992 Revendo as antas de Reguengos de Monsaraz. UNIARQ/INIC, Lisboa.

GONÇALVES, V.S. 1993a Manifestações do sagrado na Pré-História do Ocidente Peninsular. 3. A Deusa dos olhos de sol. Um primeiro olhar. Revista da Faculdade de Letras de Lisboa. 5ª série.

GONÇALVES, V.S. 1993b As práticas funerárias nas sociedades do 4º e do 3º milénios. O Megalitismo. In História de Portugal dirigida por João Medina, Vol. 1, Parte V. Ediclube, Lisboa.

GONÇALVES, V.S. 1993c A Deusa das placas de xisto. In História de Portugal dirigida por João Medina. Vol. 1. Ediclube, Lisboa.

GONÇALVES, V.S. 2003 Manifestações do sagrado na Pré-História do Ocidente Peninsular. 4. "A síndrome das placas loucas". Revista Portuguesa de Arqueologia. Vol. 6, no. 1.

GONÇALVES, V.S. 2004 Manifestações do sagrado na Pré-História do Ocidente peninsular. 5. O explícito e o implícito. Breve dissertação, invocando os limites fluidos do figurativo, a propósito do significado das placas de xisto gravadas do terceiro milénio. Revista Portuguesa de Arqueologia. Vol. 7, no. 1.

GONÇALVES, V.S. 2006 Manifestações do sagrado na Pré-História do Ocidente Peninsular. 7. As placas híbridas. Definição do conceito. Alguns poucos exemplos. De novo, os possíveis significados das placas. Revista Portuguesa de Arqueologia. Vol. 9, no. 2.

HODDER, I. 1982 Symbols in Action. Cambridge University Press, Cambridge.

HURTADO, V. 1986 El Calcolítico en la cuenca media del Guadiana y la necrópolis de la Pijotilla. Actas de la mesa redonda sobre megalitismo peninsular.

LEISNER, G.; LEISNER, V. 1943a Die Megalithgräber der Iberischen Halbinsel I: Der Suden – Text.

LEISNER, G.; LEISNER, V. 1943b Die Megalithgräber der Iberischen Halbinsel I: Der Suden – Images.

LEISNER, G.; LEISNER, V. 1951 As Antas do Concelho de Reguengos de Monsaraz (reeditado pelo INIC/UNIARQ, Lisboa, 1985). Instituto de Alta Cultura, Lisboa. .

LEISNER, V.; ZBYSEWSKI, G.; FERREIRA, O.V. 1969 Les monuments préhistoriques de Praia das Maçãs e Casaínhos. Serviços Geológicos de Portugal, Lisboa.

LILLIOS, K. 2002 Some new views of the engraved slate plaques of southwest Iberia. Revista Portuguesa de Arqueologia, 5:2, pp. 135–52. Lisboa.

LILLIOS, K. 2008 Heraldry for the Dead. Memory, Identity and the Engraved Stone Plaques of Neolithic Iberia. University of Texas Press, Austin, TX.

LISBOA, I. 1985 Meaning and messages: mapping style in the Iberian Chalcolithic. Archeological Review from Cambridge.

RENFREW, C.; BAHN, P. 1991 Archeology. Thames and Hudson, London.

RENFREW, C.; SHENNAN, S.J. (eds) 1982 Ranking, Resource and Exchange. Cambridge University Press, Cambridge.

SHANKS, M.; TILLEY, C. 1987 Reconstructing Archeology: Theory and Practice. Cambridge University Press, Cambridge.

TRIGGER, B.G. 1989 A History of Archeological Thought. Cambridge University Press, Cambridge.

ANTHROPOZOOMORPHIC FIGURES AND OTHER MONSTERS: MYTHICAL-FANTASTIC FIGURES IN ALPINE ROCK ART

Umberto SANSONI

CCSP, Centro Camuno di Studi Preistorici, Italy

Abstract: *The imaginary representations and the scenes with explicit unreal features are those which directly bear witness to one of the essential reasons for rock art: the myth and the symbolic projection world, and we can often presuppose ecstatic practices and altered or oneiric visions.*

In alpine art this type of image is relatively limited, but not rare, and normally it is really difficult to be able to understand what particular scope answers the set of images: for example if a ridden deer is evidence of a shaman practice or an element of the myth, like the anthropozoomorphic figures or the fantastic animals. But at least some clues help to sharpen the hypothesis: clues of comparisons, in particular those concerning a serious analysis of the field characteristics which give us religious-symbolic phenomenology and the fundamental nature of the shamanic ecstatic-type phenomena. So, among the Iron Age figures, the hybrid man-deer are interpreted, thanks to convincing comparisons, as representations of the god Kernunnos and the bird-shaped boats as images with a psychopomp role.

But who could tell us that the figures characterized by a complete apparent normality are not included in the same field?

Regarding many of them the doubt is very great, since there is evidence in different cultural contexts, but at the moment it is advisable to temporize about them.

The paper shows a series of images where the monstrosity or the figurative anomalies in the alpine rock art offer interpretative cues, in particular psychological ones, by a projection identification process, and symbolic ones, according to phenomenological comparisons.

BELIEFS AND PRACTICES CONNECTED WITH MEGALITHIC BURIAL CUSTOMS IN EASTERN INDIA

Ranjana RAY

Professor Emeritus
Formerly of the Department of Anthropology, Calcutta University
E-mail: prof.ranjana.ray@gmail.com

INTRODUCTION

Death is a unique and traumatic experience for human beings. Mankind survives through its gregarious nature, by forming societies. The organization of society is bound through norms and values. Death brings the loss of a member of a society. From a very early stage man looked at life in awe. Life and death are closely related. Life and death have led to certain beliefs. Such beliefs are expressed in practices. It is apparent from a very early time that death played an important role in the development of spirituality among men. The study of mortuary practices has special reconstructive value. It gives certain idea about the intangible aspects of prehistoric culture.

It is evident that careful disposal of dead came into existence at a very early stage of human evolution. Rituals and beliefs connected with mortuary practices are important landmarks for calibrating human intellectual levels in the scale of human evolution. Perhaps the concept of soul and spirit coincides with the phase of careful disposal of the dead among human beings. Graves and grave goods are indices for the belief in the soul and the afterlife. From the Paleolithic period onwards such evidence is available. The methods of disposal of the dead for understanding beliefs and rituals have been studied by various scholars (Childe 1957; Renfrew 1984; Chisholm 1993, Bator 2003).

In India careful inhumation of the human body comes from Mesolithic levels at Mahadah, Adamgarh, Langhnaj, Bagor, Sarai-Nahar-Rai and other such sites (Agrawal 1982). The erection of megaliths is an important part of the cult of the dead in India. Megaliths are reported from the Neolithic sites of Burzahom in the Kashmir valley (Agrawal 1982), from Brahmagiri in Deccan Plateau (Wheeler 1948) and many other places. With the data available so far it may be said that the megalithic burial custom goes as far back as 1000 B.C. if not earlier in eastern India (Ray 2000).

There are a large number of megaliths found all over India. Megaliths not only belong to the past but are a trait which is continuing even at present among many tribal communities. Diverse types of megaliths are found, from monolithic menhirs to dolmens, cists, capstone and rock-cut caves. Usually the erection over the remains of the dead is of stone, but in some cases especially among the tribal peoples of central India, wooden structures are found.

MEGALITHIC BURIAL PRACTICES IN EASTERN INDIA

Megalithic burial customs prevail mainly among the tribal communities of central, eastern and north-eastern regions. Tribal people in India in general live in comparative isolation in the plateaux, hills and forests. The conditions often provide scope for the study of prehistoric and primitive continuity, especially of some of the intangible traits of a culture. The tribal people in India are characterized by lack of stratification, with their worldview limited to their own culture and by lack of personal ethics and supernaturalism (Sinhala 1957). The tribal people are distinguished from the peasants by means of the essentially egalitarian and non-puritanical system of the former, as opposed to the settled agricultural economy based on surplus, social stratification, ethical religion and the puritanical value system of the latter (Sinhala 1957).

Many scholars have given detailed accounts of various methods of disposal of the dead practised by different tribes of India (Dalton 1872: Elwin 1950: Ghost 1975). The present study was conducted among a tribal community, known as Bhumij, inhabiting plateau regions of eastern India. These people have been practising megalithic burial since time immemorial. They practise settled agriculture. The term 'Bhumij' means born out of soil. The name also indicates that they were a group that owned a vast tract of land forming a kingdom until the British subjugated them. The Bhumij attracted the notice of the British Raj from a very early time (Dalton 1872). Bhumij people are mainly distributed in the districts of Manbhum and Singhbhum in the state of Bihar, in the Mayurbhanj district of Orissa and in the districts of Purulia and Medinipur in West Bengal. Dalton and others classed them as Kolarian mainly on linguistic grounds. Risley (1892) believed that the Bhumij were a branch of the Mundas. Risley (1892) recorded an enormous number of Mundari graveyards in the region. Some of them might have existed from the very early times of settlement. They speak the Mundari language, call themselves Mundas and observe all the customs present among the

Figure 1 – A Bhumij gentleman from eastern India

tribal communities living on the plateau of Chotanagpur. Similar to all the Kolarian population in the area they do not build any temples, but worship Buro, the primeval god, in the form of a stone smeared with vermilion, which is set in a sacred grove known by the name sarna, located near the village. A sarna is composed of purely jungle trees, such as sal (Shorea robusta) and others. These can very well be recognized with certainty as a fragment of the primeval forest, left standing to form an abiding place for the aboriginal deities. They observe the same festivals at the same time and in the same way as other Mundari-speaking tribes of the area. They have their own priest, locally known as laya, for conducting spiritual and ritualistic activities.

METHODOLOGY

Archaeologists frequently encounter burials at the time of site excavation. Hence the study of mortuary institution has become an important aspect of archeological discussion (Renfrew 1984). For the present study anthropological methods are largely followed. For selection of the megalithic sites along with the villages, the random sampling method is followed based on the concentration of the data. The method that is widely used in the investigation is the extensive survey and site exploration. By the method of exploration, the megalithic sites are explored. The census survey of the villages has given a detailed account about the demographic information of the villages. Specific methods such as observation, interview and case study were followed. Both structured and unstructured schedules were followed for interview. Interpretation is another technique by which the megalithic burials are considered, with special reference to the different types of existing cultural elements and their diffusion in time and space. In order to understand continuity and change in cultures, the way of life of the people and their social organization are taken into cognition.

DISPOSAL OF THE DEAD

Among the Bhumij, the cremation of the body and the erection of a megalithic structure over a secondary burial are the predominant methods of disposal of the dead. The custom described here is mainly of the disposal in case of natural death among the Bhumij community (Figure 1). When a person dies in the village the body is laid on the courtyard and prepared for the last rites. The body of the dead person is cleaned and in case of an adult male it is shaven. Female members of the dead person's family smear the body with oil and turmeric paste and wrap it in a new piece of cloth, used as a shroud. Garlands made of flowers are placed on the body and the face is often decorated with pastes of sandalwood. Then the body is laid on a wooden bed, which sometimes acts as a bier. Usually a bier is made from bamboo strips. Male members carry the bier on their shoulders. They pick up handfuls of dirt from the courtyard from the four corners of the bed or the bier which was placed on the ground. The dust is placed on the bier. Meanwhile a woman cooks some rice in an earthen pot. The pall-bearers carry the body to the burning place. Women with broomsticks and cow-dung solution in an earthen pot proceed in front of the funeral procession. They clean the way by brushing with their broomstick and sprinkling the cow-dung solution. Some women throw down the rice, known as khoi, on the way to the burning place. The rice and cow-dung are considered auspicious. No female member accompanies the funeral procession to the cremation ground. They go up to the end of the village or up to the end of the deceased's homestead.

CREMATION

The Bhumij primarily cremate the body. There is no fixed cremation ground. In most of the villages the dead may be cremated at any available space. The burning place is

Figure 2 – Cremation of the dead

Figure 3 – The ash from which charred bones are collected

usually selected near a body of water. It could very well be at the back of the dead man's house. A pit is dug at the place of cremation. Some dry wood is placed inside the pit. The body, covered in a shroud of new cloth, is laid on the wood. Some more wood is piled over the body to cover it. Usually the eldest son of the deceased first touches the face of the dead with a flaming torch. In the absence of the eldest son the youngest son may do the duty. In case a man does not have a son, any male member from the father's side will do the ritual. Some elder male members tear a part of the dead man's shroud and tie it loosely around the neck of the person who puts fire to the face of the dead, who is then led out from the cremation spot and other male members set fire to the pyre. A fowl is then killed by breaking its neck. The blood is poured over the burning pyre. They believe that it propitiates the spirit of the dead. The fowl is then cooked and eaten with rice beer in the cremation ground. After the body is burnt men carry water in pitchers and pour it over the pyre and put out the fire. They take the ashes, charcoal and charred bones out of the pit and put out the fire completely. After the cremation they join the person who has lit the face of the dead and take a dip in the body of water nearby. They then return to the house of the deceased. On the way back from the burning place they pick up a jujup branch, place a stone on it and all the members spit on it. This ensures that the soul of the dead will not follow them nor harm them. If there is a pipul tree at a crossroads they embrace the tree and take a bit of its bark. At the house of the deceased they touch fire and take rice and lentil with water. The Bhumij observe mourning for ten days. The relatives consider themselves as unclean on those days.

Next day the female relatives of the deceased, mainly the daughters-in-law, go back to the cremation ground accompanied by the village priest, laya. They carry a new earthen pot with them. Charred bones are picked up from the assumed regions of the knee, neck, forehead, breast and elbow. The bones are then smeared with oil and turmeric paste. An effigy of the dead man is made on the ground with the help of the ashes. They place the bones on the legs, navel pit and neck of the effigy. Then the women address the dead man loudly and ask, 'Who has put turmeric on your bones?' The bones are then wrapped in a piece of yellow cloth and placed very carefully in the clay pot. They say that the bones are raised with extreme care, as much care as is given while lifting a newborn child. The pot is closed with a clay lid. A cloth is tied over it. The pot is then taken back to the deceased's house. The pot is either kept buried under the soil near the tulsi, the sacred plant of the house, or hung tied from the eves of the roof of the house. Later on the pot is carried to the appropriate place of megalithic burial. Sometimes people place an elongated piece of rock on the hole of the pyre to mark the spot.

POST-CREMATION RITUALS

The relatives on the father's side of the deceased do not take cooked rice until the third day, when they take bitter rice, boiled with margosa leaves. For the next ten days only boiled rice and vegetables are taken by them. On the second day the son who lit the face of the dead goes to a water body, picks a koosh grass, and plants it by the pond. Relatives place food and other favourite items of the deceased at the base of the koosh. This is done every day until the tenth day. On that day son person sits by the water and offers ten rice balls to the deceased by throwing them in the water. Then he takes a dip and comes up. The barber shaves him and he puts on new clothes given to him by his maternal uncle.

Between the tenth and twelfth days of the death a ritual known as Purak Pindadan takes place, when a barber, a washer man and a Brahmin priest are invited to perform the mourning rituals. These people belong to Hindu caste communities. This part of the ceremony is a trait taken over from Hindu customs. The barber shaves the heads of the male members and also pares the nails of both the male and female mourners. The washer man washes the clothes of the mourners. The Brahmin priest performs the ceremony of offering food, clothes and other necessities of the afterlife to the ancestors. The barber, the washer man and the Brahmin are paid in cash and kind according to the same jajmani system as the neighbouring Hindu community. The person who performed the Mukhagni or the touching of the face at the time of the cremation does the ceremony of Purak Pindadan. In the evening, the priest accompanies the person to the nearby water. On the water bank, the priest makes a small heap of clay on the northern corner. At the same time, he also prepares ten rice balls with unsalted butter. The rice balls are placed on the mound. Before this, the person bathes and puts on new clothes. After performing Purak Pindadan he takes vegetarian food.

On the thirteenth day after death the sradh or mourning ceremony takes place. On this day all the relatives are invited. The relatives cook food in the courtyard in an earthen pot. After cooking, the pot is broken and thrown away. The same day, the priest performs a ritual called Sorash dan, meaning that gifts of sixteen objects are offered to the departed and to the ancestors. These are beetle nut, clothes, shoes, umbrellas, utensils, water, rice, etc. The next stage is the Pindadan. The son or an equivalent relation offers rice made into small balls mixed with, honey, milk and ghee (unsalted butter) to the deceased and to the ancestors. It is performed in the courtyard of the deceased. After performing all the rituals, the relatives and the other invited villagers participate in a communal feast in the courtyard.

ERECTION OF THE MEGALITHIC STRUCTURE

The Bhumij tribe is divided into a number of exogamous totemic clans. Clan organization is very important among the Bhumij. Every clan has a designated burial ground where the bones collected in the earthen pot are buried and a megalithic structure is erected on it. The bones are

Figure 4 – A megalith under which the pot with bones and ash are buried

not buried immediately after cremation but mostly within three days after. As mentioned earlier, for these three days they take only bitter rice. The pot is carried by a male member of the family to the sasan. The man is accompanied by the tribal priest, the laya, and other menfolk of the family.

The Bhumij call the burial ground for the bones *sasan*. The menfolk of the family first select the place in the sasan where the megalithic structure is to be placed. The selection of the place is made according to the descent line of the dead person. There is a hereditary keeper for each megalithic burial ground known as rakhdar. He enjoys the freehold of the land in return for his services. He shows the menfolk the family line. The megaliths are erected one after the other in a linear fashion according to clan, family and descent. At the selected place a hole is dug in the ground. Water mixed with cow-dung is sprayed on the hole to purify it. The essential food items of daily life, such as, rice, lentil, onion, potato, etc, along with a few coins, are then placed in the hole. The pot containing the bones is then placed in the hole. Meanwhile some clan members go to the nearby outcrops in search of suitable stone slabs. They select a stone slab and three or four smaller pieces, which serve as support to the slab. They carry them to the burial ground. The stone slab is cleaned with water and purified by sacrificing a fowl on top of it. They place the stone slab over the hole. The slab is supported by three corner stones, like a dolmen. Near the mouth of the hole balls made of cooked rice paste are placed.

The megaliths are mostly dolmenoid in structure among the Bhumij, but some menhir types of monoliths are also found. The Bhumij who live in the fringe area of plain and plateau in West Bengal at present are constructing brick and mortar structures over the pit in which the bones are buried.

CONCLUSION

The Bhumij tribe has retained many of the early customs, especially in relation to the rituals connected with the disposal of the dead. In eastern India though, the tribal group has undergone much cultural change in the form of Sanskritisation (Das 1931; Sinha 1959). The Bhumij people have retained Mundari beliefs and practices about the disposal of the dead. In spite of the large-scale Hindu influence, two important factors come up in their belief system: their close connection with the ancestors and the sense of strong solidarity through clan organization.

The presence of the sacred grove suggests an early form of naturalistic worship. They believe in a primeval god, which is represented by a stone. Belief in the soul and the spirit plays an important part in the life of a Bhumij. Such belief is expressed in the offering of grave goods. They keep the remains of their ancestors in the land near their agricultural field but a little way from the villages. This points out that they wish that the agricultural field should be protected by the spirits of the departed ancestors. They do not want to deprive the ancestors of the proximity to the field that had provided sustenance to them when they were alive. It may be said that the ancestors are placed in a specific place so that they may preserve the ground for the Bhumij and protect the harvest.

They do not want the spirits to leave the ground. For that reason they place food items in front of the megalithic structures not only right after the interment but also annually on festive occasions, so that the soul may not wander away but stay nearby and give protection to those the soul has left behind. This also indicates the awe and fear that leads the people to keep the spirit inside the structure.

The burial practices may also be connected to fertility rites, as suggested by scholars concerning urn burial (Chisholm 1993; Rajan 1998). This is also evident in the way the charred bones are treated while placing them in the pot. The task is given to the women. They are instructed by the tribal priest to pick up the bones in the same way as one would pick up a newly born.

At the same time the custom of clan designation in the megalithic burial ground makes sure that the dead spirit stays close to the other spirits belonging to the same clan group. Social identity and group solidarity form an important part of the belief system. It also emerges that among early man nature, the spirit and the relationship between man and the land relationship were very strong. The group's subsistence, identity, social organization, economy, worldview and philosophy rested on its outlook towards the dead, the ancestors. Strict adherence to the clan through the rituals through the life cycle of a Bhumij, especially for the selection of the last resting place, points to its strong sense of social identity (Ray and Dey 2003). Although there is a strong influence of Hindu rituals as is evident in the so called sradh ceremony, they have their ancient customs and for that they do not rely on the Hindu Brahmin priest but the tribal priest laya. To the Bhumij death is not a disconnection nor is the idea that the reincarnation of the soul is validated by their beliefs and practices in connection with the dead.

References

AGRAWAL, D.P. 1982 The Archaeology of India. Scandinavian Institute of Asian Studies, Monograph series no. 46.

BATOR, Mark 2003 Dialogues with the dead. Authorhouse, Bloomington, IN.

CHILDE, V.G. 1957 The Dawn of European Civilization (6th edn). Routledge and Kegan Paul, London.

CHISHOLM, James S. 1993 Death, Hope and Sex, *Current Anthropology*, 34(1), pp. 1–24.

DALTON, E.T. 1872 Descriptive Ethnology of Bengal. Calcutta (Office of the Superintendent, Government Printing), VI – 327.

DAS, T.C. 1931 The Bhumijas of Seraikella. Calcutta, University of Calcutta, Anthropological papers, N.S., 2.

ELWIN, V. 1950 Bondo Highlander, XIX-290. Oxford University Press, Madras.

GHOSH, A.K. 1975 Prehistoric religion from Indian megaliths. *Valcamonica Symposium 1972-Actes du symposium international sur les religions de la prehistorie*, pp. 443–52. Edizioni del Centro, Capo di Ponte.

RAJAN, K. 1988 Archaeology of South Arcot region with special reference to megalithic burial Complex. *Man and Environment*, XXIII (1), pp. 93–105.

RAY, Ranjana 2000 Some notes on the megalithic burial practice found among the Bhumij communities from eastern India. *Prehistoria,* 1, 1, pp. 82–90.

RAY, Ranjana; Subhra DEY 2003 Bhumij burial practices: A study on caste tribal interaction. *Journal of the Indian Anthropological Society,* 38 (243), pp. 363-73.

RENFREW, C. 1984 Megaliths, Territories and Population. *Approaches of Social Anthropology*, C. Renfrew ed. Edinburgh University Press, Edinburgh.

RISLEY, H.H. 1891 *The Tribes and Castes of Bengal*, Vol. I, pp. 116–26, Vol. 2. Bengal Secretariat Press, Calcutta.

SINHA, Surajit Chandra 1957 The media and nature of Hindu-Bhumij interactions. *Journal of the Asiatic Society*, 23(1): 23-37.

WHEELER, R.E.M. 1948 Brahmagiri and Chandravalli 1947: Megalithic and other cultures in Mysore state, *Ancient India*, 4, pp. 180–310.

SUBSTRATS NEOLITHIQUES AUX ARTS TRADITIONNELS DES BALKANS

Marcel OTTE

Professeur de Préhistoire, Université de Liège, Belgium

NEOLITHIC SUBSTRATES FOR TRADITIONAL BALKAN ARTS

Abstract: *The rural civilizations of the modern Balkans possess a popular mythology and an extremely rich craft art with a strong persistence of the traditional. The effect of Christianization is felt only very superficially, in particular by the superposition of annual festivals with the actions of certain saints and cults of the Virgin Mary. The profound significance of these rituals, still well known, also coincides with seasonal rhythms. Modern decorative motifs clearly recall them, passing from figured themes (trees, horses, snakes, for example) to plastic patterns. Original religious motifs (pagan) are thus maintained as decorative elements, sometimes even without the knowledge of the peasants who still use them. We can thus read the fundamental motifs articulated by the regional Neolithic metaphysics, itself extremely powerful and of much longer duration than Christianization. The same challenges, moreover, traverse the Balkan peasantry that the Neolithic apparently put in place.*

Résumé: *Les civilisations paysannes des Balkans actuels possèdent une mythologie populaire et un art artisanal extrêmement riches, à forte persistance traditionnelle. L'effet de la christianisation ne se fait sentir que très superficiellement, en particulier par la superposition des fêtes calendaires aux actions de certains saints et aux cultes de la Vierge. La signification profonde de ces rituels, encore bien connue, coïncide d'ailleurs avec les rythmes saisonniers. Les motifs décoratifs actuels les rappellent clairement, en passant des thèmes figurés (arbres, chevaux, serpents, par exemple) aux schémas par dérive plastique. Les motifs religieux originels (« païens ») se maintiennent donc au titre d'éléments « décoratifs », parfois même à l'insu des paysans qui les utilisent encore. On peut donc y « lire » les motifs fondamentaux articulés par la métaphysique néolithique régionale, elle aussi extrêmement puissante et de beaucoup plus longue durée que la christianisation. Les mêmes défis traversent d'ailleurs la paysannerie balkanique qu'au néolithique apparemment forgé sur place.*

INTRODUCTION

Comme l'ont brillamment démontré Mircea Éliade (1976) et Claude Lévi-Strauss (1962), les articulations religieuses se placent à la jonction des coutumes traditionnelles et des phénomènes cycliques où ils s'inscrivent. Les coutumes constituent des ensembles de relations symboliques choisies par un peuple dans un certain milieu. Ces systèmes de relations sont si puissants qu'ils se maintiennent quasi-intacts malgré l'écoulement du temps ou les transformations du milieu. Leur ultime justification se place en effet dans la sphère métaphysique et accroche les règles de la vie sociale aux raisons même de l'existence. Ainsi, via ses symboles, la vie sociale porte un sens et peut être poursuivie, garantie, justifiée, pour soi-même comme par rapport aux rythmes naturels, tels les mouvements astraux, le rythme des saisons, les cycles de naissance et de mort. Un « ordre » est dès lors apporté à la fois à l'existence de l'univers et aux fonctions sociales qui s'y accordent. L'exclusion ou la mise hors circuit, plus ou moins explicite, d'individus enfreignant ces règles porte dès lors une sorte de valeur sacrée correspondant inconsciemment au maintien de cet ordre grâce auquel le groupe aurait « toujours » survécu. Le conditionnel s'impose ici car autant les fonctionnements traditionnels peuvent être variés dans le même milieu, autant les « marginaux » ainsi définis peuvent-ils, au risque de leur vie, faire admettre des lois du changement et le déterminisme futile d'une civilisation.

Cet ordre existe de manière si puissante à travers les millénaires qu'on peut en suivre la trace par les expressions matérielles laissées par les rituels qui le perpétuent. Ces expressions apparaissent avec d'autant plus de netteté qu'elles s'appliquent à des phénomènes accessoires, là où l'emprise de la technicité laisse le champ libre aux harmonies plastiques, tels les costumes, les décors muraux, les textiles éphémères ou les masques d'usages occasionnels. Ces reflets lointains d'une métaphysique disparue se perpétuent discrètement grâce à une pirouette propre aux mécanismes historiques : ils sont rangés parmi les activités « folkloriques » c'est-à-dire extraits en quelque sorte de l'histoire en marche : ils sont tous devenus « marginaux ». Par l'ironie du temps, ce qui fut sacré devient dérisoire, ou considéré comme tel.

Les manifestations mythiques les plus fondamentales, celles qui renouent les liens entre la société et l'univers, furent le plus souvent exprimées par une gestuelle et par des discours éphémères : les voies du sacré répugnent à la fixité et à l'accessibilité qu'impose l'écriture. Elles doivent rester secrètes afin de garder toute leur force et leur cohésion. Transmises oralement, elles s'inscrivent dans les coutumes et y prennent racine, puis se développent, à l'abri de toute remise en cause. Mais chaque manifestation ritualisée s'exprime aussi par la vue où viennent jouer les expressions plastiques, autant chargées de sacralité que le rituel lui-même, mais le rendant en quelque sorte plus puissant par sa permanence. C'est ainsi que si, par exemple, les rites agraires possèdent des structures analogues de la Chine à la Méditerranée et jusqu'aux Amériques, l'infinie variation des thèmes décoratifs qui les accompagnent permet à cour sûr de distinguer les régions et les traditions au premier regard. Car, le plus souvent, le poids des valeurs pèse davantage sur les variations stylistiques que sur les structures universelles : c'est en effet là où se réfugie la singularité d'un groupe, donc l'auto-reconnaissance individuelle.

Le cas des Balkans néolithiques est spécialement éloquent car les sociétés y sont puissantes, anciennes, longues et diversifiées (Gimbutas, 1991 ; Kozlowski, 1993), de telle sorte que leurs valeurs imprègnent encore les campagnes où elles furent parfois approchées par des études ethnographiques récentes. Dès lors, la mise en perspective des symboles graphiques néolithiques y gagne une infinie richesse.

LES RYTHMES SAISONNIERS

L'étude de Nicolaï Nikov (2004) illustre parfaitement cette relation entre les rythmes naturels et les rituels sociaux préservés dans les campagnes de l'actuelle Bulgarie. L'année s'amorce par un jeu de masques aux références animales et agressives, telles les cornes de béliers (Figure 10). Ils incarnent et expriment la rudesse de l'hiver à combattre. Des rameaux d'arbustes décorés y sont opposés, intermédiaires entre sacré et réel, ils rétablissent la fécondité (Figure 8). Durant les débuts de l'année solaire, l'eau est glorifiée pour sa force purificatrice et magique, sous la forme d'une croix jetée à la rivière. C'est aussi le moment de la fraternité au sein du groupe, spécialement les grands-mères accoucheuses. Ensuite, les rituels portent sur le renouveau du soleil levant et de la renaissance des défunts. Les relations parentales sont ensuite renouvelées au printemps. Les animaux de trait (bovidés) sont honorés. Des feux sont allumés et des flèches lancées. Cette période est aussi celle des masques et déguisements pour chasser les mauvais esprits des champs et les rendre fertiles. Les chevaux sont ensuite honorés afin d'assurer leur santé et fertilité (Figure 5). Au mois de mars, les champs sont ensemencés après y avoir enfoncé des branches incandescentes. Le retour du soleil est annoncé par l'arrivée des hirondelles et des cigognes, accompagnées par des champs et des sacrifices. Le mois d'avril est dédié aux femmes non mariées qui exhibent leurs plus beaux apparats, en insistant sur la couronne, le décolleté et le tablier (Figure 4). En avril, les dragons viennent tourmenter les jeunes filles, qui sortent vainqueurs évidemment de ces « combats »... Les œufs sont peints et les deux premiers pondus sont teints en rouge, couleur du dieu des foudres ; ils sont gardés toute l'année car chargés de vertus curatives (Figure 3). À nouveau, les décors des œufs peints évoquent les formes dominantes de la décoration : l'arbre floral établissant le lien avec les cieux, les croix, les spirales et les fleurs (Figures 9 et 12). Le mois de mai est consacré aux serpents, animaux redoutés, étranges et dissimulés dans les sols (Figures 11 et 1). Ils en sont chassés par des martèlements répétés sur

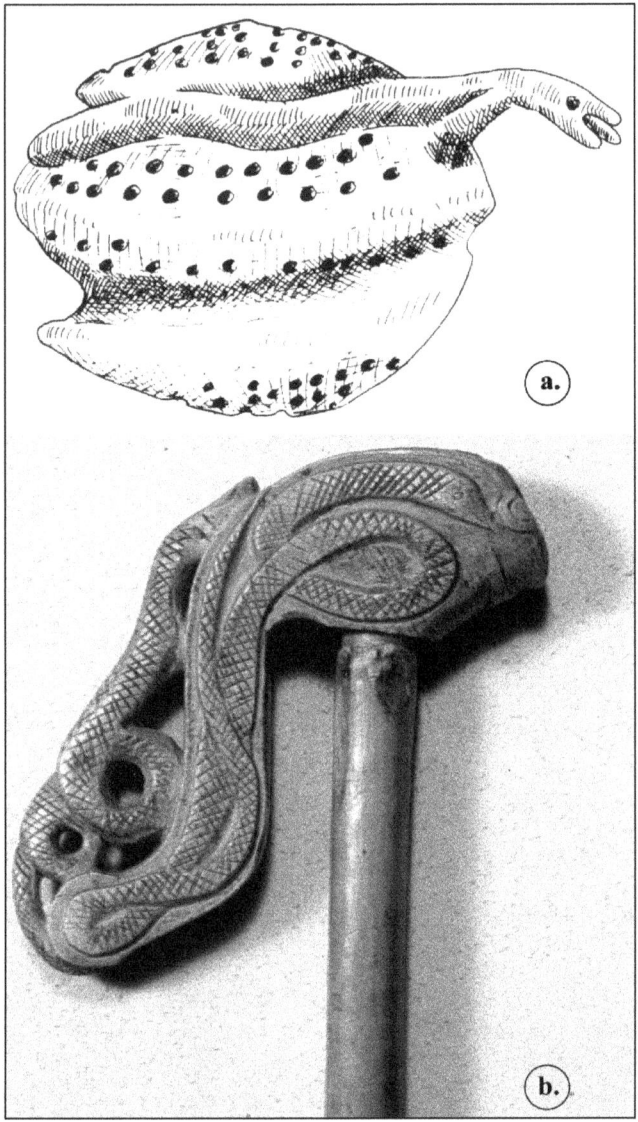

Figure 1 – Le thème du serpent apparaît dans le folklore sous la forme de forces terrestres. Ici sous le manche de canne (b) et dès le néolithique sous la forme d'anse de vase (a). (a) Gimbutas, 1991. p. 49, fig. 85. (b) Kovacheva-Kostadinova et al., 1994, p. 78, fig. 138

les récipients. La grêle est redoutée aussi dans ce mois et écartée par des tirs sur les aigles, censés l'apporter aux champs ensemencés. La grêle est aussi écartée par des statuettes d'argile, des deux sexes, enterrées aux entrées des villages pour en interdire l'accès au dieu de la grêle. Les défunts sont alors commémorés par des ablutions d'eau et de vin et des dépôts de feuilles de noyers. Au mois de juin, une sorte d'initiation sélectionne les jeunes hommes, honnêtes, sains et forts. Ils sont isolés et laissés à jeun durant une semaine. Les danses et les fêtes consacrées à la bonne récolte se succèdent aux sons de la flûte et du tambour. Le calendrier mythologique divise l'année au solstice d'été, cette date est marquée par de nombreux rituels. Le mois de juin est parcouru par de nombreuses festivités afin de protéger et d'augmenter la moisson. En juillet, les malades vont aux eaux curatives et y déposent des bouts de vêtements, censés emporter la maladie. À nouveau, un arbrisseau est dressé afin d'y

Figure 2 – Le thème de l'arbre de vie perpétuelle apparaît dès le néolithique. Il se retrouve sous forme schématique dans le folklore actuel. (a) Komitska, Borissova, 2000. (b) Nikov, 2004, p. 95

accrocher ces colifichets, d'où la maladie s'envole, emportée par le vent (Figure 2). Le mois de juillet est consacré au dieu de la foudre et du tonnerre, afin qu'il épargne les récoltes des ravages provoqués par les torrents et les inondations. Au mois d'août, consacré aux récoltes, les fêtes s'y succèdent, telle celle de l'adieu aux champs durant laquelle les derniers épis sont solennellement fauchés par de jeunes filles. Ils sont arrosés d'eau fraîche et fertilisés avec du pain. À la fin du mois d'août, les blés sont engrenés rituellement sur des aires battues par des bœufs. À la même période, le jour est égal à la nuit, l'eau est également coupée et on ne peut plus se baigner : les dragons rentrent chez eux. En septembre, les eaux sont « bénites », mêlées à la farine, elles forment des galettes destinées à nourrir les bœufs qui entament l'ouverture des premiers sillons, où les œufs sacralisés seront déposés (Figure 3). En septembre, des galettes en forme de croix sont façonnées et enterrées devant des poteaux. Les malades sacrifient une poupée enduite de miel et couronnée. En octobre, les journaliers rentrent chez eux, avec un bélier, les maisons en cours de construction sont consacrées par le sacrifice d'un mouton (Figure 10). En novembre, les fêtes sont consacrées aux défunts, les tombes arrosées, un repas y est organisé où chacun laisse une part aux défunts, afin qu'il « vive » dans l'au-delà. Le mois de novembre est consacré à honorer le loup, puis l'ours, où des rituels écartent les mauvais sorts que ces animaux dangereux pourraient faire aux villageois. En décembre débutent les fêtes pour saluer la nouvelle année, par d'autres rituels liés à la purification des étables et toute une série d'actions destinées à faire fructifier les futures récoltes, le bétail et les hommes. C'est aussi le mois des morts et de la renaissance : un porc est sacrifié car ses entrailles sont assimilées à l'utérus de la moisson. De la fin décembre au début janvier, on évite de quitter la maison car le diable rôde.

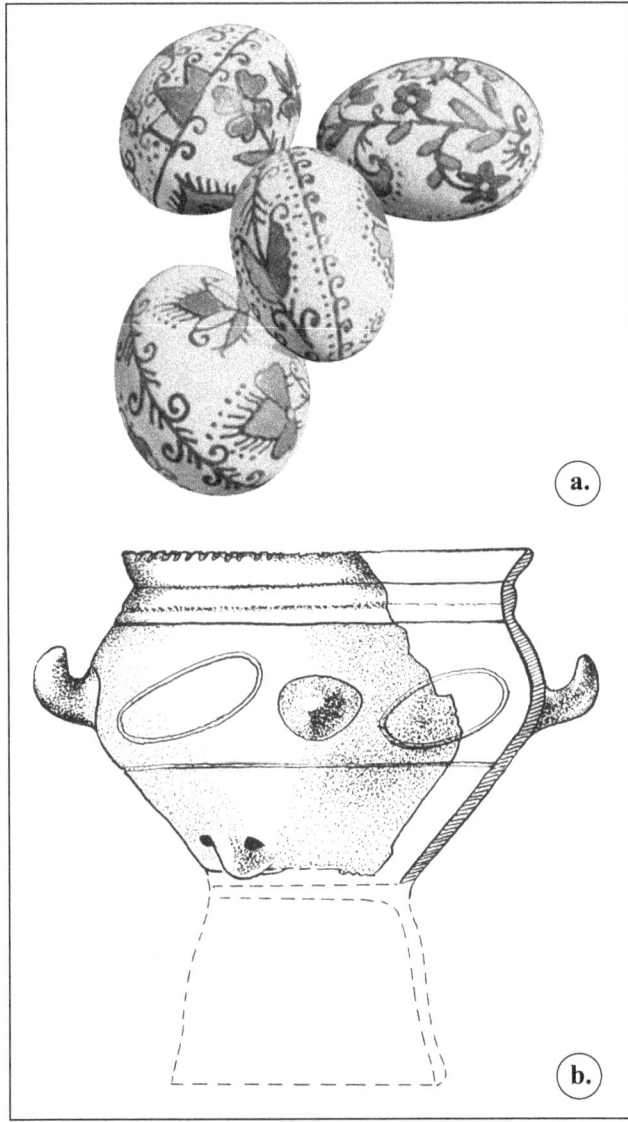

Figure 3 – L'œuf, comme symbole de vie ultérieure, est un thème chargé d'espoir de vie dès le néolithique (b) et toujours dans le folklore actuel (a). (a) Nikov, 2004, p. 39. (b) Gimbutas, 1991, p. 215, fig. 333

Des êtres maléfiques (vampires) cherchent à sucer le sang des moissons et la fertilité des sols (Figure 11). L'ail, cousu aux vêtements, est utilisé pour ses vertus protectrices.

Chacune de ces cérémonies requiert les costumes et les coiffes appropriées où les signes de leur consécration sont brodés. L'arbre de vie y est spécialement fréquent, ainsi que les spirales, signes de perpétuité (Figure 6). Les masques, les couleurs, les gâteaux, les vaisselles employées, tous portent la marque de leurs fonctions magiques étalées au fil de l'année. Les libations sont fréquentes, et ne laissent aucune trace. Les choix des fleurs, des feuilles et des branches reflètent le sens de ces fêtes. Les broderies de tabliers portent des schémas issus des animaux honorés ou redoutés : serpents ou béliers. Les œufs décorés, les couronnes de fleurs, au symbolisme puissant ne laissent subsister aucune trace également, pas plus que les feux, le gestes et les danses pourtant si

Figure 4 – Les motifs décoratifs observés sur les statuettes néolithiques (a) évoquent les costumes traditionnels des campagnes bulgares (b). Gimbutas, 1991, p. 173, fig. 274. (b) Nikov, 2004, p. 37

fervents et chargés de pouvoirs magiques, de signification protectrice ou plein d'espérance. Ce cas particulier nous ramène aux situations analogues, vécues en préhistoire dont pourtant les fondements économiques et les cultes astraux furent si proches (Figure 7).

RICHESSE ET SYMBOLES DES COSTUMES ACTUELS

Un ouvrage spécial fut consacré aux diversités des décors vestimentaires, cérémoniels et aux caractères fortement traditionnels (Komitska et Borissova, 2000). Les symboles y abondent à foison et on y retrouve facilement

Figure 5 – Le thème du cheval correspond dans le folklore actuel à la force de traction de l'araire (c), si fondamentale pour le renouvellement de la vie. On le voit sous forme réaliste ou schématique dans le folklore actuel (a et b). (a) Kovacheva-Kostadinova *et al.*, 1994, p. 45, fig. 32. (b) Kovacheva-Kostadinova *et al.*, 1994, p. 80, fig. 143. (c) Nikov, 2004, p. 29

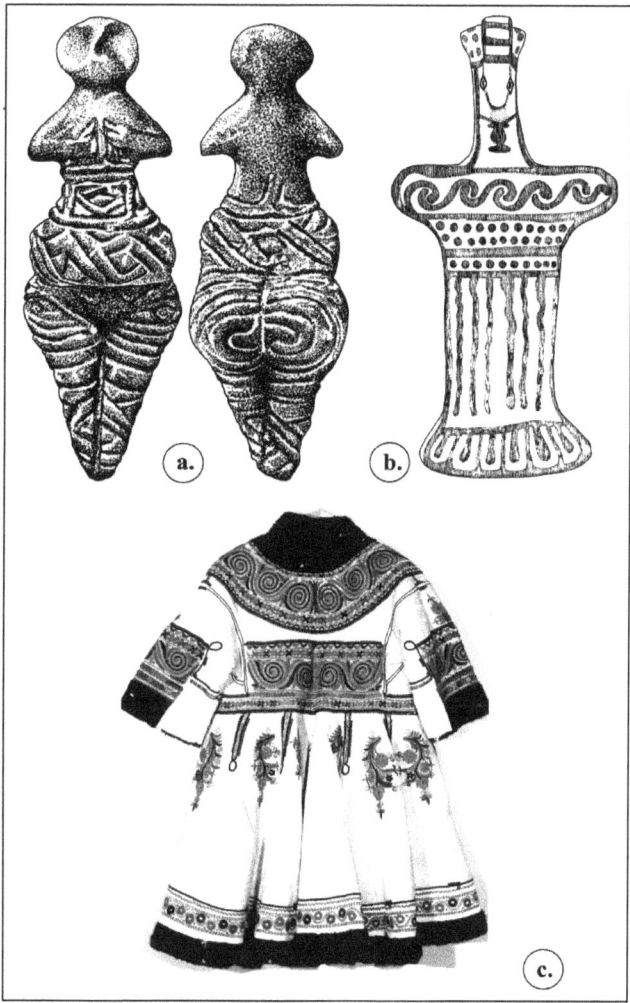

Figure 6 – Le thème de la spirale, signe de vie, de renouvellement par l'eau et la renaissance, se trouve aussi bien au néolithique (a et b) que dans les robes actuelles (c). (a) Gimbutas, 1991, p. 165, fig. 257. (b) Gimbutas, 1991, p. 131, fig. 213. (c) Kovacheva-Kostadinova *et al.*, 1994, p. 82, fig. 152

la relation aux sens des fêtes : l'oiseau qui emporte les vœux, les cercles solaires, les sinuosités des serpents et, surtout, l'image ambigüe de l'arbre sacré liant la terre et le ciel, mais dont la silhouette évoque tout autant un homme aux bras dressés (Figure 8). En outre, ces costumes sont absolument somptueux. Par leur fraîcheur et portés avec fierté, ils restituent un pan de la conscience religieuse néolithique régionale : le même « esprit » y règne, dans les rapports texturaux, le jeu des formes amples, le choix des couleurs, les jeux des schémas (Figure 9). Ils disent comment la foi s'est transformée en formes. Ils expriment à quel point l'expression d'une appartenance ethnique se matérialise dans l'élégance. Ils montrent l'aspect vital des cérémonies à respecter rigoureusement. Mais ils désignent aussi l'importance de la perte du document archéologique qui a perdu la brillance, les couleurs, et, surtout, la fierté dégagée par les regards des femmes ainsi sacralisées (Figure 12).

La signification religieuse des signes à ce point schématisés était peut-être déjà perdue dès la préhistoire : ils étaient devenus, comme nos lettres de l'alphabet, de pures formes abstraites mais investis de valeur sacrée, codée, significative. Ils donnent une leçon d'humilité, autant sur nos créations artistiques contemporaines que sur la splendeur fanée des documents retrouvés en préhistoire.

ARTISANATS

Avec la même constance (Kovacheva-Kostadinova et al. 1994), on voit réapparaître les motifs mythologiques sur les ustensiles d'usages les plus banals. De la boîte à la cuillère, des masques rituels aux décors des cannes aux crosses de bergers (Figure 1), les thèmes d'animaux mythiques, à peine schématisés, traversent les contraintes mécaniques les plus diverses, autant que les nécessités fonctionnelles, d'apparence si contraignante. La même symétrie et les mêmes accords de tons structurent les décors brodés des étoffes familières, nappes, couvertures, décorations murales (Figure 2). Une grammaire semble s'imposer aux formes aussitôt que la contrainte technique

Figure 7 – Le thème de la femme décorée apparaît sur les céramiques néolithiques peintes (a) et sur les robes actuelles (b). (a) Gimbutas, 1991. p. 239, fig. 373. (b) Kovacheva-Kostadinova *et al.*, 1994, p. 50, fig. 49

est satisfaite et laisse libre cours aux « décors secondaires », telles les tasses en bois, ou les têtes de quenouilles, les poires à poudre ou les chandeliers. Toujours, la rosace domine, l'arbre sacré s'impose et les spirales s'enroulent telle la vitalité spontanée de l'univers et des hommes (Figure 6). Les monstres et les masques surgissent du décor, sinueux et coloré (Figure 11). Jusque dans les décors les plus contraints par les lois mécaniques, les plus dépouillés, tels les croix et les losanges, la même harmonie réunit les teintes, les textures, les rythmes, comme s'ils transperçaient les nécessités fonctionnelles pour rejoindre les mondes obscurs des symboles oubliés dont seuls les schémas démystifiés subsistaient.

QUELQUES EXEMPLES COMPARATIFS AU NEOLITHIQUE

La documentation consacrée aux mêmes effets de style se trouve dans une littérature archéologique mille fois plus importante, paradoxalement, que celle consacrée aux récits mythologiques contemporains. L'abondance des fouilles, la richesse de ces civilisations, leur immense diversité et la durée multimillénaire de ces productions expliquent et justifient cette abondance de l'information archéologique issue des Balkans néolithiques. Parmi l'ample moisson de travaux édités, nous n'avons sélectionné ici que quelques synthèses significatives (Kruta, 1992 ; Gimbutas, 1991). Tout comme dans les récits mythiques actuels, certains thèmes fixes abondent, telle la spirale et les méandres (Figure 9). Le plus souvent, les schémas décoratifs sont portés sur des statuettes, essentiellement féminines, comme s'il s'agissait de motifs portés aujourd'hui sur les robes et les costumes rituels (Figure 12). La relation à l'eau y est aussi constante par exemple par les statuettes où s'assemblent le récipient et la figurine, ou les méandres et les spirales (Figure 7). La schématisation y est du même style qu'aujourd'hui, sur la vaisselle ou sur les robes, bien qu'il s'agisse ici de contraintes mécaniques toutes différentes (peintures ou gravures sur statuettes). Les thèmes des oiseaux (ascension des vœux) et des serpents (fertilité et dangerosité des sous-sols) figurent non seulement au titre de décoration mais aussi comme statuettes, ou les deux animaux, aux fonctions opposées mais complémentaires, furent parfois associés. Les béliers, si souvent employés comme thèmes agressifs dans les masques rituels actuels, abondent aussi sous forme de statuettes ou de décors gravés (Figure 10). Les losanges horizontaux figurent autant sur les robes des statuettes d'argile que sur les robes et tabliers actuels (Figure 7). Bien entendu, l'image de la femme est abondamment reproduite, dans toutes les positions, y comprises celles d'accouchement, de « déesses » trônant ou hiératiques, figées comme en réponse à une pose fixée (Figure 6). Elles rappellent alors toutes les images où les femmes actuelles, dès qu'elles portent les costumes rituels, se dressent et exposent les attributs de leur fonction sacrée, comme une affirmation, une exhibition de leur raison d'être et comme porteuses du destin du groupe (Figure 4). Les monstres, démons et êtres composites annoncent l'esprit du « dragon » des contes populaires actuels, courant la nuit dans les champs morts,

Figure 8 – Le thème de l'orant aux bras dressés se retrouve comme un fidèle qui implore ses dieux. (a) Kovacheva-Kostadinova *et al.*, 1994, p. 66, fig. 96. (b) Kovacheva-Kostadinova *et al.*, 1994, p. 70, fig. 107. (c) Nikov, 2004, p. 12

au cœur de l'hiver (Figure 11). Les taureaux et les oiseaux rapaces, si courants dans les rituels ethnographiques, forment la base de décors et de modelages dès le néolithique. Des statuettes, interprétées comme symboles de mort et de résurrection par l'opposition symétrique de leur décor, évoquent la célébration coutumière de cette phase au creux de l'hiver solaire (solstice). Les œufs, sacralisés aujourd'hui (peinture et offrandes aux sillons), chargés de symbolique spontanée de la reproduction en germe, sont aussi un motif fréquent de décors gravés ou peints (Figure 3).

CONCLUSION

Ainsi, trop souvent réduites au niveau anecdotique, les activités dites « folkloriques » reflètent en fait des formes d'équilibre multimillénaires qu'une société s'est structurée pour se forger une identité. Les repères fondamentaux de la conscience collective y restent liés à des schémas dont le sens originel fut le plus souvent perdu, en dépit d'une répétition perpétuelle. Les fêtes, les rituels, les costumes s'articulent aux rythmes des phénomènes saisonniers, des moments-clefs des activités économiques, des cycles biologiques de la vie (mariages, naissances, morts et rappels des défunts). Tout cela fonctionne en harmonie avec les mouvements célestes, les jeux des planètes et des étoiles. Autant de solutions forgées aux palpitations de l'existence, terrestres, célestes et humaines, ont déterminé des formules, considérées comme « païennes » mais dont les valeurs n'ont jamais vraiment quitté l'esprit d'un peuple. Si on y est sensible et attentif, ces formules s'imposent à l'évidence, tant leur goût est prononcé et largement distribué. Dans le cas des Balkans néolithiques, la permanence des signes fut si puissante qu'elle absorba les modifications sociales inévitables lors des introductions successives des métaux (or, cuivre, bronze, fer) car elles n'altéraient pas en profondeur les fondements d'une économie restée majoritairement agricole. C'est aussi pour cela que leurs témoignages actuels s'expriment principalement dans les campagnes. Les activités urbaines ont brisé le statut mythique des décors et des masques : elles les ont transformées en une matière morte, abandonnée sous la poussière des musées et de l'oubli. Des pratiques rituelles renouvelées dans les rues de Sofia, de Bucarest ou de Belgrade, ne seraient que des curiosités sans âme. Les mêmes, transposées en contexte campagnard susciteraient une sourde nostalgie et y acquerraient aussitôt le prestige d'une ambiance en résonance avec une foi profonde. Les motifs chrétiens, comme superposés au titre de prétexte, y constituent, à l'inverse, des singularités immédiatement repérées par leur contraste sur un fond dominé par l'esprit traditionnel. Il est d'ailleurs significatif que, parmi tous les thèmes offerts par la chrétienté, celui qui y fut prélevé préférentiellement est celui de saint Georges dominant le dragon, comme s'il entrait plus facilement que d'autres dans une mythologie païenne où le dragon combat les forces de la terre afin de les rendre stériles. Cet être composite, formé par les composantes d'animaux dangereux (serpent, félidé, rapace) rappelle d'ailleurs l'exact équivalent du néolithique chinois où il incarne les forces du mal à combattre annuellement à dates fixes. Lui aussi, d'héritage lointain, semble incarner le vestige du voyage extatique du shaman paléolithique. Il se superpose, dans les deux cas, aux expressions naturelles maîtrisées, tels les taureaux, les béliers et les chevaux de trait. La solide harmonie des millénaires prospères du néolithique y oppose aussi les thèmes astraux (soleils, étoiles, cycles saisonniers) comme si les rituels d'organisation rythmique en récupéraient la force, la constance et la régularité. En ethnographie, comme en préhistoire balkanique, tout se passe comme si les rituels et les signes exhibés précédaient et annonçaient les évènements astronomiques, plutôt que de s'y confondre. Ce « décalage » chronologique et symbolique, soigneusement calculé et maintenu, implique que ces rituels provoquent les mouvements saisonniers plutôt que les célébrer. Telle est la force réelle des rituels périodiques et la raison pour laquelle les rythmes du mariage ou de la consécration des morts sont si

Figure 9 – La structure du décor vestimentaire traverse tous les temps en marquant la distinction entre le plastron et la jupe, et en insistant sur les motifs rayonnants, spiralés et en étoile. (a) Gimbutas, 1991, p. 205, fig. 323. (b) Kruta, 1992, p. 144, fig. 109. (c) Kruta, 1992, p. 143, fig. 108. (d) Komitska, Borissova, 2000

Figure 10 – Le thème du bélier, symbole de la force animale vaincue, apparaît dès le néolithique (a et b) et se poursuit dans les fêtes du printemps actuelles sous forme de masques (c et d). (a) Gimbutas, 1991. p. 78, fig. 123. (b) Gimbutas, 1991. p. 77, fig. 121. (c) Nikov, 2004, p. 26. (d) Kovacheva-Kostadinova *et al.*, 1994, p. 85, fig. 161

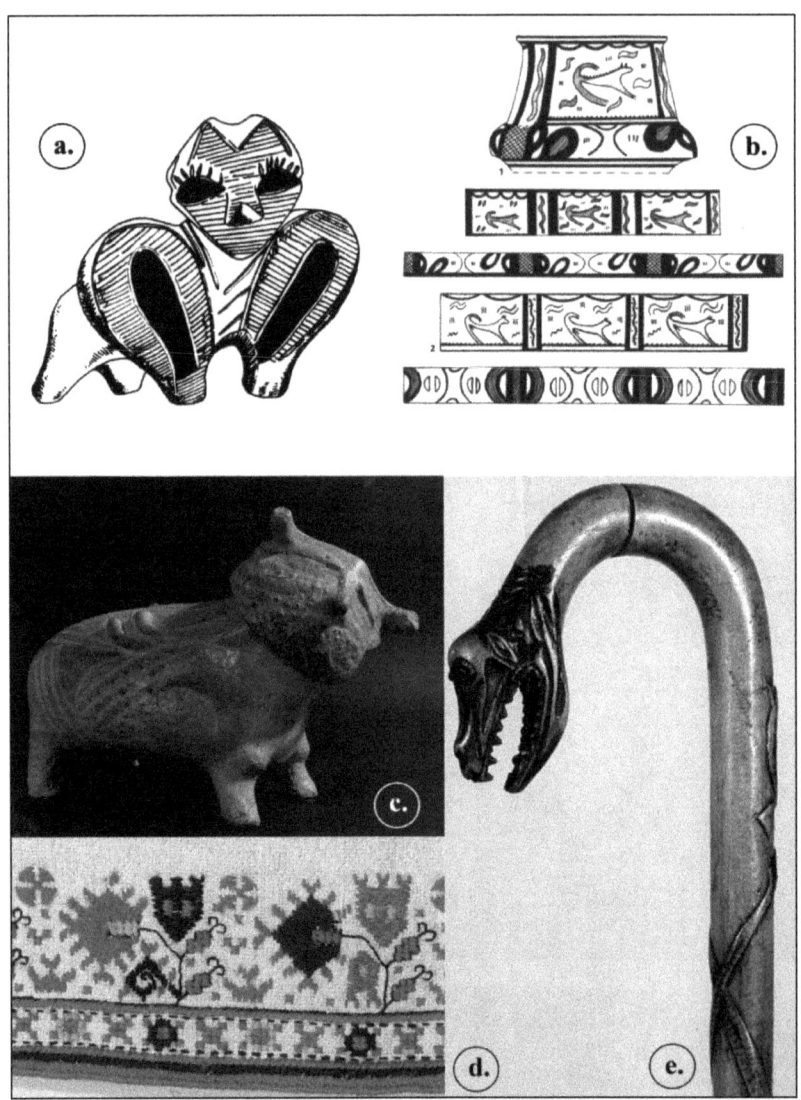

Figure 11 – Le dragon combine différents signes d'animaux dangereux, comme les carnassiers, le rapace et le serpent. On le retrouve aussi bien dans des décors peints néolithiques (b) et dans la statuaire (a et c) que dans les crosses de berger actuelles (e). (a) Gimbutas, 1991, p. 180, fig. 279. (b) Gimbutas, 1991, p. 233, fig. 362. (c) Kruta, 1992, p. 94, fig. 70. (d) Kovacheva-Kostadinova *et al.*, 1994, p. 72, fig. 113. (e) Kovacheva-Kostadinova *et al.*, 1994, p. 78, fig. 139

strictement définis. Par cette mise en harmonie céleste, les consécrations humaines se rattachent aux cycles astronomiques perpétuels. Ainsi, la vie sociale, comme la vie économique se trouvent-elles garanties par les forces célestes. C'est pourquoi aussi les symboles de cette harmonie persistent avec une telle puissance jusqu'à nous et pourquoi aussi leur revitalisation actuelle laisse froid le citadin et comble d'émotion le paysan. Les voies de la mythologie ethnographique restituent la vocation religieuse des arts protohistoriques, en leur rendant un peu d'âme et de dignité. Inversement, la profondeur prise sur le temps par les documents archéologiques, offre une garantie de stabilité aux éléments du « folklore » actuel. Globalement enfin, si cette référence à la continuité des symboles, des signes et des rites était remise en cause, l'ethnographie actuelle s'ouvrirait sur une béance absurde, car elle deviendrait sans passé donc sans signification. Si on accepte de considérer la cohérence de l'esprit humain, y compris dans la permanence de sa quête métaphysique, alors les sources matérielles livrées par l'archéologie doivent trouver un écho dans les pratiques actuelles. Parmi les plus profondes convictions se placent les rapports aux cycles perpétuels de l'univers et, plus discrètement, tous les reflets décoratifs de cette harmonie intellectuelle. Directement sensibles à l'âme et en écho à la métaphysique, les harmonies esthétiques en restituent aussitôt la saveur, comme l'âme d'un peuple restituée, portée par les générations successives qui y ont trouvé leurs raisons d'exister.

Références

ÉLIADE, M. 1976 Histoire des croyances et des idées religieuses. Payot, Paris.

GIMBUTAS, M. 1991 The Language of the Goddess. Harper, San Francisco, CA.

Figure 12 – La vaztika est un signe de vitalité par l'empennage donné à la croix qui lui donne son mouvement. Il se retrouve à l'identique sur les décors des robes néolithiques (a) et des robes actuelles (b).
(a) Kruta, 1992, p. 142, fig. 107. (b) Komitska, Borissova, 2000

KOMITSKA, A.; BORISSOVA, V. 2000 Bulgarian folk costumes. Borina Publishing House, Sofia.

KOVACHEVA-KOSTADINOVA, V.; SARAFONA, M.; CHERKEZOVA, M.; TENEVA, N. 1994 Traditional Bulgarian costumes and folk arts, Bulgarian Academy of Sciences, Sofia.

KOZLOWKI, J. (dir.) 1993 Atlas du Néolithique Européen. L'Europe orientale, 1, ERAUL 45, Liège.

KRUTA, V. 1992 L'Europe des origines. La Protohistoire 6000-500 avant J.-C. Gallimard, Paris.

LEVI-STRAUSS, C. 1962 La Pensée sauvage. Plon, Paris.

NIKOV, N. 2004 Les fêtes bulgares à travers les mythes et les légendes. Musée National du Livre, Sofia.

www.ingramcontent.com/pod-product-compliance
Lightning Source LLC
Chambersburg PA
CBHW041707290426
44108CB00027B/2881